Get the eBook FREE!
(PDF, ePub, Kindle, and liveBook all included)

We believe that once you buy a book from us, you should be able to read it in any format we have available. To get electronic versions of this book at no additional cost to you, purchase and then register this book at the Manning website.

Go to https://www.manning.com/freebook and follow the instructions to complete your pBook registration.

That's it!
Thanks from Manning!

Machine Learning
with TensorFlow

NISHANT SHUKLA
KENNETH FRICKLAS, SENIOR TECHNICAL EDITOR

MANNING

SHELTER ISLAND

For online information and ordering of this and other Manning books, please visit
www.manning.com. The publisher offers discounts on this book when ordered in quantity.
For more information, please contact

  Special Sales Department
  Manning Publications Co.
  20 Baldwin Road
  PO Box 761
  Shelter Island, NY 11964
  Email: orders@manning.com

Manning Publications Co.
20 Baldwin Road
PO Box 761
Shelter Island, NY 11964

Development editor:	Toni Arritola
Technical development editor:	Jerry Gaines
Review editor:	Aleksandar Dragosavljević
Project editor:	Tiffany Taylor
Copy editor:	Sharon Wilkey
Proofreader:	Katie Tennant
Technical proofreader:	David Fombella Pombal
Typesetter:	Dennis Dalinnik
Cover designer:	Marija Tudor

ISBN: 9781617293870
Printed in the United States of America

brief contents

contents

preface

Like many people of my generation, I've always been addicted to the latest online trends. Around 2005, I remember endlessly refreshing FARK, YTMND, and Delicious for entertainment and news. Now, I shuffle between Reddit and Hacker News, which led me to witness TensorFlow's ceremonious debut on November 9, 2015. The post appeared at the top of the front page on Hacker News and received hundreds of comments—that energy overshadowed anything else on the website.

At that time, machine-learning tools were already fragmented into a zoo of libraries; the ecosystem relied on experimental software packages from academic labs and proprietary solutions from industry giants. When Google revealed TensorFlow, the community's responses were mixed. Despite Google's history of retiring beloved services (such as Google Reader, iGoogle, Knol, and Google Wave), the company also had a history of nurturing open source projects (such as Android, Chromium, Go, and Protobuf).

Bets had to be made right then and there about whether to adopt TensorFlow. Although many chose to wait until the library developed, a few dived right in. I sprinted through the official documentation, mastered the basics, and was ready to apply the technology to my doctoral research at UCLA. I accumulated notes diligently, having no idea that the pages I wrote for myself to navigate the TensorFlow documentation would develop into a book.

Around that time, an acquisitions editor at Manning Publications contacted me for a second opinion on a new Haskell book—part of their due diligence procedure, because I'm the author of *Haskell Data Analysis Cookbook* (Packt Publishing, 2014). The journey of writing the book you're reading right now began with my reply: "On another note, have you heard about Google's new machine-learning library called TensorFlow?"

Machine Learning with TensorFlow started with a traditional table of contents, featuring subjects you might expect in any machine-learning book, but it evolved to cover topics that lacked online tutorials. For example, it's difficult to find online TensorFlow implementations of hidden Markov models (HMMs) and reinforcement learning (RL). Each iteration of editing the book introduced more concepts like these that didn't have sufficient existing sources.

Online TensorFlow tutorials are often too brief or too advanced for a beginner who wants to explore the art of machine learning. The purpose of this book is to fill those gaps, and I believe it does exactly that. If you're new to machine learning or TensorFlow, you'll appreciate the book's down-to-earth teaching style.

acknowledgments

The deep gratification of writing this book traces back to the support of my family: Suman (Mom), Umesh (Dad), and Natasha (Sis). Their happiness and pride are always contagious.

Moral support throughout the months of writing came from my close college friends, the Awesomest Turntable DJs: Alex Katz, Anish Simhal, Jasdev Singh, John Gillen, Jonathon Blonchek, Kelvin Green, Shiv Sinha, and Vinay Dandekar.

Thank you, Barbara Blumenthal, my best friend and more, for tying the galaxies, nebulas, and whales with your pink ribbons. You've been my escape, the cure to my writer's block.

I would like to acknowledge the tremendous feedback I've received from online communities: my posts on Reddit (r/artificial, r/machinelearning, r/Python, r/Tensor-Flow, and r/Programming) and Hacker News received fruitful attention. I thank those who posted on the official book forum and contributed to the GitHub repository. In addition, my thanks go to the amazing group of technical peer reviewers led by Aleksandar Dragosavljević: Nii Attoh-Okine, Thomas Ballinger, John Berryman, Gil Biraud, Mikaël Dautrey, Hamish Dickson, Miguel Eduardo, Peter Hampton, Michael Jensen, David Krief, Nat Luengnaruemitchai, Thomas Peklak, Mike Staufenberg, Ursin Stauss, Richard Tobias, William Wheeler, Brad Wiederholt, and Arthur Zubarev. Their contributions included catching technical mistakes, errors in terminology, and typos, and making topic suggestions. Each pass through the review process and each piece of feedback implemented through the forum topics shaped and molded the manuscript.

Special thanks go to Ken Fricklas, who served as the book's senior technical editor; Jerry Gaines, the book's technical development editor; and David Fombella Pombal, the book's technical proofreader. They are the best technical editors I could have hoped for.

Finally, I want to thank the people at Manning Publications who made this book possible: publisher Marjan Bace and everyone on the editorial and production teams, including Janet Vail, Tiffany Taylor, Sharon Wilkey, Katie Tennant, Dennis Dalinnik, and many others who worked behind the scenes. Of all the interactions with the many individuals at Manning, I extend my greatest gratitude to Toni Arritola, the book's development editor. Her persistent guidance and education throughout the process opened the book to a much wider audience.

about this book

Whether you're new to machine learning or just new to TensorFlow, this book will be your ultimate guide. You'll need working knowledge of object-oriented programming in Python to understand some of the code listings, but other than that, this book covers introductory machine learning from the basics.

Roadmap

The book is divided into three parts:

- Part 1 starts by exploring what machine learning is and highlighting Tensor-Flow's crucial role. Chapter 1 introduces the terminology and theory of machine learning, and chapter 2 tells you everything you need to know to begin using TensorFlow.
- Part 2 covers fundamental algorithms that have withstood the test of time. Chapters 3–6 discuss regression, classification, clustering, and hidden Markov models, respectively. You'll find these algorithms everywhere in the field of machine learning.
- Part 3 unveils the true power of TensorFlow: neural networks. Chapters 7–12 introduce you to autoencoders, reinforcement learning, convolutional neural networks, recurrent neural networks, sequence-to-sequence models, and utility, respectively.

Unless you're an experienced TensorFlow user with a fair amount of machine-learning experience under your belt, I highly recommend reading chapters 1 and 2 first. Other than that, feel free to skip around in the book as you wish.

Source code

The ideas in this book are timeless; and, thanks to the community, the code listings are, too. They're available at the book's website, www.manning.com/books/machine-learning-with-tensorflow; and the software will be kept up to date on the book's official GitHub repository, https://github.com/BinRoot/TensorFlow-Book. You're encouraged to contribute to the repo by sending pull requests or submitting new issues through GitHub.

Note to print book readers

Some graphics in this book are best viewed in color. The eBook versions display the color graphics, so they should be referred to as you read. To get your free eBook in PDF, ePub, and Kindle formats, go to https://manning.com/books/machine-learning-with-tensorflow to register your print book.

Book forum

Purchase of *Machine Learning with TensorFlow* includes free access to a private web forum run by Manning Publications where you can make comments about the book, ask technical questions, and receive help from the author and from other users. To access the forum, go to https://forums.manning.com/forums/machine-learning-with-tensorflow. You can also learn more about Manning's forums and the rules of conduct at https://forums.manning.com/forums/about.

Manning's commitment to our readers is to provide a venue where a meaningful dialogue between individual readers and between readers and the author can take place. It is not a commitment to any specific amount of participation on the part of the author, whose contribution to the forum remains voluntary (and unpaid). We suggest you try asking him some challenging questions lest his interest stray! The forum and the archives of previous discussions will be accessible from the publisher's website as long as the book is in print.

about the author

Nishant Shukla (http://shukla.io) is a doctorate researcher at UCLA, focusing on machine learning and computer vision techniques with robotics. He holds a BS in Computer Science and a BA in Mathematics from the University of Virginia. There, he was a founding member of Hack.UVA (http://hackuva.io), and he lectured for a widely attended course on Haskell (http://shuklan.com/haskell). Nishant has worked as a developer for Microsoft, Facebook, and Foursquare, and as a machine-learning engineer for SpaceX, and he is the author of *Haskell Data Analysis Cookbook* (http://haskelldata .com). In addition, he has published research papers on topics ranging from analytical chemistry to natural-language processing (http://mng.bz/e9sk). In his free time, he occasionally loses at Settlers of Catan and Gwent.

about the cover

The figure on the cover of *Machine Learning with TensorFlow* is captioned "Man from the island Pag, Dalmatia, Croatia." The illustration is taken from the reproduction, published in 2006, of a nineteenth-century collection of costumes and ethnographic descriptions entitled *Dalmatia* by Professor Frane Carrara (1812–1854), an archaeologist and historian, and the first director of the Museum of Antiquity in Split, Croatia. The illustrations were obtained from a helpful librarian at the Ethnographic Museum (formerly the Museum of Antiquity), itself situated in the Roman core of the medieval center of Split: the ruins of Emperor Diocletian's retirement palace from around AD 304. The book includes finely colored illustrations of figures from different regions of Dalmatia, accompanied by descriptions of the costumes and of everyday life.

Dress codes have changed since the nineteenth century, and the diversity by region, so rich at the time, has faded away. It is now hard to tell apart the inhabitants of different continents, let alone different towns or regions. Perhaps we have traded cultural diversity for a more varied personal life—certainly for a more varied and fast-paced technological life.

At a time when it's hard to tell one computer book from another, Manning celebrates the inventiveness and initiative of the computer business with book covers based on the rich diversity of regional life of two centuries ago, brought back to life by illustrations from collections such as this one.

Part 1

Your machine-learning rig

Learning to parallel park a car for the first time is typically an intimidating challenge. The first few days are spent getting familiar with the buttons, assisting cameras, and engine sensitivity. Machine learning and the TensorFlow library follow a similar curriculum. Before applying state-of-the-art strategies for solving face detection or stock-market predictions, you must first tinker with your tools.

There are two aspects to establishing a reputable machine-learning rig. First, as covered in chapter 1, you must understand the lingo and theory of machine learning. Researchers have manifested precise terminology and formulations into the literature for a common way to communicate in this field, so we'd better do the same to avoid confusion. Second, chapter 2 covers everything you need to know to start operating TensorFlow. Samurai have katanas, musicians have instruments, and machine-learning practitioners have TensorFlow.

A machine-learning
odyssey

1

Have you ever wondered if there are limits to what computer programs can solve? Nowadays, computers appear to do a lot more than unravel mathematical equations. In the last half-century, programming has become the ultimate tool to automate tasks and save time, but how much can we automate, and how do we go about doing so?

Can a computer observe a photograph and say, "Aha, I see a lovely couple walking over a bridge under an umbrella in the rain"? Can software make medical decisions as accurately as trained professionals can? Can software predictions about the stock market perform better than human reasoning? The achievements of the past decade hint that the answer to all these questions is a resounding yes, and the implementations appear to share a common strategy.

Recent theoretical advances coupled with newly available technologies have enabled anyone with access to a computer to attempt their own approach at solving these incredibly hard problems. Okay, not just anyone, but that's why you're reading this book, right?

A programmer no longer needs to know the intricate details of a problem to solve it. Consider converting speech to text: a traditional approach may involve understanding the biological structure of human vocal chords to decipher utterances by using many hand-designed, domain-specific, un-generalizable pieces of code. Nowadays, it's possible to write code that looks at many examples and figures out how to solve the problem, given enough time and examples.

Algorithms learn from data, similar to the way humans learn from experience. Humans learn by reading books, observing situations, studying in school, exchanging conversations, and browsing websites, among other means. How can a machine possibly develop a brain capable of learning? There's no definitive answer, but world-class researchers have developed intelligent programs from different angles. Among the implementations, scholars have noticed recurring patterns in solving these kinds of problems that has led to a standardized field that we today label *machine learning* (ML).

As the study of ML matures, the tools have become more standardized, robust, high-performing, and scalable. This is where TensorFlow comes in. This software library has an intuitive interface that lets programmers dive into using complex ML ideas. The next chapter presents the ins and outs of this library, and every chapter thereafter explains how to use TensorFlow for each of the various ML applications.

Trusting machine-learning output

Pattern detection is a trait that's no longer unique to humans. The explosive growth of computer clock speed and memory has led us to an unusual situation: computers now can be used to make predictions, catch anomalies, rank items, and automatically label images. This new set of tools provides intelligent answers to ill-defined problems, but at the subtle cost of trust. Would you trust a computer algorithm to dispense vital medical advice such as whether to perform heart surgery?

There's no place for mediocre machine-learning solutions. Human trust is too fragile, and our algorithms must be robust against doubt. Follow along closely and carefully in this chapter.

1.1 Machine-learning fundamentals

Have you ever tried to explain to someone how to swim? Describing the rhythmic joint movements and fluid patterns is overwhelming in its complexity. Similarly, some software problems are too complicated for us to easily wrap our minds around. For this, machine learning may be just the tool to use.

Handcrafting carefully tuned algorithms to get the job done was once the only way of building software. From a simplistic point of view, traditional programming assumes a deterministic output for each input. Machine learning, on the other hand, can solve a class of problems for which the input-output correspondences aren't well understood.

Full speed ahead!

Machine learning is a relatively young technology, so imagine you're a geometer in Euclid's era, paving the way to a newly discovered field. Or consider yourself a physicist during the time of Newton, possibly pondering something equivalent to general relativity for the field of machine learning.

Machine learning is characterized by software that learns from previous experiences. Such a computer program improves performance as more and more examples are available. The hope is that if you throw enough data at this machinery, it'll learn patterns and produce intelligent results for newly fed input.

Another name for machine learning is *inductive learning*, because the code is trying to infer structure from data alone. It's like going on vacation in a foreign country, and reading a local fashion magazine to mimic how to dress. You can develop an idea of the culture from images of people wearing local articles of clothing. You're learning *inductively*.

You might never before have used such an approach when programming, because inductive learning isn't always necessary. Consider the task of determining whether the sum of two arbitrary numbers is even or odd. Sure, you can imagine training a machine-learning algorithm with millions of training examples (outlined in figure 1.1), but you certainly know that's overkill. A more direct approach can easily do the trick.

Input		Output
$x_1 = (2, 2)$	$\rightarrow$	$y_1 = $ Even
$x_2 = (3, 2)$	$\rightarrow$	$y_2 = $ Odd
$x_3 = (2, 3)$	$\rightarrow$	$y_3 = $ Odd
$x_4 = (3, 3)$	$\rightarrow$	$y_4 = $ Even
...		...

Figure 1.1   **Each pair of integers, when summed, results in an even or odd number. The input and output correspondences listed are called the *ground-truth dataset*.**

For example, the sum of two odd numbers is always an even number. Convince yourself: take any two odd numbers, add them, and check whether the sum is an even number. Here's how you can prove that fact directly:

- For any integer n, the formula $2n + 1$ produces an odd number. Moreover, any odd number can be written as $2n + 1$ for some value n. The number 3 can be written as $2(1) + 1$. And the number 5 can be written as $2(2) + 1$.
- Let's say we have two odd numbers, $2n + 1$ and $2m + 1$, where n and m are integers. Adding two odd numbers yields $(2n + 1) + (2m + 1) = 2n + 2m + 2 = 2(n + m + 1)$. This is an even number because 2 times anything is even.

Likewise, we see that the sum of two even numbers is also an even number: $2m + 2n = 2(m + n)$. And lastly, we also deduce that the sum of an even with an odd is an odd number: $2m + (2n + 1) = 2(m + n) + 1$. Figure 1.2 presents this logic more clearly.

That's it! With absolutely no use of machine learning, you can solve this task on any pair of integers someone throws at you. Directly applying mathematical rules can solve this problem. But in ML algorithms, we can treat the inner logic as a *black box*, meaning the logic happening inside might not be obvious to interpret, as depicted in figure 1.3.

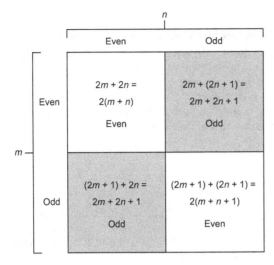

Figure 1.2 This table reveals the inner logic behind how the output response corresponds to the input pairs.

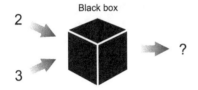

Figure 1.3 An ML approach to solving problems can be thought of as tuning the parameters of a black box until it produces satisfactory results.

1.1.1 Parameters

Sometimes, the best way to devise an algorithm that transforms an input to its corresponding output is too complicated. For example, if the input were a series of numbers representing a grayscale image, you can imagine the difficulty in writing an algorithm to label every object in the image. Machine learning comes in handy when the inner workings aren't well understood. It provides us with a toolset to write software without defining every detail of the algorithm. The programmer can leave some values undecided and let the machine-learning system figure out the best values by itself.

The undecided values are called *parameters*, and the description is referred to as the *model*. Your job is to write an algorithm that observes existing examples to figure out how to best tune parameters to achieve the best model. Wow, that's a mouthful! Don't worry, this concept will be a reoccurring motif.

Machine learning might solve a problem without much insight

By mastering the art of inductive problem solving, we wield a double-edged sword. Although ML algorithms may perform well when solving specific tasks, tracing the steps of deduction to understand why a result is produced may not be as immediate. An elaborate machine-learning system learns thousands of parameters, but untangling the meaning behind each parameter is sometimes not the prime directive. With that in mind, I assure you there's a world of magic to unfold.

EXERCISE 1.1

Suppose you've collected three months' worth of stock market prices. You'd like to predict future trends to outsmart the system for monetary gains. Without using ML, how would you go about solving this problem? (As you'll see in chapter 8, this problem becomes approachable with ML techniques.)

ANSWER

Believe it or not, hard-designed rules are a common way to define stock market trading strategies. For example, an algorithm as simple as "if the price drops 5%, buy some stocks" is often used. Notice that there's no machine learning involved, just traditional logic.

1.1.2   *Learning and inference*

Suppose you're trying to bake desserts in an oven. If you're new to the kitchen, it can take days to come up with both the right combination and perfect ratio of ingredients to make something that tastes great. By recording recipes, you can remember how to quickly repeat the dessert if you happen to discover the ultimate tasty meal.

Similarly, machine learning shares this idea of recipes. Typically, we examine an algorithm in two stages: *learning* and *inference*. The objective of the learning stage is to describe the data, which is called the *feature vector*, and summarize it in a *model*. The model is our recipe. In effect, the model is a program with a couple of open interpretations, and the data helps disambiguate it.

> **NOTE**   A *feature vector* is a practical simplification of data. You can think of it as a sufficient summary of real-world objects into a list of attributes. The learning and inference steps rely on the feature vector instead of the data directly.

Similar to the way recipes can be shared and used by other people, the learned model is reused by other software. The learning stage is the most time consuming. Running an algorithm may take hours, if not days or weeks, to converge into a useful model. Figure 1.4 outlines the learning pipeline.

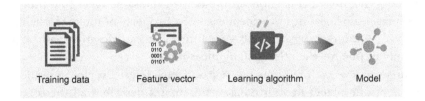

Figure 1.4   **The learning approach generally follows a structured recipe. First, the dataset needs to be transformed into a representation, most often a list of features, which can be used by the learning algorithm. The learning algorithm chooses a model and efficiently searches for the model's parameters.**

The inference stage uses the model to make intelligent remarks about never-before-seen data. It's like using a recipe you found online. The process of inference typically takes orders of magnitude less time than learning; inference can be fast enough to work on real-time data. Inference is all about testing the model on new data and observing performance in the process, as shown in figure 1.5.

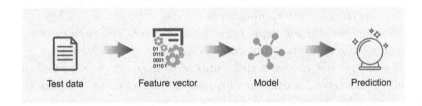

Figure 1.5   **The inference approach generally uses a model that has already been either learned or given. After converting data into a usable representation, such as a feature vector, it uses the model to produce intended output.**

1.2 *Data representation and features*

Data is a first-class citizen of machine learning. Computers are nothing more than sophisticated calculators, and so the data we feed our machine-learning systems must be mathematical objects such as vectors, matrices, or graphs.

The basic theme in all forms of representation is the concept of *features*, which are observable properties of an object:

- *Vectors* have a flat and simple structure and are the typical embodiment of data in most real-world machine-learning applications. They have two attributes: a natural number representing the *dimension* of the vector, and a *type* (such as real numbers, integers, and so on). Just as a refresher, some examples of two-dimensional vectors of integers are (1, 2) and (–6, 0). Some examples of three-dimensional vectors of real numbers are (1.1, 2.0, 3.9) and (π, π/2, π/3).

You get the idea: a collection of numbers of the same type. In a program that uses machine learning, a vector measures a property of the data, such as color, density, loudness, or proximity—anything you can describe with a series of numbers, one for each thing being measured.

- Moreover, a vector of vectors is a *matrix*. If each feature vector describes the features of one object in your dataset, the matrix describes all the objects; each item in the outer vector is a node that's a list of features of one object.

- *Graphs*, on the other hand, are more expressive. A graph is a collection of objects (*nodes*) that can be linked together with *edges* to represent a network. A graphical structure enables representing relationships between objects, such as in a friendship network or a navigation route of a subway system. Consequently, they're tremendously harder to manage in machine-learning applications. In this book, our input data will rarely involve a graphical structure.

Feature vectors are practical simplifications of real-world data, which can be too complicated to deal with. Instead of attending to every little detail of a data item, a feature vector is a practical simplification. For example, a car in the real world is much more than the text used to describe it. A car salesman is trying to sell you the car, not the intangible words spoken or written. Those words are just abstract concepts, similar to the way feature vectors are just summaries of the data.

The following scenario will explain this further. When you're in the market for a new car, keeping tabs on every minor detail of different makes and models is essential. After all, if you're about to spend thousands of dollars, you may as well do so diligently. You'd likely record a list of features about each car and compare them back and forth. This ordered list of features is the feature vector.

When shopping for cars, you might find comparing mileage to be more lucrative than comparing something less relevant to your interest, such as weight. The number of features to track also must be just right: not too few, or you'll lose information you care about, and not too many, or they'll be unwieldy and time consuming to keep track of. This tremendous effort to select both the number of measurements and which measurements to compare is called *feature engineering*. Depending on which features you examine, the performance of your system can fluctuate dramatically. Selecting the right features to track can make up for a weak learning algorithm.

For example, when training a model to detect cars in an image, you'll gain an enormous performance and speed improvement if you first convert the image to grayscale. By providing some of your own bias when preprocessing the data, you end up helping the algorithm, because it won't need to learn that colors don't matter when detecting cars. The algorithm can instead focus on identifying shapes and textures, which will lead to much faster learning than trying to process colors as well.

The general rule of thumb in ML is that more data produces better results. But the same isn't always true of having more features. Perhaps counterintuitively, if the number of features you're tracking is too high, performance may suffer. Populating the space of all data with representative samples requires exponentially more data as the dimension of the feature vector increases. As a result, feature engineering, as depicted in figure 1.6, is one of the most significant problems in ML.

Figure 1.6   Feature engineering is the process of selecting relevant features for the task.

Curse of dimensionality

To accurately model real-world data, we clearly need more than one or two data points. But how much data depends on a variety of things, including the number of dimensions in the feature vector. Adding too many features causes the number of data points required to describe the space to increase exponentially. That's why we can't just design a 1,000,000-dimension feature vector to exhaust all possible factors and then expect the algorithm to learn a model. This phenomenon is called the *curse of dimensionality*.

You may not appreciate it right away, but something consequential happens when you decide which features are worth observing. For centuries, philosophers have pondered the meaning of *identity*; you may not immediately realize this, but you've come up with a definition of *identity* by your choice of specific features.

Imagine writing a machine-learning system to detect faces in an image. Let's say one of the necessary features for something to be a face is the presence of two eyes. Implicitly, a face is now defined as something with eyes. Do you realize the kind of trouble this can get you into? If a photo of a person shows them blinking, your detector won't find a face, because it can't find two eyes. The algorithm would fail to detect a face when a person is blinking. The definition of a face was inaccurate to begin with, and it's apparent from the poor detection results.

The identity of an object is decomposed into the features from which it's composed. For example, if the features you're tracking of one car exactly match the corresponding features of another car, they may as well be indistinguishable from your perspective. You'd need to add another feature to the system in order to tell them apart, or you'll think they're the same item. When handcrafting features, you must take great care not to fall into this philosophical predicament of identity.

EXERCISE 1.2

Let's say you're teaching a robot how to fold clothes. The perception system sees a shirt lying on a table, as shown in the following figure. You'd like to represent the shirt as a vector of features so you can compare it with different clothes. Decide which features would be most useful to track. (Hint: What types of words do retailers use to describe their clothing online?)

A robot is trying to fold a shirt. What are good features of the shirt to track?

ANSWER

The width, height, x-symmetry score, y-symmetry score, and flatness are good features to observe when folding clothes. Color, cloth texture, and material are mostly irrelevant.

EXERCISE 1.3

Now, instead of detecting clothes, you ambitiously decide to detect arbitrary objects; the following figure shows some examples. What are some salient features that can easily differentiate objects?

Here are images of three objects: a lamp, a pair of pants, and a dog. What are some good features that you should record to compare and differentiate objects?

ANSWER

Observing brightness and reflection may help differentiate the lamp from the other two objects. The shape of pants often follows a predictable template, so shape would be another good feature to track. Lastly, texture may be a salient feature to differentiate the picture of a dog from the other two classes.

Feature engineering is a refreshingly philosophical pursuit. For those who enjoy thought-provoking escapades into the meaning of self, we invite you to meditate on feature selection, because it's still an open problem. Fortunately for the rest of you, to alleviate extensive debates, recent advances have made it possible to automatically determine which features to track. You'll be able to try it out for yourself in chapter 7.

Feature vectors are used in both learning and inference

The interplay between learning and inference provides a complete picture of a machine-learning system, as shown in the following figure. The first step is to represent real-world data in a feature vector. For example, we can represent images by a vector of numbers corresponding to pixel intensities. (We'll explore how to represent images in greater detail in future chapters.) We can show our learning algorithm the ground-truth labels (such as Bird or Dog) along with each feature vector. With enough data, the algorithm generates a learned model. We can use this model on other real-world data to uncover previously unknown labels.

(continued)

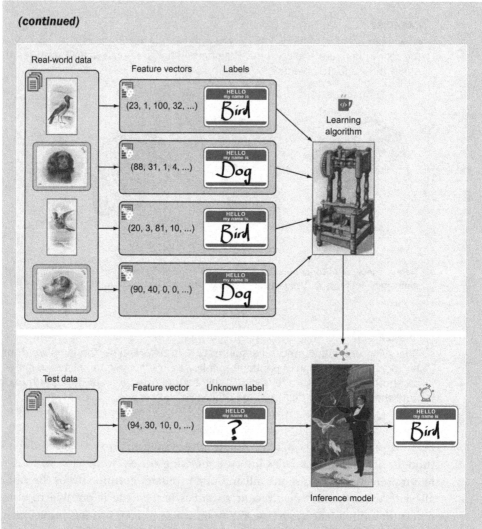

Feature vectors are a representation of real-world data used by both the learning and inference components of machine learning. The input to the algorithm isn't the real-world image directly, but instead its feature vector.

1.3 Distance metrics

If you have feature vectors of cars you may potentially want to buy, you can figure out which two are most similar by defining a distance function on the feature vectors. Comparing similarities between objects is an essential component of machine learning. Feature vectors allow us to represent objects so that we may compare them in a variety of ways. A standard approach is to use the *Euclidian distance*, which is the geometric interpretation you may find most intuitive when thinking about points in space.

Let's say we have two feature vectors, $x = (x_1, x_2, ..., x_n)$ and $y = (y_1, y_2, ..., y_n)$. The Euclidian distance $\|x - y\|$ is calculated by

$$\sqrt{(x_1 - y_1)^2 + (x_2 - y_2)^2 + ... + (x_n - y_n)^2}$$

For example, the Euclidian distance between $(0, 1)$ and $(1, 0)$ is

$$\|(0,1) - (1,0)\|$$

$$= \|(-1,1)\|$$

$$= \sqrt{(-1)^2 + 1^2}$$

$$= \sqrt{2} = 1.414...$$

Scholars call this the *L2 norm*. But that's just one of many possible distance functions. The L0, L1, and L-infinity norms also exist. All these norms are valid ways to measure distance. Here they are in more detail:

- The *L0 norm* counts the total number of nonzero elements of a vector. For example, the distance between the origin $(0, 0)$ and vector $(0, 5)$ is 1, because there's only one nonzero element. The L0 distance between $(1, 1)$ and $(2, 2)$ is 2, because neither dimension matches up. Imagine that the first and second dimensions represent username and password, respectively. If the L0 distance between a login attempt and the true credentials is 0, the login is successful. If the distance is 1, then either the username or password is incorrect, but not both. Lastly, if the distance is 2, both username and password aren't found in the database.
- The *L1 norm*, shown in figure 1.7, is defined as $\Sigma |x_n|$. The distance between two vectors under the L1 norm is also referred to as the *Manhattan distance*. Imagine living in a downtown area like Manhattan, New York, where the streets form a grid. The shortest distance from one intersection to another is along the blocks. Similarly, the L1 distance between two vectors is along the orthogonal directions.

The distance between (0, 1) and (1, 0) under the L1 norm is 2. Computing the L1 distance between two vectors is the sum of absolute differences at each dimension, which is a useful measure of similarity.

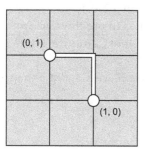

Figure 1.7   The L1 distance is also called the *Manhattan distance* (also referred to as the *taxicab metric*), because it resembles the route of a car in a grid-like neighborhood such as Manhattan. If a car is traveling from point (0,1) to point (1,0), the shortest route requires a length of 2 units.

- The *L2 norm*, shown in figure 1.8, is the Euclidian length of a vector, $(\Sigma(x_n)^2)^{1/2}$. It's the most direct route you can possibly take on a geometric plane to get from one point to another. For the mathematically inclined, this is the norm that implements the least square estimation as predicted by the Gauss-Markov theorem. For the rest of you, it's the shortest distance between two points in space.

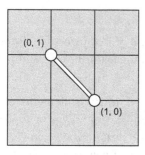

Figure 1.8   The L2 norm between points (0,1) and (1,0) is the length of a single straight-line segment between both points.

- The *L-N norm* generalizes this pattern, resulting in $(\Sigma|x_n|^N)^{1/N}$. We rarely use finite norms above L2, but it's here for completeness.
- The *L-infinity norm* is $(\Sigma|x_n|^\infty)^{1/\infty}$. More naturally, it's the largest magnitude among each element. If the vector is (−1, −2, −3), the L-infinity norm is 3. If a feature vector represents costs of various items, minimizing the L-infinity norm of the vector is an attempt to reduce the cost of the most expensive item.

> **When do I use a metric other than the L2 norm in the real world?**
>
> Let's say you're working for a new search-engine startup trying to compete with Google. Your boss assigns you the task of using machine learning to personalize the search results for each user.
>
> A good goal might be that users shouldn't see five or more incorrect search results per month. A year's worth of user data is a 12-dimensional vector (each month of the year is a dimension), indicating the number of incorrect results shown per month. You're trying to satisfy the condition that the L-infinity norm of this vector must be less than 5.
>
> Suppose instead that your boss changes the requirements, saying that fewer than five erroneous search results are allowed for the entire year. In this case, you're trying to achieve an L1 norm below 5, because the sum of all errors in the entire space should be less than 5.
>
> Now, your boss changes the requirements again: the number of months with erroneous search results should be fewer than 5. In that case, you're trying to achieve an L0 norm less than 5, because the number of months with a nonzero error should be fewer than 5.

1.4 Types of learning

Now that you can compare feature vectors, you have the tools necessary to use data for practical algorithms. Machine learning is often split into three perspectives: supervised learning, unsupervised learning, and reinforcement learning. Let's examine each.

1.4.1 Supervised learning

By definition, a *supervisor* is someone higher up in the chain of command. When we're in doubt, our supervisor dictates what to do. Likewise, *supervised learning* is all about learning from examples laid out by a supervisor (such as a teacher).

A supervised machine-learning system needs labeled data to develop a useful understanding, which we call its *model.* For example, given many photographs of people and their recorded corresponding ethnicity, we can train a model to classify the ethnicity of a never-before-seen individual in an arbitrary photograph. Simply put, a model is a function that assigns a label to data. It does so by using a collection of previous examples, called a *training dataset,* as reference.

A convenient way to talk about models is through mathematical notation. Let x be an instance of data, such as a feature vector. The corresponding label associated with x is $f(x)$, often referred to as the *ground truth* of x. Usually, we use the variable $y = f(x)$ because it's quicker to write. In the example of classifying the ethnicity of a person through a photograph, x can be a 100-dimensional vector of various relevant features, and y is one of a couple of values to represent the various ethnicities. Because y is discrete with few values, the model is called a *classifier*. If y can result in many values, and the values have a natural ordering, then the model is called a *regressor*.

Let's denote a model's prediction of *x* as *g(x)*. Sometimes you can tweak a model to change its performance drastically. Models have parameters that can be tuned either by a human or automatically. We use the vector θ to represent the parameters. Putting it all together, $g(x|\theta)$ more completely represents the model, read "g of x given θ."

> **NOTE**   Models may also have *hyperparameters*, which are extra ad hoc properties about a model. The term *hyper* in *hyperparameter* seems a bit strange at first. If it helps, a better name could be *metaparameter*, because the parameter is akin to metadata about the model.

The success of a model's prediction $g(x|\theta)$ depends on how well it agrees with the ground truth *y*. We need a way to measure the distance between these two vectors. For example, the L2 norm may be used to measure how close two vectors lie. The distance between the ground truth and the prediction is called the *cost*.

The essence of a supervised machine-learning algorithm is to figure out the parameters of a model that result in the least *cost*. Mathematically put, we're looking for a θ* (Theta star) that minimizes the cost among all data points $x \in X$. One way of formalizing this optimization problem is the following:

$$\theta^* = \arg\min_\theta Cost(\theta|X)$$

$$\text{where } Cost(\theta|X) = \sum_{x \in X} \|g(x|\theta) - f(x)\|$$

Clearly, brute forcing every possible combination of θs (also known as a *parameter space*) will eventually find the optimal solution, but at an unacceptable runtime. A major area of research in machine learning is about writing algorithms that efficiently search through this parameter space. Some of the early algorithms include *gradient descent, simulated annealing,* and *genetic algorithms.* TensorFlow automatically takes care of the low-level implementation details of these algorithms, so we won't get into them in too much detail.

After the parameters are learned one way or another, you can finally evaluate the model to figure out how well the system captured patterns from the data. A rule of thumb is to not evaluate your model on the same data you used to train it, because you already know it works for the training data; you need to tell whether it works for data that *wasn't* part of the training set, to make sure your model is general purpose and not *biased* to the data used to train it. Use the majority of the data for training, and the remaining for testing. For example, if you have 100 labeled data points, randomly select 70 of them to train a model, and reserve the other 30 to test it.

Why split the data?

If the 70-30 split seems odd to you, think about it like this. Let's say your physics teacher gives you a practice exam and tells you the real exam will be no different. You might as well memorize the answers and earn a perfect score without understanding the concepts. Similarly, if you test your model on the training dataset, you're not doing yourself any favors. You risk a false sense of security, because the model may merely be memorizing the results. Now, where's the intelligence in that?

Instead of the 70-30 split, machine-learning practitioners typically divided their dataset 60-20-20. Training consumes 60% of the dataset, and testing uses 20%, leaving the other 20% for *validation*, which is explained in the next chapter.

1.4.2 Unsupervised learning

Unsupervised learning is about modeling data that comes without corresponding labels or responses. The fact that we can make any conclusions at all on raw data feels like magic. With enough data, it may be possible to find patterns and structure. Two of the most powerful tools that machine-learning practitioners use to learn from data alone are clustering and dimensionality reduction.

Clustering is the process of splitting the data into individual buckets of similar items. In a sense, clustering is like classification of data without knowing any corresponding labels. For instance, when organizing your books on three shelves, you likely place similar genres together, or maybe you group them by the authors' last names. You might have a Stephen King section, another for textbooks, and a third for "anything else." You don't care that they're all separated by the same feature, just that each has something unique about it that allows you to break it into roughly equal, easily identifiable groups. One of the most popular clustering algorithms is *k-means*, which is a specific instance of a more powerful technique called the *E-M algorithm*.

Dimensionality reduction is about manipulating the data to view it under a much simpler perspective. It's the ML equivalent of the phrase, "Keep it simple, stupid." For example, by getting rid of redundant features, we can explain the same data in a lower-dimensional space and see which features matter. This simplification also helps in data visualization or preprocessing for performance efficiency. One of the earliest algorithms is *principle component analysis* (PCA), and a newer one is *autoencoders*, which we cover in chapter 7.

1.4.3 Reinforcement learning

Supervised and unsupervised learning seem to suggest that the existence of a teacher is all or nothing. But in one well-studied branch of machine learning, the environment acts as a teacher, providing hints as opposed to definite answers. The learning system receives feedback on its actions, with no concrete promise that it's progressing in the right direction, which might be to solve a maze or accomplish an explicit goal.

Exploration vs. exploitation—the heart of reinforcement learning

Imagine playing a video game that you've never seen before. You click buttons on a controller and discover that a particular combination of strokes gradually increases your score. Brilliant—now you repeatedly exploit this finding in hopes of beating the high score. In the back of your mind, you think that maybe there's a better combination of button clicks that you're missing out on. Should you exploit your current best strategy, or risk exploring new options?

Unlike supervised learning, where training data is conveniently labeled by a "teacher," *reinforcement learning* trains on information gathered by observing how the environment reacts to actions. Reinforcement learning is a type of machine learning that interacts with the environment to learn which combination of actions yields the most favorable results. Because we're already anthropomorphizing algorithms by using the words *environment* and *action*, scholars typically refer to the system as an autonomous *agent*. Therefore, this type of machine learning naturally manifests itself in the domain of robotics.

To reason about agents in the environment, we introduce two new concepts: states and actions. The status of the world frozen at a particular time is called a *state*. An agent may perform one of many *actions* to change the current state. To drive an agent to perform actions, each state yields a corresponding *reward*. An agent eventually discovers the expected total reward of each state, called the *value* of a state.

Like any other machine-learning system, performance improves with more data. In this case, the data is a history of previous experiences. In reinforcement learning, we don't know the final cost or reward of a series of actions until it's executed. These situations render traditional supervised learning ineffective, because we don't know exactly which action in the history of action sequences is to blame for ending up in a low-value state. The only information an agent knows for certain is the cost of a series of actions that it has already taken, which is incomplete. The agent's goal is to find a sequence of actions that maximizes rewards.

EXERCISE 1.4

Would you use supervised, unsupervised, or reinforcement learning to solve the following problems? (a) Organize various fruits in three baskets based on no other information. (b) Predict the weather based on sensor data. (c) Learn to play chess well after many trial-and-error attempts.

ANSWER

(a) Unsupervised, (b) Supervised, (c) Reinforcement

1.5   *TensorFlow*

Google open-sourced its machine-learning framework, TensorFlow, in late 2015 under the Apache 2.0 license. Before that, it was used proprietarily by Google in its speech recognition, Search, Photos, and Gmail, among other applications.

> **A bit of history**
>
> A former scalable distributed training and learning system called DistBelief is the primary influence on TensorFlow's current implementation. Ever written a messy piece of code and wished you could start all over again? That's the dynamic between DistBelief and TensorFlow.

The library is implemented in C++ and has a convenient Python API, as well as a lesser appreciated C++ API. Because of the simpler dependencies, TensorFlow can be quickly deployed to various architectures.

Similar to Theano (a popular numerical computation library for Python you may already be familiar with), computations are described as flowcharts, separating design from implementation. With little-to-no hassle, this dichotomy allows the same design to be implemented on not just large-scale training systems with thousands of processors, but also mobile devices. The single system spans a broad range of platforms.

One of the fanciest properties of TensorFlow is its *automatic differentiation* capabilities. You can experiment with new networks without having to redefine many key calculations.

> **NOTE** Automatic differentiation makes it much easier to implement back-propagation, which is a computationally heavy calculation used in a branch of machine learning called *neural networks*. TensorFlow hides the nitty-gritty details of back-propagation so you can focus on the bigger picture. Chapter 7 covers an introduction to neural networks with TensorFlow.

All the mathematics is abstracted away and unfolded under the hood. It's like using WolframAlpha for a calculus problem set.

Another feature of this library is its interactive visualization environment called *TensorBoard*. This tool shows a flowchart of the way data transforms, displays summary logs over time, and traces performance. Figure 1.9 shows an example of what TensorBoard looks like when in use. The next chapter covers using it in greater detail.

Prototyping in TensorFlow is much faster than in Theano (code initiates in a matter of seconds as opposed to minutes) because many of the operations come precompiled. It becomes easy to debug code due to subgraph execution; an entire segment of computation can be reused without recalculation.

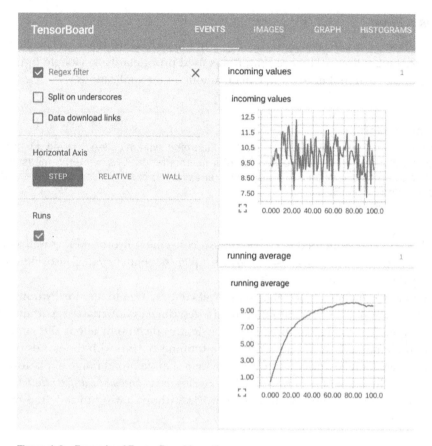

Figure 1.9   Example of TensorBoard in action

Because TensorFlow isn't only about neural networks, it also has out-of-the-box matrix computation and manipulation tools. Most libraries such as Torch and Caffe are designed solely for deep neural networks, but TensorFlow is more flexible as well as scalable.

The library is well documented and officially supported by Google. Machine learning is a sophisticated topic, so having an exceptionally well-reputed company behind TensorFlow is comforting.

1.6   *Overview of future chapters*

Chapter 2 demonstrates how to use various components of TensorFlow (see figure 1.10). Chapters 3–6 show how to implement classic machine-learning algorithms in Tensor-Flow, and chapters 7–12 cover algorithms based on neural networks. The algorithms solve a wide variety of problems such as prediction, classification, clustering, dimensionality reduction, and planning.

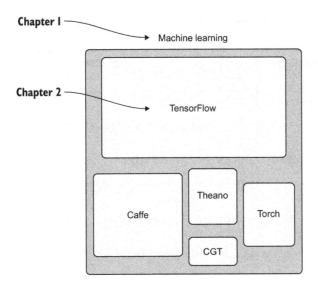

Figure 1.10 This chapter introduced fundamental machine-learning concepts, and the next chapter begins your journey into TensorFlow. Other tools to apply machine-learning algorithms (such as Caffe, Theano, and Torch) are available, but you'll see in chapter 2 why TensorFlow is the way to go.

Many algorithms can solve the same real-world problem, and many real-world problems can be solved by the same algorithm. Table 1.1 covers the ones laid out in this book.

Table 1.1 Many real-world problems can be solved using the corresponding algorithm found in its respective chapter.

Real-world problem	Algorithm	Chapter
Predicting trends, fitting a curve to data points, describing relationships between variables	Linear regression	3
Classifying data into two categories, finding the best way to split a dataset	Logistic regression	4
Classifying data into multiple categories	Softmax regression	4
Revealing hidden causes of observations, finding the most likely hidden reason for a series of outcomes	Hidden Markov model (Viterbi)	5
Clustering data into a fixed number of categories, automatically partitioning data points into separate classes	K-means	6
Clustering data into arbitrary categories, visualizing high-dimensional data into a lower-dimensional embedding	Self-organizing map	6

Table 1.1   Many real-world problems can be solved using the corresponding algorithm found in its respective chapter. *(continued)*

Real-world problem	Algorithm	Chapter
Reducing dimensionality of data, learning latent variables responsible for high-dimensional data	Autoencoder	7
Planning actions in an environment using neural networks (reinforcement learning)	Q-policy neural network	8
Classifying data using supervised neural networks	Perceptron	9
Classifying real-world images using supervised neural networks	Convolution neural network	9
Producing patterns that match observations using neural networks	Recurrent neural network	10
Predicting natural language responses to natural language queries	Seq2seq model	11
Learning to rank items by learning their utility	Ranking	12

TIP   If you're interested in the intricate architecture details of TensorFlow, the best available source is the official documentation at www.tensorflow.org/extend/architecture. This book will sprint ahead and use TensorFlow without slowing down for the breadth of low-level performance tuning. For those interested in cloud services, you may consider Google's solution for professional-grade scale and speed: https://cloud.google.com/products/machine-learning/.

1.7   Summary

- TensorFlow has become the tool of choice among professionals and researchers to implement machine-learning solutions.
- Machine learning uses examples to develop an expert system that can make useful statements about new inputs.
- A key property of ML is that performance tends to improve with more training data.
- Over the years, scholars have crafted three major archetypes that most problems fit: supervised learning, unsupervised learning, and reinforcement learning.
- After a real-world problem is formulated in a machine-learning perspective, several algorithms become available. Out of the many software libraries and frameworks to accomplish an implementation, we chose TensorFlow as our silver bullet. Developed by Google and supported by its flourishing community, TensorFlow gives us a way to easily implement industry-standard code.

TensorFlow essentials

2

This chapter covers

- Understanding the TensorFlow workflow
- Creating interactive notebooks with Jupyter
- Visualizing algorithms by using TensorBoard

Before implementing machine-learning algorithms, let's first get familiarized with how to use TensorFlow. You're going to get your hands dirty writing simple code right away! This chapter covers some essential advantages of TensorFlow to convince you it's the machine-learning library of choice.

As a thought experiment, let's see what happens when we use Python code without a handy computing library. It'll be like using a new smartphone without installing any additional apps. The functionality will be there, but you'd be so much more productive if you had the right tools.

Suppose you're a private business owner tracking the flow of sales for your products. Your inventory consists of 100 items, and you represent each item's price in a vector called `prices`. Another 100-dimensional vector called `amounts` represents the inventory count of each item. You can write the chunk of Python code shown in the following listing to calculate the revenue of selling all products. Keep in mind that this code doesn't import any libraries.

Listing 2.1 Computing the inner product of two vectors without using a library

```
revenue = 0
for price, amount in zip(prices, amounts):
    revenue += price * amount
```

That's a lot of code just to calculate the inner product of two vectors (also known as the *dot product*). Imagine how much code would be required for something more complicated, such as solving linear equations or computing the distance between two vectors.

When installing the TensorFlow library, you also install a well-known and robust Python library called NumPy, which facilitates mathematical manipulation in Python. Using Python without its libraries (NumPy and TensorFlow) is like using a camera without auto mode: you gain more flexibility, but you can easily make careless mistakes (for the record, we have nothing against photographers who micromanage aperture, shutter, and ISO). It's easy to make mistakes in machine learning, so let's keep our camera on autofocus and use TensorFlow to help automate tedious software development.

The following listing shows how to concisely write the same inner product using NumPy.

Listing 2.2 Computing the inner product using NumPy

```
import numpy as np
revenue = np.dot(prices, amounts)
```

Python is a succinct language. Fortunately for you, that means this book doesn't have pages and pages of cryptic code. On the other hand, the brevity of the Python language also implies that a lot is happening behind each line of code, which you should familiarize yourself with carefully as you follow along in this chapter.

Machine-learning algorithms require many mathematical operations. Often, an algorithm boils down to a composition of simple functions iterated until convergence. Sure, you may use any standard programming language to perform these computations, but the secret to both manageable and high-performing code is the use of a well-written library, such as TensorFlow (which officially supports Python and C++).

> **TIP** Detailed documentation about various functions for the Python and C++ APIs are available at www.tensorflow.org/api_docs/.

The skills you learn in this chapter are geared toward using TensorFlow for computations, because machine learning relies on mathematical formulations. After going through the examples and code listings, you'll be able to use TensorFlow for arbitrary tasks, such as computing statistics on big data. The focus here is entirely on how to use TensorFlow, as opposed to machine learning. That sounds like a gentle start, right?

Later in this chapter, you'll use TensorFlow's flagship features that are essential for machine learning. These include representation of computation as a dataflow graph, separation of design and execution, partial subgraph computation, and autodifferentiation. Without further ado, let's write your first TensorFlow code!

2.1 *Ensuring that TensorFlow works*

First, you should ensure that everything is working correctly. Check the oil level in your car, repair the blown fuse in your basement, and ensure that your credit balance is zero. Just kidding; we're talking about TensorFlow.

Before you begin, follow the procedures in the appendix for step-by-step installation instructions. Create a new file called test.py for your first piece of code. Import TensorFlow by running the following script:

```
import tensorflow as tf
```

Having technical difficulty?

An error commonly occurs at this step if you installed the GPU version and the library fails to search for CUDA drivers. Remember, if you compiled the library with CUDA, you need to update your environment variables with the path to CUDA. Check the CUDA instructions on TensorFlow. (See http://mng.bz/QUMh for further information.)

This single import prepares TensorFlow to do your bidding. If the Python interpreter doesn't complain, you're ready to start using TensorFlow!

Sticking with TensorFlow conventions

The TensorFlow library is usually imported with the `tf` alias. Generally, qualifying TensorFlow with `tf` is a good idea to remain consistent with other developers and open source TensorFlow projects. Of course, you may use another alias (or no alias at all), but then successfully reusing other people's snippets of TensorFlow code in your own projects will be an involved process.

2.2   *Representing tensors*

Now that you know how to import TensorFlow into a Python source file, let's start using it! As covered in the previous chapter, a convenient way to describe an object in the real world is through listing its properties, or features. For example, you can describe a car by its color, model, engine type, mileage, and so on. An ordered list of features is called a *feature vector,* and that's exactly what you'll represent in TensorFlow code.

Feature vectors are one of the most useful devices in machine learning because of their simplicity (they're just a list of numbers). Each data item typically consists of a feature vector, and a good dataset has hundreds, if not thousands, of these feature vectors. No doubt, you'll often be dealing with more than one vector at a time. A matrix concisely represents a list of vectors, where each column of a matrix is a feature vector.

The syntax to represent matrices in TensorFlow is a vector of vectors, each of the same length. Figure 2.1 is an example of a matrix with two rows and three columns, such as [[1, 2, 3], [4, 5, 6]]. Notice that this is a vector containing two elements, and each element corresponds to a row of the matrix.

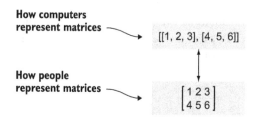

Figure 2.1   The matrix in the lower half of the diagram is a visualization from its compact code notation in the upper half of the diagram. This form of notation is a common paradigm in most scientific computing libraries.

We access an element in a matrix by specifying its row and column indices. For example, the first row and first column indicate the very first top-left element. Sometimes it's convenient to use more than two indices, such as when referencing a pixel in a color image not only by its row and column, but also by its red/green/blue channel. A *tensor* is a generalization of a matrix that specifies an element by an arbitrary number of indices.

Example of a tensor

Suppose an elementary school enforces assigned seating for all its students. You're the principal, and you're terrible with names. Luckily, each classroom has a grid of seats, and you can easily nickname a student by their row and column index.

The school has multiple classrooms, so you can't simply say, "Good morning 4,10! Keep up the good work." You need to also specify the classroom: "Hi 4,10 from classroom 2." Unlike a matrix, which needs only two indices to specify an element, the students in this school need three numbers. They're all a part of a rank-3 tensor!

The syntax for tensors is even more nested vectors. For example, as shown in figure 2.2, a 2 × 3 × 2 tensor is [[[1,2], [3,4], [5,6]], [[7,8], [9,10], [11,12]]], which can be thought of as two matrices, each of size 3 × 2. Consequently, we say this tensor has a *rank* of 3. In general, the rank of a tensor is the number of indices required to specify an element. Machine-learning algorithms in TensorFlow act on tensors, so it's important to understand how to use them.

How a tensor is represented in code — [[[1, 2], [3, 4], [5, 6], [[7, 8], [9, 10], [11, 12]]]

How we visualize a tensor —

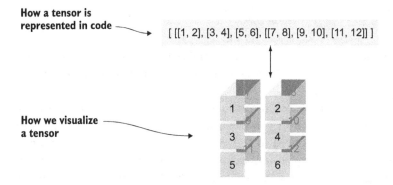

Figure 2.2 This tensor can be thought of as multiple matrices stacked on top of each other. To specify an element, you must indicate the row and column, as well as which matrix is being accessed. Therefore, the rank of this tensor is 3.

It's easy to get lost in the many ways to represent a tensor. Intuitively, three lines of code in listing 2.3 are trying to represent the same 2×2 matrix. This matrix represents two feature vectors of two dimensions each. It could, for example, represent two people's ratings of two movies. Each person, indexed by the row of the matrix, assigns a number to describe their review of the movie, indexed by the column. Run the code to see how to generate a matrix in TensorFlow.

Listing 2.3   Different ways to represent tensors

```
import tensorflow as tf                    You'll use NumPy
import numpy as np                         matrices in TensorFlow.

m1 = [[1.0, 2.0],
      [3.0, 4.0]]

m2 = np.array([[1.0, 2.0],                 Defines a 2 × 2
               [3.0, 4.0]], dtype=np.float32)   matrix in three
                                               ways
m3 = tf.constant([[1.0, 2.0],
                  [3.0, 4.0]])

print(type(m1))         Prints the type
print(type(m2))         for each matrix
print(type(m3))

t1 = tf.convert_to_tensor(m1, dtype=tf.float32)   Creates tensor
t2 = tf.convert_to_tensor(m2, dtype=tf.float32)   objects out of
t3 = tf.convert_to_tensor(m3, dtype=tf.float32)   the various types

print(type(t1))         Notice that the
print(type(t2))         types will be the
print(type(t3))         same now.
```

The first variable (m1) is a list, the second variable (m2) is an ndarray from the NumPy library, and the last variable (m3) is TensorFlow's constant Tensor object that you initialize using tf.constant.

All operators in TensorFlow, such as negative, are designed to operate on tensor objects. A convenient function you can sprinkle anywhere just to make sure you're dealing with tensors as opposed to the other types is tf.convert_to_tensor(...). Most functions in the TensorFlow library already perform this function (redundantly) even if you forget to do so. Using tf.convert_to_tensor(...) is optional, but we show it here because it helps demystify the implicit type system being handled across the library. Listing 2.3 outputs the following three times:

```
<class 'tensorflow.python.framework.ops.Tensor'>
```

> **TIP**   You can find these code listings on the book's website, to make copying and pasting easier: www.manning.com/books/machine-learning-with-tensor-flow.

Let's take another look at defining tensors in code. After importing the TensorFlow library, you can use the `tf.constant` operator as follows. Here are a couple of tensors of various dimensions.

Listing 2.4   Creating tensors

```
import tensorflow as tf

m1 = tf.constant([[1., 2.]])        Defines a
                                    2 × 1 matrix

m2 = tf.constant([[1],              Defines a
                  [2]])             1 × 2 matrix

m3 = tf.constant([ [[1,2],
                    [3,4],
                    [5,6]],
                   [[7,8],
                    [9,10],          Defines a
                    [11,12]] ])      rank-3 tensor

print(m1)               Try printing
print(m2)               the tensors.
print(m3)
```

Running listing 2.4 produces the following output:

```
Tensor( "Const:0",
        shape=TensorShape([Dimension(1), Dimension(2)]),
        dtype=float32 )
Tensor( "Const_1:0",
        shape=TensorShape([Dimension(2), Dimension(1)]),
        dtype=int32 )
Tensor( "Const_2:0",
        shape=TensorShape([Dimension(2), Dimension(3), Dimension(2)]),
        dtype=int32 )
```

As you can see from the output, each tensor is represented by the aptly named `Tensor` object. Each `Tensor` object has a unique label (name), a dimension (shape) to define its structure, and a data type (dtype) to specify the kind of values you'll manipulate. Because you didn't explicitly provide a name, the library automatically generated the names: `Const:0`, `Const_1:0`, and `Const_2:0`.

Tensor types

Notice that each element of `m1` ends with a decimal point. The decimal point tells Python that the data type of the elements isn't an integer, but instead a float. You can pass in explicit `dtype` values. Much like NumPy arrays, tensors take on a data type that specifies the kind of values you'll manipulate in that tensor.

TensorFlow also comes with a few convenient constructors for some simple tensors. For example, tf.zeros(shape) creates a tensor with all values initialized at zero of a specific shape. Similarly, tf.ones(shape) creates a tensor of a specific shape with all values initialized at once. The shape argument is a one-dimensional (1D) tensor of type int32 (a list of integers) describing the dimensions of the tensor.

EXERCISE 2.1

Initialize a 500 × 500 tensor with all elements equaling 0.5.

ANSWER

```
tf.ones([500,500]) * 0.5
```

2.3   *Creating operators*

Now that you have a few starting tensors ready to be used, you can apply more-interesting operators such as addition or multiplication. Consider each row of a matrix representing the transaction of money to (positive value) and from (negative value) another person. Negating the matrix is a way to represent the transaction history of the other person's flow of money. Let's start simple and run a negation op (short for *operation*) on the m1 tensor from listing 2.4. Negating a matrix turns the positive numbers into negative numbers of the same magnitude, and vice versa.

Negation is one of the simplest operations. As shown in listing 2.5, negation takes only one tensor as input, and produces a tensor with every element negated. Try running the code. If you master how to define negation, it'll provide a stepping stone to generalize that skill to all other TensorFlow operations.

NOTE *Defining* an operation, such as negation, is different from *running* it. So far, you've *defined* how operations should behave. In section 2.4, you'll *evaluate* (or *run*) them to compute their value.

Listing 2.5   Using the negation operator

```
import tensorflow as tf

x = tf.constant([[1, 2]])        Defines an arbitrary tensor
negMatrix = tf.negative(x)       Negates the tensor
print(negMatrix)                 Prints the object
```

Listing 2.5 generates the following output:

```
Tensor("Neg:0", shape=TensorShape([Dimension(1), Dimension(2)]), dtype=int32)
```

Notice that the output isn't [[-1, -2]]. That's because you're printing out the definition of the negation op, not the actual evaluation of the op. The printed output shows that the negation op is a `Tensor` class with a name, shape, and data type. The name was automatically assigned, but you could've provided it explicitly as well when using the `tf.negative` op in listing 2.5. Similarly, the shape and data type were inferred from the `[[1, 2]]` that you passed in.

Useful TensorFlow operators

The official documentation carefully lays out all available math ops: www.tensorflow .org/api_guides/python/math_ops. Specific examples of commonly used operators include the following:

`tf.add(x, y)`—Adds two tensors of the same type, $x + y$

`tf.subtract(x, y)`—Subtracts tensors of the same type, $x - y$

`tf.multiply(x, y)`—Multiplies two tensors element-wise

`tf.pow(x, y)`—Takes the element-wise x to the power of y

`tf.exp(x)`—Equivalent to $pow(e, x)$, where e is Euler's number (2.718 ...)

`tf.sqrt(x)`—Equivalent to $pow(x, 0.5)$

`tf.div(x, y)`—Takes the element-wise division of x and y

`tf.truediv(x, y)`—Same as `tf.div`, except casts the arguments as a float

`tf.floordiv(x, y)`—Same as `truediv`, except rounds down the final answer into an integer

`tf.mod(x, y)`—Takes the element-wise remainder from division

EXERCISE 2.2

Use the TensorFlow operators you've learned so far to produce the Gaussian distribution (also known as the normal distribution). See figure 2.3 for a hint. For reference, you can find the probability density of the normal distribution online: https://en.wikipedia.org/wiki/Normal_distribution.

ANSWER

Most mathematical expressions such as ×, –, +, and so on are just shortcuts for their TensorFlow equivalent, for brevity. The Gaussian function includes many operations, so it's cleaner to use shorthand notations as follows:

```
from math import pi
mean = 0.0
sigma = 1.0
(tf.exp(tf.negative(tf.pow(x - mean, 2.0) /
        (2.0 * tf.pow(sigma, 2.0) ))) *
  (1.0 / (sigma * tf.sqrt(2.0 * pi) )))
```

2.4 Executing operators with sessions

A *session* is an environment of a software system that describes how the lines of code should run. In TensorFlow, a session sets up how the hardware devices (such as CPU and GPU) talk to each other. That way, you can design your machine-learning algorithm without worrying about micromanaging the hardware it runs on. You can later configure the session to change its behavior without changing a line of the machine-learning code.

To execute an operation and retrieve its calculated value, TensorFlow requires a session. Only a registered session may fill the values of a `Tensor` object. To do so, you must create a session class by using `tf.Session()` and tell it to run an operator, as shown in the following listing. The result will be a value you can later use for further computations.

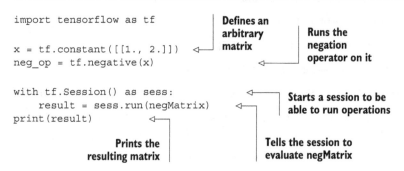

Listing 2.6 Using a session

```
import tensorflow as tf                    Defines an
                                           arbitrary        Runs the
                                           matrix           negation
x = tf.constant([[1., 2.]])  ⟵                              operator on it
neg_op = tf.negative(x)                        ⟵

with tf.Session() as sess:                          ⟵      Starts a session to be
    result = sess.run(negMatrix)        ⟵                  able to run operations
print(result)                    ⟵

            Prints the                         Tells the session to
            resulting matrix                   evaluate negMatrix
```

Congratulations! You've just written your first full TensorFlow code. Although all it does is negate a matrix to produce `[[-1, -2]]`, the core overhead and framework are just the same as everything else in TensorFlow. A session not only configures *where* your code will be computed on your machine, but also crafts *how* the computation will be laid out in order to parallelize computation.

Code performance seems a bit slow

You may have noticed that running your code took a few more seconds than expected. It may appear unnatural that TensorFlow takes seconds to negate a small matrix. But substantial preprocessing occurs to optimize the library for larger and more complicated computations.

Every `Tensor` object has an `eval()` function to evaluate the mathematical operations that define its value. But the `eval()` function requires defining a session object for the library to understand how to best use the underlying hardware. In listing 2.6, we used sess.run(…), which is equivalent to invoking the Tensor's eval() function in the context of the session.

When you're running TensorFlow code through an interactive environment (for debugging or presentation purposes), it's often easier to create the session in interactive mode, where the session is implicitly part of any call to eval(). That way, the session variable doesn't need to be passed around throughout the code, making it easier to focus on the relevant parts of the algorithm, as seen in the following listing.

Listing 2.7   Using the interactive session mode

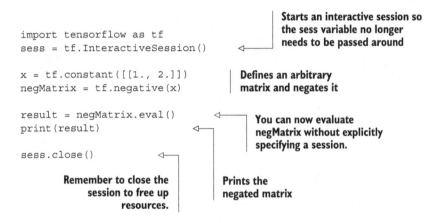

```
import tensorflow as tf
sess = tf.InteractiveSession()
```
Starts an interactive session so the sess variable no longer needs to be passed around

```
x = tf.constant([[1., 2.]])
negMatrix = tf.negative(x)
```
Defines an arbitrary matrix and negates it

```
result = negMatrix.eval()
print(result)
```
You can now evaluate negMatrix without explicitly specifying a session.

```
sess.close()
```
Remember to close the session to free up resources.

Prints the negated matrix

2.4.1   *Understanding code as a graph*

Consider a doctor who predicts the expected weight of a newborn to be 7.5 pounds. You'd like to figure out how that differs from the actual measured weight. Being an overly analytical engineer, you design a function to describe the likelihood of all possible weights of the newborn. For example, 8 pounds is more likely than 10 pounds.

You can choose to use the Gaussian (otherwise known as normal) probability distribution function. It takes as input a number, and outputs a non-negative number describing the probability of observing the input. This function shows up all the time in machine learning and is easy to define in TensorFlow. It uses multiplication, division, negation, and a couple of other fundamental operators.

Think of every operator as a node in a graph. Whenever you see a plus symbol (+) or any mathematical concept, just picture it as one of many nodes. The edges between these nodes represent the composition of mathematical functions. Specifically, the negative operator we've been studying is a node, and the incoming/outgoing edges of this node are how the Tensor transforms. A tensor flows through the graph, which is why this library is called TensorFlow!

Here's a thought: every operator is a strongly typed function that takes input tensors of a dimension and produces output of the same dimension. Figure 2.3 is an example of how the Gaussian function can be designed using TensorFlow. The function is represented as a graph in which operators are nodes and edges represent interactions between nodes. This graph, as a whole, represents a complicated mathematical function (specifically, the Gaussian function). Small segments of the graph represent simple mathematical concepts, such as negation or doubling.

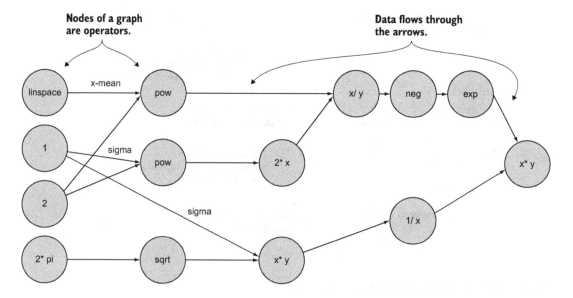

Figure 2.3   The graph represents the operations needed to produce a Gaussian distribution. The links between the nodes represent how data flows from one operation to the next. The operations themselves are simple, but the complexity arises from the way they intertwine.

TensorFlow algorithms are easy to visualize. They can be simply described by flowcharts. The technical (and more correct) term for such a flowchart is a *dataflow graph*. Every arrow in a dataflow graph is called an *edge*. In addition, every state of the dataflow graph is called a *node*. The purpose of the session is to interpret your Python code into a dataflow graph, and then associate the computation of each node of the graph to the CPU or GPU.

2.4.2   Setting session configurations

You can also pass options to tf.Session. For example, TensorFlow automatically determines the best way to assign a GPU or CPU device to an operation, depending on what's available. You can pass an additional option, log_device_placements=True, when creating a session, as shown in the following listing, which will show you exactly where on your hardware the computations are evoked.

Listing 2.8 Logging a session

```
import tensorflow as tf

x = tf.constant([[1., 2.]])            Defines a matrix
negMatrix = tf.negative(x)             and negates it

with tf.Session(config=tf.ConfigProto(log_device_placement=True)) as sess:   ◄──
    result = sess.run(negMatrix)   ◄──

print(result)   ◄──
```

Starts the session with a special config passed into the constructor to enable logging

Evaluates negMatrix

Prints the resulting value

This outputs info about which CPU/GPU devices are used in the session for each operation. For example, running listing 2.8 results in traces of output like the following to show which device was used to run the negation op:

```
Neg: /job:localhost/replica:0/task:0/cpu:0
```

Sessions are essential in TensorFlow code. You need to call a session to "run" the math. Figure 2.4 maps out how the components on TensorFlow interact with the machine-learning pipeline. A session not only runs a graph operation, but also can take placeholders, variables, and constants as input. We've used constants so far, but in later sections we'll start using variables and placeholders. Here's a quick overview of these three types of values:

- *Placeholder*—A value that's unassigned but will be initialized by the session wherever it's run. Typically, placeholders are the input and output of your model.
- *Variable*—A value that can change, such as parameters of a machine-learning model. Variables must be initialized by the session before they're used.
- *Constant*—A value that doesn't change, such as hyperparameters or settings.

The entire pipeline for machine learning with TensorFlow follows the flow of figure 2.4. Most of the code in TensorFlow consists of setting up the graph and session. After you design a graph and hook up the session to execute it, your code is ready to use!

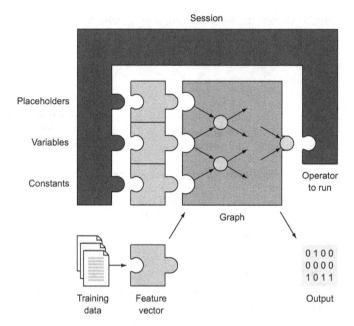

Session

Placeholders

Variables

Constants

Operator
to run

Graph

Training
data

Feature
vector

0 1 0 0
0 0 0 0
1 0 1 1

Output

**Figure 2.4   The session dictates how the hardware will be used to
process the graph most efficiently. When the session starts, it assigns
the CPU and GPU devices to each of the nodes. After processing, the
session outputs data in a usable format, such as a NumPy array.
A session optionally may be fed placeholders, variables, and constants.**

2.5   *Writing code in Jupyter*

Because TensorFlow is primarily a Python library, you should make full use of Python's interpreter. *Jupyter* is a mature environment for exercising the interactive nature of the language. It's a web application that displays computation elegantly so that you can share annotated interactive algorithms with others to teach a technique or demonstrate code.

You can share your Jupyter notebooks with others to exchange ideas and download others' to learn about their code. See the appendix to get started with installing the Jupyter Notebook.

From a new terminal, change the directory to the location where you want to practice TensorFlow code, and start a notebook server:

```
$ cd ~/MyTensorFlowStuff
$ jupyter notebook
```

Running this command should launch a new browser window with the Jupyter Notebook dashboard. If no window automatically opens, you can manually navigate to http://localhost:8888 from any browser. You'll see a web page similar to the one in figure 2.5.

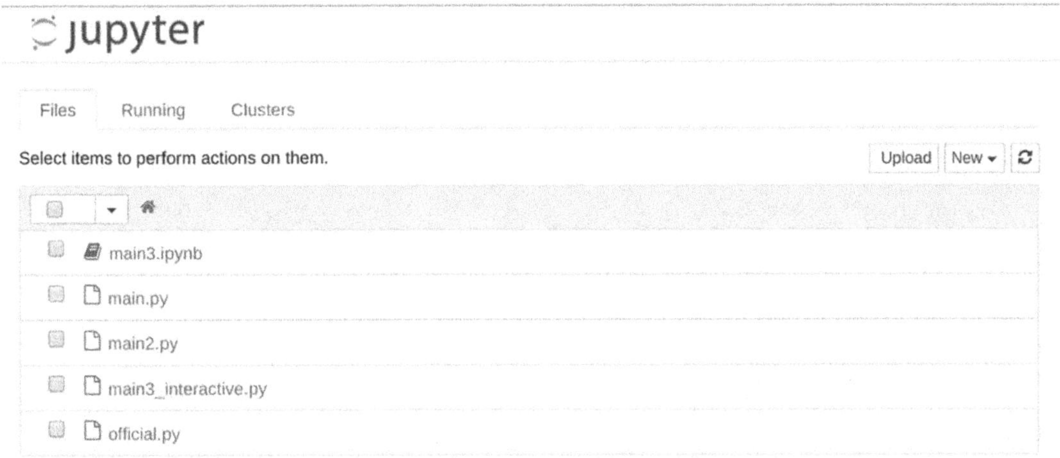

Figure 2.5   Running the Jupyter Notebook will launch an interactive notebook on http://localhost:8888.

Create a new notebook by clicking the New drop-down menu at upper right; then choose Notebooks > Python 3. This creates a new file called Untitled.ipynb, which you can immediately start editing through the browser interface. You can change the name of the notebook by clicking the current Untitled name and typing in something more memorable, such as TensorFlow Example Notebook.

Everything in the Jupyter Notebook is an independent chunk of code or text called a *cell*. Cells help divide a long block of code into manageable pieces of code snippets and documentation. You can run cells individually, or choose to run everything at once, in order. There are three common ways to evaluate cells:

- Pressing Shift-Enter on a cell executes the cell and highlights the next cell below.
- Pressing Ctrl-Enter maintains the cursor on the current cell after executing it.
- Pressing Alt-Enter executes the cell and then inserts a new empty cell directly below.

You can change the cell type by clicking the drop-down in the toolbar, as shown in figure 2.6. Alternatively, you can press Esc to leave edit mode, use the arrow keys to highlight a cell, and press Y to change to code mode or M for markdown mode.

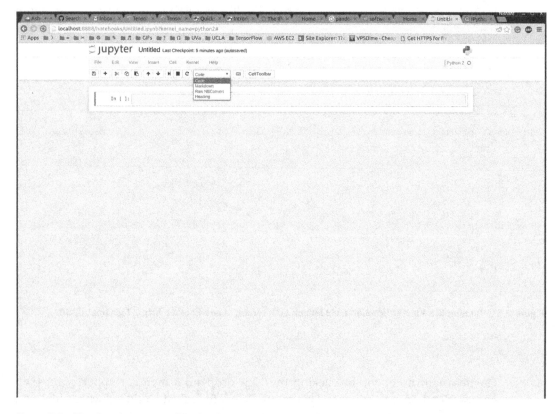

Figure 2.6   The drop-down menu changes the type of cell in the notebook. The Code cell is for Python code, whereas the Markdown code is for text descriptions.

Finally, you can create a Jupyter notebook that elegantly demonstrates TensorFlow code by interlacing code and text cells as shown in figure 2.7.

EXERCISE 2.3
If you look closely at figure 2.7, you'll notice that it uses `tf.neg` instead of `tf.neg-ative`. That's strange. Could you explain why we might have done that?

ANSWER
You should be aware that the TensorFlow library changed naming conventions, and you may run into these artifacts when following old TensorFlow tutorials online.

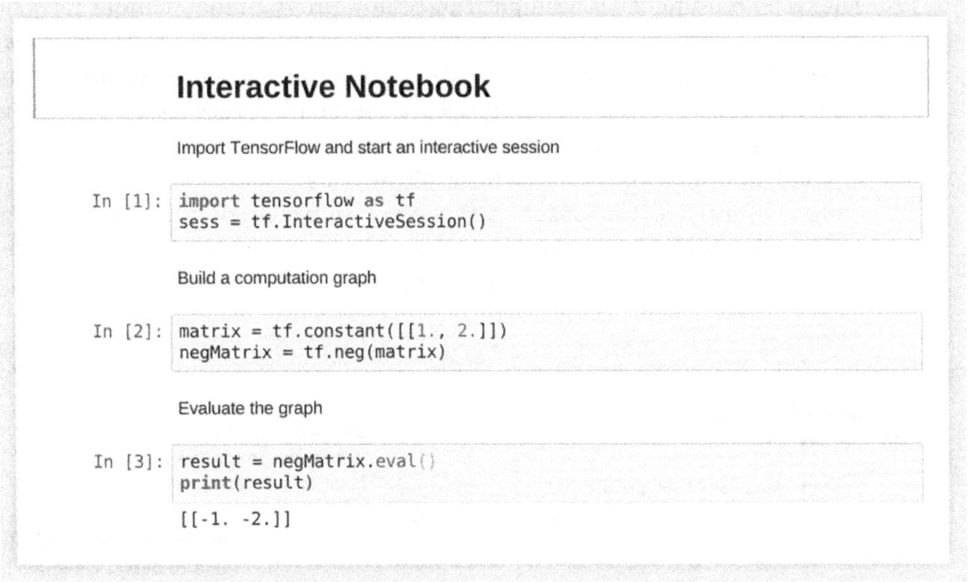

```
                    Interactive Notebook

          Import TensorFlow and start an interactive session

In [1]:   import tensorflow as tf
          sess = tf.InteractiveSession()


          Build a computation graph

In [2]:   matrix = tf.constant([[1., 2.]])
          negMatrix = tf.neg(matrix)


          Evaluate the graph

In [3]:   result = negMatrix.eval()
          print(result)

          [[-1. -2.]]
```

Figure 2.7   An interactive Python notebook presents both code and comments grouped for readability.

2.6   *Using variables*

Using TensorFlow constants is a good start, but most interesting applications require data to change. For example, a neuroscientist may be interested in detecting neural activity from sensor measurements. A spike in neural activity could be a Boolean variable that changes over time. To capture this in TensorFlow, you can use the `Variable` class to represent a node whose value changes over time.

Example of using a Variable object in machine learning

Finding the equation of a line that best fits many points is a classic machine-learning problem that's discussed in greater detail in the next chapter. The algorithm starts with an initial guess, which is an equation characterized by a few numbers (such as the slope or y-intercept). Over time, the algorithm generates increasingly better guesses for these numbers, which are also called *parameters*.

So far, we've been manipulating only constants. Programs with only constants aren't that interesting for real-world applications, so TensorFlow allows richer tools such as variables, which are containers for values that may change over time. A machine-learning algorithm updates the parameters of a model until it finds the optimal value for each variable. In the world of machine learning, it's common for parameters to fluctuate until eventually settling down, making variables an excellent data structure for them.

The code in listing 2.9 is a simple TensorFlow program that demonstrates how to use variables. It updates a variable whenever sequential data abruptly increases in value. Think about recording measurements of a neuron's activity over time. This piece of code can detect when the neuron's activity suddenly spikes. Of course, the algorithm is an oversimplification for didactic purposes.

Start with importing TensorFlow. TensorFlow allows you to declare a session by using `tf.InteractiveSession()`. When you've declared an interactive session, TensorFlow functions don't require the session attribute they would otherwise, which makes coding in Jupyter Notebooks easier.

Listing 2.9   Using a variable

Let's say you have some raw data like this.

Starts the session in interactive mode so you won't need to pass around sess

```
import tensorflow as tf
sess = tf.InteractiveSession()
```

Creates a Boolean variable called spike to detect a sudden increase in a series of numbers

```
raw_data = [1., 2., 8., -1., 0., 5.5, 6., 13]
spike = tf.Variable(False)
spike.initializer.run()
```

Because all variables must be initialized, initialize the variable by calling run() on its initializer.

```
for i in range(1, len(raw_data)):
    if raw_data[i] - raw_data[i-1] > 5:
        updater = tf.assign(spike, True)
        updater.eval()
    else:
        tf.assign(spike, False).eval()
    print("Spike", spike.eval())

sess.close()
```

To update a variable, assign it a new value using tf.assign(<var name>, <new value>). Evaluate it to see the change.

Remember to close the session after it'll no longer be used.

Loops through the data (skipping the first element) and updates the spike variable when there's a significant increase

The expected output of listing 2.9 is a list of spike values over time:

```
('Spike', False)
('Spike', True)
('Spike', False)
('Spike', False)
('Spike', True)
('Spike', False)
('Spike', True)
```

2.7 Saving and loading variables

Imagine writing a monolithic block of code, of which you'd like to individually test a tiny segment. In complicated machine-learning situations, saving and loading data at known checkpoints makes it much easier to debug code. TensorFlow provides an elegant interface to save and load variable values to disk; let's see how to use it for that purpose.

Let's revamp the code that you created in listing 2.9 to save the spike data to disk so you can load it elsewhere. You'll change the spike variable from a simple Boolean to a vector of Booleans that captures the history of spikes (listing 2.10). Notice that you'll explicitly name the variables so they can be loaded later with the same name. Naming a variable is optional but highly encouraged to organize your code.

Try running this code to see the results.

Listing 2.10   Saving variables

Defines a Boolean vector called spikes to locate a sudden spike in raw data

Imports TensorFlow and enables interactive sessions

```
import tensorflow as tf
sess = tf.InteractiveSession()
```

Let's say you have a series of data like this.

```
raw_data = [1., 2., 8., -1., 0., 5.5, 6., 13]
spikes = tf.Variable([False] * len(raw_data), name='spikes')
spikes.initializer.run()
```

Don't forget to initialize the variable.

```
saver = tf.train.Saver()
```

Loop through the data and update the spikes variable when there's a significant increase.

```
for i in range(1, len(raw_data)):
    if raw_data[i] - raw_data[i-1] > 5:
        spikes_val = spikes.eval()
        spikes_val[i] = True
        updater = tf.assign(spikes, spikes_val)
        updater.eval()
```

Updates the value of spikes by using the tf.assign function

Don't forget to evaluate the updater; otherwise, spikes won't be updated.

```
save_path = saver.save(sess, "spikes.ckpt")
print("spikes data saved in file: %s" % save_path)
```

Saves the variable to disk

Prints out the relative file path of the saved variables

```
sess.close()
```

The saver op will enable saving and restoring variables. If no dictionary is passed into the constructor, then it saves all variables in the current program.

You'll notice a couple of files generated, one of them being spikes.ckpt, in the same directory as your source code. It's a compactly stored binary file, so you can't easily modify it with a text editor. To retrieve this data, you can use the `restore` function from the `saver` op, as demonstrated in the following listing.

Listing 2.11   Loading variables

```
import tensorflow as tf
sess = tf.InteractiveSession()


spikes = tf.Variable([False]*8, name='spikes')
# spikes.initializer.run()
saver = tf.train.Saver()


saver.restore(sess, "./spikes.ckpt")
print(spikes.eval())


sess.close()
```

Creates a variable of the same size and name as the saved data

You no longer need to initialize this variable because it'll be directly loaded.

Creates the saver op to restore saved data

Restores data from the spikes.ckpt file

Prints the loaded data

2.8   *Visualizing data using TensorBoard*

In machine learning, the most time-consuming part isn't programming, but it's waiting for code to finish running. For example, a famous dataset called ImageNet contains over 14 million images prepared to be used in a machine-learning context. Sometimes it can take up to days or weeks to finish training an algorithm using a large dataset. TensorFlow's handy dashboard, TensorBoard, affords you a quick peek into the way values are changing in each node of the graph, giving you some idea of how your code is performing.

Let's see how to visualize variable trends over time in a real-world example. In this section, you'll implement a moving-average algorithm in TensorFlow, and then you'll carefully track the variables you care about for visualization in TensorBoard.

2.8.1   *Implementing a moving average*

In this section, you'll use TensorBoard to visualize how data changes. Suppose you're interested in calculating the average stock price of a company. Typically, computing the average is just a matter of adding up all the values and dividing by the total number seen: mean = $(x_1 + x_2 + ... + x_n)$ / n. When the total number of values is unknown, you can use a technique called *exponential averaging* to estimate the average value of an unknown number of data points. The exponential average algorithm calculates the current estimated average as a function of the previous estimated average and the current value.

More succinctly, $Avg_t = f(Avg_{t-1}, x_t) = (1 - \alpha)\ Avg_{t-1} + \alpha\ x_t$. Alpha ($\alpha$) is a parameter that will be tuned, representing how strongly recent values should be biased in the calculation of the average. The higher the value of α, the more dramatically the calculated average will differ from the previously estimated average. Figure 2.8 (shown after listing 2.16) shows how TensorBoard visualizes the values and corresponding running average over time.

When you code this, it's a good idea to think about the main piece of computation that takes place in each iteration. In this case, each iteration will compute $Avg_t = (1 - \alpha)$ $Avg_{t-1} + \alpha\ x_t$. As a result, you can design a TensorFlow operator (listing 2.12) that does exactly as the formula says. To run this code, you'll have to eventually define `alpha`, `curr_value`, and `prev_avg`.

Listing 2.12 Defining the average update operator

```
update_avg = alpha * curr_value + (1 - alpha) * prev_avg          ⟵───┐
                                                                       │
                          alpha is a tf.constant, curr_value is a      │
                          placeholder, and prev_avg is a variable.     │
```

You'll define the undefined variables later. The reason you're writing code in such a backward way is that defining the interface first forces you to implement the peripheral setup code to satisfy the interface. Skipping ahead, let's jump right to the session part to see how your algorithm should behave. The following listing sets up the primary loop and calls the `update_avg` operator on each iteration. Running the `update_avg` operator depends on the `curr_value`, which is fed using the `feed_dict` argument.

Listing 2.13 Running iterations of the exponential average algorithm

```
raw_data = np.random.normal(10, 1, 100)

with tf.Session() as sess:
    for i in range(len(raw_data)):
        curr_avg = sess.run(update_avg, feed_dict={curr_value:raw_data[i]})
        sess.run(tf.assign(prev_avg, curr_avg))
```

Great, the general picture is clear, because all that's left to do is to write out the undefined variables. Let's fill in the gaps and implement a working piece of TensorFlow code. Copy the following listing so you can run it.

Listing 2.14   **Filling in missing code to complete the exponential average algorithm**

```
import tensorflow as tf
import numpy as np

raw_data = np.random.normal(10, 1, 100)

alpha = tf.constant(0.05)
curr_value = tf.placeholder(tf.float32)
prev_avg = tf.Variable(0.)
update_avg = alpha * curr_value + (1 - alpha) * prev_avg

init = tf.global_variables_initializer()

with tf.Session() as sess:
    sess.run(init)
    for i in range(len(raw_data)):
        curr_avg = sess.run(update_avg, feed_dict={curr_value: raw_data[i]})
        sess.run(tf.assign(prev_avg, curr_avg))
        print(raw_data[i], curr_avg)
```

Creates a vector of 100 numbers with a mean of 10 and standard deviation of 1

Defines alpha as a constant

Initializes the previous average to zero

Loops through the data one by one to update the average

A placeholder is just like a variable, but the value is injected from the session.

2.8.2   *Visualizing the moving average*

Now that you have a working implementation of a moving-average algorithm, let's visualize the results by using TensorBoard. Visualization using TensorBoard is usually a two-step process:

1. Pick out which nodes you care about measuring by annotating them with a *summary op*.
2. Call add_summary on them to queue up data to be written to disk.

For example, let's say you have an img placeholder and a cost op, as shown in the following listing. You can annotate them (by giving each a name such as img or cost) so that they're capable of being visualized in TensorBoard. You'll do something similar with your moving-average example.

Listing 2.15   **Annotating with a summary op**

```
img = tf.placeholder(tf.float32, [None, None, None, 3])
cost = tf.reduce_sum(...)

my_img_summary = tf.summary.image("img", img)
my_cost_summary = tf.summary.scalar("cost", cost)
```

More generally, to communicate with TensorBoard, you must use a summary op, which produces serialized strings used by a SummaryWriter to save updates to a directory.

Every time you call the add_summary method from SummaryWriter, TensorFlow will save data to disk for TensorBoard to use.

> **WARNING** Be careful not to call the add_summary function too often! Although doing so will produce higher-resolution visualizations of your variables, it'll be at the cost of more computation and slightly slower learning.

Run the following command to make a directory called logs in the same folder as this source code:

```
$ mkdir logs
```

Run TensorBoard with the location of the logs directory passed in as an argument:

```
$ tensorboard --logdir=./logs
```

Open a browser and navigate to http://localhost:6006, which is the default URL for TensorBoard. The following listing shows how to hook up the SummaryWriter to your code. Run it and refresh the TensorBoard to see the visualizations.

Listing 2.16 Writing summaries to view in TensorBoard

```
import tensorflow as tf
import numpy as np


raw_data = np.random.normal(10, 1, 100)              Creates a
                                                   summary node
                                                   for the averages
alpha = tf.constant(0.05)
curr_value = tf.placeholder(tf.float32)                           Creates a
prev_avg = tf.Variable(0.)                                        summary
update_avg = alpha * curr_value + (1 - alpha) * prev_avg          node for
                                                                 the values
avg_hist = tf.summary.scalar("running_average", update_avg)   ◁
value_hist = tf.summary.scalar("incoming_values", curr_value)   ◁
merged = tf.summary.merge_all()                     ◁
writer = tf.summary.FileWriter("./logs")         ◁      Merges the summaries
init = tf.global_variables_initializer()                to make it easier to
                                                        run all at once
with tf.Session() as sess:
    sess.run(init)
    sess.add_graph(sess.graph)                  Passes in the logs directory's
    for i in range(len(raw_data)):              location to the writer

Optional, but allows you to
visualize the computation
graph in TensorBoard
```

```
summary_str, curr_avg = sess.run([merged, update_avg],
    feed_dict={curr_value: raw_data[i]})
sess.run(tf.assign(prev_avg, curr_avg))
print(raw_data[i], curr_avg)
writer.add_summary(summary_str, i)
```

Runs the merged op and the update_avg op at the same time

Adds the summary to the writer

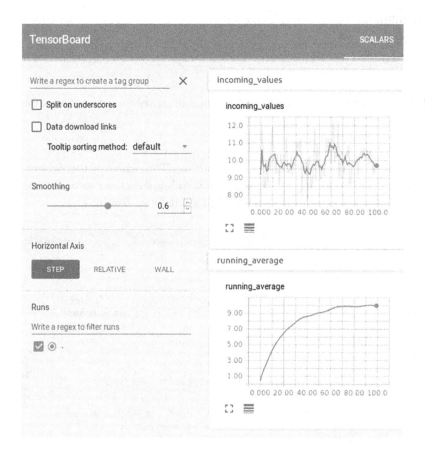

Figure 2.8 The summary display in TensorBoard created in listing 2.16. TensorBoard provides a user-friendly interface to visualize data produced in TensorFlow.

TIP You may need to ensure that the TensorFlow session has ended before starting TensorBoard. If you rerun listing 2.16, you'll need to remember to clear the logs directory.

2.9 *Summary*

- You should start thinking of mathematical algorithms in terms of a flowchart of computation. When you consider each node as an operation, and edges as data flow, writing TensorFlow code becomes trivial. After you define your graph, you evaluate it under a session, and you have your result.

- No doubt, there's more to TensorFlow than representing computations as a graph. As you'll see in the coming chapters, some of the built-in functions are tailored to the field of machine learning. In fact, TensorFlow has some of the best support for convolutional neural networks, a currently popular type of model for processing images (with promising results in audio and text as well).

- TensorBoard provides an easy way to visualize the way data changes in Tensor-Flow code as well as troubleshoot bugs by inspecting trends in data.

- TensorFlow works wonderfully with Jupyter notebooks, which are an elegant interactive medium for sharing and documenting Python code.

Part 2

Core learning algorithms

When former US President Barack Obama said, "You can put lipstick on a pig, but it's still a pig," he wasn't referring to how most complex ideas in machine learning boil down to just a few foundational ideas, but he might as well have been. For example, the core algorithms are regression, classification, clustering, and hidden Markov models. The concepts are each detailed in their respective chapters, in the order listed.

After you master these four chapters, you'll see how most real-world problems can be solved using similar techniques. What were once foreign or unintuitive complications can now be untangled using the formulations from these core learning algorithms.

Linear regression
and beyond

3

This chapter covers

- Fitting a line to data points
- Fitting arbitrary curves to data points
- Testing performance of regression algorithms
- Applying regression to real-world data

Remember science courses back in high school? It might have been a while ago, or who knows—maybe you're in high school now, starting your journey in machine learning early. Either way, whether you took biology, chemistry, or physics, a common technique to analyze data is to plot how changing one variable affects another.

Imagine plotting the correlation between rainfall frequency and agriculture production. You may observe that an increase in rainfall produces an increase in agriculture production rate. Fitting a line to these data points enables you to make predictions about the production rate under different rain conditions. If you discover the underlying function from a few data points, then that learned function empowers you to make predictions about the values of unseen data.

Regression is a study of how to best fit a curve to summarize your data. It's one of the most powerful and well-studied types of supervised-learning algorithms. In regression, we try to understand the data points by discovering the curve that might have generated them. In doing so, we seek an explanation for why the given data is scattered the way it is. The best-fit curve gives us a model for explaining how the dataset might have been produced.

This chapter shows you how to formulate a real-world problem to use regression. As you'll see, TensorFlow is just the right tool that delivers some of the most powerful predictors.

3.1   *Formal notation*

If you have a hammer, every problem looks like a nail. This chapter demonstrates the first major machine-learning tool, regression, and formally defines it by using precise mathematical symbols. Learning regression first is a great idea, because many of the skills you'll develop will carry over to other types of problems in future chapters. By the end of this chapter, regression will become the "hammer" in your box of machine-learning tools.

Let's say you have data about how much money people spent on bottles of beer. Alice spent $4 on 2 bottles, Bob spent $6 on 3 bottles, and Clair spent $8 on 4 bottles. You want to find an equation that describes how the number of bottles affects the total cost. For example, if the linear equation $y = 2x$ describes the cost of buying a particular number of bottles, then you can find out how much each bottle of beer costs.

When a line appears to fit some data points well, you might claim that your linear model performs well. But you could have tried out many possible slopes instead of choosing the value 2. The choice of slope is the *parameter*, and the equation containing the parameter is the *model*. Speaking in machine-learning terms, the equation of the best-fit curve comes from learning the parameters of a model.

As another example, the equation $y = 3x$ is also a line, except with a steeper slope. You can replace that coefficient with any real number, let's call it w, and the equation will still produce a line: $y = wx$. Figure 3.1 shows how changing the parameter w affects the model. The set of all equations you can generate this way is denoted as $M = \{y = wx \mid w \in \mathbb{R}\}$. This is read, "All equations $y = wx$ such that w is a real number."

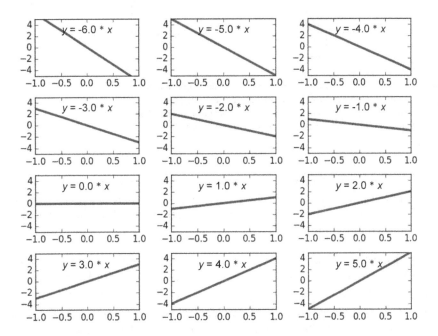

Figure 3.1 Different values of the parameter w result in different linear equations. The set of all these linear equations is what constitutes the linear model M.

M is a set of all possible models. Choosing a value for w generates a candidate model $M(w) : y = wx$. The regression algorithms that you'll write in TensorFlow will iteratively converge to progressively better values for the model's parameter w. An optimal parameter, let's call it w^* (pronounced w *star*), is the best-fit equation $M(w^*): y = w^*x$.

In the most general sense, a regression algorithm tries to design a function, let's call it f, that maps an input to an output. The function's domain is a real-valued vector $\mathbb{R}^d$, and its range is the set of real numbers $\mathbb{R}$.

NOTE   Regression can also be posed with multiple outputs, as opposed to just one real number. In that case, we call it *multivariate regression.*

The input of the function could be continuous or discrete. But the output must be continuous, as demonstrated in figure 3.2.

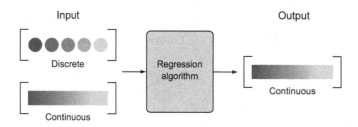

Figure 3.2   A regression algorithm is meant to produce continuous output. The input is allowed to be discrete or continuous. This distinction is important because discrete-valued outputs are handled better by classification, which is discussed in the next chapter.

NOTE   Regression predicts continuous outputs, but sometimes that's overkill. Sometimes we just want to predict a discrete output, such as 0 or 1, but nothing in between. Classification is a technique better suited for such tasks, and it's discussed in chapter 4.

We'd like to discover a function f that agrees well with the given data points, which are essentially input/output pairs. Unfortunately, the number of possible functions is infinite, so we'll have no luck trying them out one by one. Having too many options available to choose from is usually a bad idea. It behooves us to tighten the scope of all the functions we want to deal with. For example, if we look at only straight lines to fit a set of data points, the search becomes much easier.

EXERCISE 3.1
How many possible functions exist that map 10 integers to 10 integers? For example, let $f(x)$ be a function that can take numbers 0 through 9 and produce numbers 0 through 9. One example is the identity function that mimics its input—for example, $f(0) = 0$, $f(1) = 1$, and so on. How many other functions exist?

ANSWER
$10^{10} = 10,000,000,000$

3.1.1 *How do you know the regression algorithm is working?*

Let's say you're trying to sell a housing-market-predictor algorithm to a real estate firm. The algorithm predicts housing prices given properties such as the number of bedrooms and lot size. Real estate companies can easily make millions with such information, but they need some proof that the algorithm works before buying it from you.

To measure the success of the learning algorithm, you'll need to understand two important concepts, variance and bias:

- *Variance* indicates how sensitive a prediction is to the training set that was used. Ideally, how you choose the training set shouldn't matter—meaning a lower variance is desired.
- *Bias* indicates the strength of assumptions made about the training dataset. Making too many assumptions might make the model unable to generalize, so you should prefer low bias as well.

If a model is too flexible, it may accidentally memorize the training data instead of resolving useful patterns. You can imagine a curvy function passing through every point of a dataset, appearing to produce no error. If that happens, we say the learning algorithm *overfits* the data. In this case, the best-fit curve will agree with the training data well; but it may perform abysmally when evaluated on the testing data (see figure 3.3).

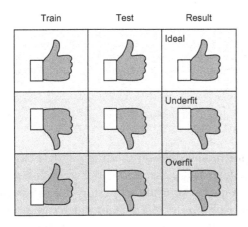

Figure 3.3 Ideally, the best-fit curve fits well on both the training data and the test data. If we witness it fitting poorly with the test data and the training data, there's a chance that our model is underfitting. On the other hand, if it performs poorly on the test data but well on the training data, we know the model is overfitting.

On the other end of the spectrum, a not-so-flexible model may generalize better to unseen testing data, but would score relatively low on the training data. That situation is called *underfitting*. A too-flexible model has high variance and low bias, whereas a too-strict model has low variance and high bias. Ideally, you want a model with both low-variance error and low-bias error. That way, it both generalizes to unseen data and captures the regularities of the data. See figure 3.4 for examples of a model underfitting and overfitting data points in 2D.

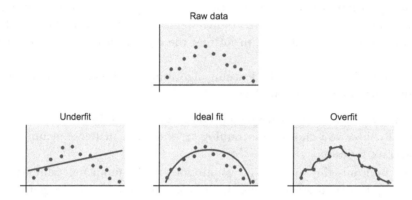

Figure 3.4   Examples of underfitting and overfitting the data

Concretely, the variance of a model is a measure of how badly the responses fluctuate, and the bias is a measure of how badly the response is offset from the ground-truth. You want your model to achieve accurate (low-bias) as well as reproducible (low-variance) results.

EXERCISE 3.2
Let's say your model is $M(w) : y = wx$. How many possible functions can you generate if the values of the weight parameter w must be integers between 0 and 9 (inclusive)?

ANSWER
Only 10: $\{y = 0,\ y = x,\ y = 2x,\ ...,\ y = 9x\}$.

In summary, measuring how well your model does on the training data isn't a great indicator of its generalizability. Instead, you should evaluate your model on a separate batch of testing data. You might find out that your model performs great on the data you trained it with, but it performs terribly on the test data, in which case your model is likely overfitting the training data. If the testing error is around the same as the training error, and both errors are similar, then your model may be fitting well, or underfitting if that error is high.

This is why, to measure success in machine learning, you partition the dataset into two groups: a training dataset and a testing dataset. The model is learned using the training dataset, and performance is evaluated on the testing dataset (exactly how you evaluate performance is described in the next section). Out of the many possible weight parameters you can generate, the goal is to find one that best fits the data. The way you measure *best fit* is by defining a cost function, which is discussed in greater detail in the following section.

3.2   *Linear regression*

Let's start by creating fake data for a leap into the heart of linear regression. Create a Python source file called regression.py, and follow along with the following listing to initialize data. The code will produce output similar to figure 3.5.

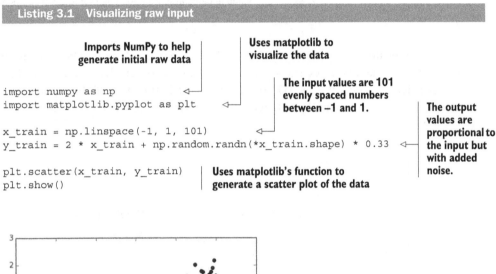

Listing 3.1   Visualizing raw input

```
import numpy as np
import matplotlib.pyplot as plt

x_train = np.linspace(-1, 1, 101)
y_train = 2 * x_train + np.random.randn(*x_train.shape) * 0.33

plt.scatter(x_train, y_train)
plt.show()
```

Imports NumPy to help generate initial raw data

Uses matplotlib to visualize the data

The input values are 101 evenly spaced numbers between −1 and 1.

The output values are proportional to the input but with added noise.

Uses matplotlib's function to generate a scatter plot of the data

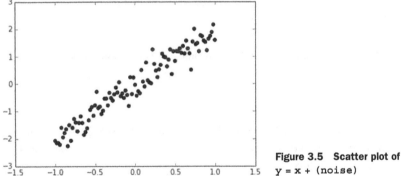

Figure 3.5   Scatter plot of y = x + (noise)

Now that you have some data points available, you can try fitting a line. At the very least, you need to provide TensorFlow with a score for each candidate parameter it tries. This score assignment is commonly called a *cost function*. The higher the cost, the worse the model parameter will be. For example, if the best-fit line is $y = 2x$, a parameter choice of 2.01 should have low cost, but the choice of −1 should have higher cost.

After you define the situation as a cost-minimization problem, as denoted in figure 3.6, TensorFlow takes care of the inner workings and tries to update the parameters in an efficient way to eventually reach the best possible value. Each step of looping through all your data to update the parameters is called an *epoch*.

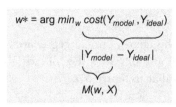

Figure 3.6   **Whichever parameter w minimizes, the cost is optimal. Cost is defined as the norm of the error between the ideal value with the model response. And, lastly, the response value is calculated from the function in the model set.**

In this example, the way you define *cost* is by the sum of errors. The error in predicting *x* is often calculated by the squared difference between the actual value $f(x)$ and the predicted value $M(w, x)$. Therefore, the cost is the sum of the squared differences between the actual and predicted values, as seen in figure 3.7.

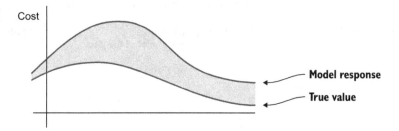

Figure 3.7   **The cost is the norm of the point-wise difference between the model response and the true value.**

Update your previous code to look like the following listing. This code defines the cost function and asks TensorFlow to run an optimizer to find the optimal solution for the model parameters.

Listing 3.2   Solving linear regression

```
import tensorflow as tf
import numpy as np
import matplotlib.pyplot as plt
```
Imports TensorFlow for the learning algorithm. You'll need NumPy to set up the initial data. And you'll use matplotlib to visualize your data.

```
learning_rate = 0.01
training_epochs = 100
```
Defines constants used by the learning algorithm. They're called hyperparameters.

```
x_train = np.linspace(-1, 1, 101)
y_train = 2 * x_train + np.random.randn(*x_train.shape) * 0.33
```
Sets up fake data that you'll use to find a best-fit line

```
X = tf.placeholder(tf.float32)        Sets up the input and output nodes as placeholders
Y = tf.placeholder(tf.float32)        because the value will be injected by x_train and y_train

def model(X, w):                       ◁─┐  Defines the model
    return tf.multiply(X, w)              │  as y = w*X

w = tf.Variable(0.0, name="weights")   ◁─┐  Sets up the
                                          │  weights variable

y_model = model(X, w)                  Defines the
cost = tf.square(Y-y_model)            cost function

train_op = tf.train.GradientDescentOptimizer(learning_rate).minimize(cost)

sess = tf.Session()                    Sets up a session and
init = tf.global_variables_initializer()   initializes all variables
sess.run(init)

for epoch in range(training_epochs):   ◁─┐  Loops through the
  for (x, y) in zip(x_train, y_train): ◁─┤  dataset multiple times
    sess.run(train_op, feed_dict={X: x, Y: y})   Loops through each
                                                 item in the dataset
w_val = sess.run(w)                    Obtains the final
                                       parameter value

sess.close()                           ◁──┐  Closes the
plt.scatter(x_train, y_train)          ◁──┤  session
y_learned = x_train*w_val
plt.plot(x_train, y_learned, 'r')      Plots the
plt.show()                             best-fit line    Plots the
                                                        original data
```

**Updates the model parameter(s) to try
to minimize the cost function**

**Defines the operation that will be called on
each iteration of the learning algorithm**

As figure 3.8 shows, you've just solved linear regression using TensorFlow! Conveniently, the rest of the topics in regression are just minor modifications of listing 3.2. The entire pipeline involves updating model parameters using TensorFlow, as summarized in figure 3.9.

You've just learned how to implement a simple regression model in TensorFlow. Making further improvements is simply a matter of enhancing the model with the right medley of variance and bias, as we discussed earlier. For example, the linear regression model you've designed so far is burdened with a strong bias; it expresses only a limited set of functions, such as linear functions. In the next section, you'll try a more flexible model. You'll notice how only the TensorFlow graph needs to be rewired, while everything else (such as preprocessing, training, evaluation) stays the same.

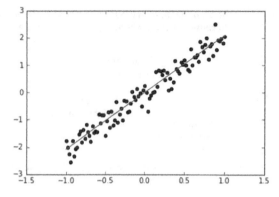

Figure 3.8   Linear regression estimate shown by running listing 3.2

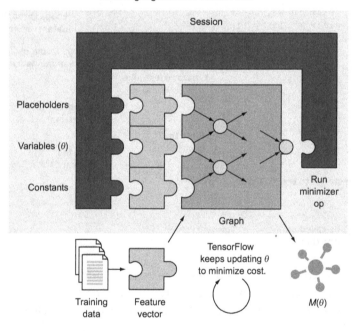

Figure 3.9   The learning algorithm updates the model's parameters to minimize the given cost function.

3.3   *Polynomial model*

Linear models may be an intuitive first guess, but rarely are real-world correlations so simple. For example, the trajectory of a missile through space is curved relative to the observer on Earth. Wi-Fi signal strength degrades with an inverse square law. The change in height of a flower over its lifetime certainly isn't linear.

When data points appear to form smooth curves rather than straight lines, you need to change your regression model from a straight line to something else. One such approach is to use a polynomial model. A *polynomial* is a generalization of a linear function. The *nth* degree polynomial looks like the following:

$$f(x) = w_n x^n + \ldots + w_1 x + w_0$$

NOTE   When $n = 1$, a polynomial is simply a linear equation $f(x) = w_1 x + w_0$.

Consider the scatter plot in figure 3.10, showing the input on the x-axis and the output on the y-axis. As you can tell, a straight line is insufficient to describe all the data. A polynomial function is a more flexible generalization of a linear function.

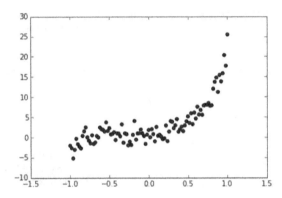

Figure 3.10   Data points like this aren't suitable for a linear model.

Let's try to fit a polynomial to this kind of data. Create a new file called polynomial.py, and follow along with the next listing.

Listing 3.3   Using a polynomial model

```
import tensorflow as tf
import numpy as np
import matplotlib.pyplot as plt           Imports the relevant
                                          libraries and initializes
                                          the hyperparameters
learning_rate = 0.01
training_epochs = 40
                                          Sets up fake raw
                                          input data
trX = np.linspace(-1, 1, 101)

num_coeffs = 6
trY_coeffs = [1, 2, 3, 4, 5, 6]           Sets up raw output
trY = 0                                   data based on a fifth-
for i in range(num_coeffs):               degree polynomial
    trY += trY_coeffs[i] * np.power(trX, i)
```

```
trY += np.random.randn(*trX.shape) * 1.5
```
⟵⌐ **Adds noise**

```
plt.scatter(trX, trY)
plt.show()
```
| **Shows a scatter plot of the raw data**

```
X = tf.placeholder(tf.float32)
Y = tf.placeholder(tf.float32)
```
| **Defines the nodes to hold values for input/output pairs**

```
def model(X, w):
    terms = []
    for i in range(num_coeffs):
        term = tf.multiply(w[i], tf.pow(X, i))
        terms.append(term)
    return tf.add_n(terms)
```
Defines your polynomial model

```
w = tf.Variable([0.] * num_coeffs, name="parameters")
y_model = model(X, w)
```
| **Sets up the parameter vector to all zeros**

Defines the cost function just as before
```
cost = (tf.pow(Y-y_model, 2))
train_op = tf.train.GradientDescentOptimizer(learning_rate).minimize(cost)
```

```
sess = tf.Session()
init = tf.global_variables_initializer()
sess.run(init)
```

```
for epoch in range(training_epochs):
    for (x, y) in zip(trX, trY):
        sess.run(train_op, feed_dict={X: x, Y: y})
```
Sets up the session and runs the learning algorithm just as before

```
w_val = sess.run(w)
print(w_val)
```

```
sess.close()
```
⟵———— **Closes the session when done**

```
plt.scatter(trX, trY)
trY2 = 0
for i in range(num_coeffs):
    trY2 += w_val[i] * np.power(trX, i)
```
Plots the result

```
plt.plot(trX, trY2, 'r')
plt.show()
```

The final output of this code is a fifth-degree polynomial that fits the data, as shown in figure 3.11.

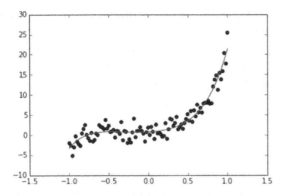

Figure 3.11 The best-fit curve smoothly aligns with the nonlinear data.

3.4 Regularization

Don't be fooled by the wonderful flexibility of polynomials, as shown in the previous section. Just because higher-order polynomials are extensions of lower ones doesn't mean you should always prefer to use the more flexible model.

In the real world, raw data rarely forms a smooth curve mimicking a polynomial. Imagine you're plotting house prices over time. The data likely will contain fluctuations. The goal of regression is to represent the complexity in a simple mathematical equation. If your model is too flexible, the model may be overcomplicating its interpretation of the input.

Take, for example, the data presented in figure 3.12. You try to fit an eighth-degree polynomial into points that appear to follow the equation $y = x^2$. This process fails miserably as the algorithm tries its best to update the nine coefficients of the polynomial.

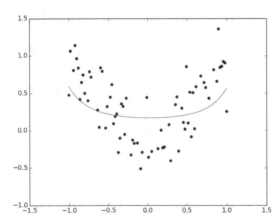

Figure 3.12 When the model is too flexible, a best-fit curve can look awkwardly complicated or unintuitive. We need to use regularization to improve the fit, so that the learned model performs well against test data.

Regularization is a technique to structure the parameters in a form you prefer, often to solve the problem of overfitting. In this case, you anticipate the learned coefficients to be 0 everywhere except for the second term, thus producing the curve $y = x^2$. The regression algorithm has no idea about this, so it may produce curves that score well but look strangely overcomplicated.

To influence the learning algorithm to produce a smaller coefficient vector (let's call it w), you add that penalty to the loss term. To control how significantly you want to weigh the penalty term, you multiply the penalty by a constant non-negative number, λ, as follows:

$$Cost(X, Y) = Loss(X, Y) + \lambda|\omega|$$

If λ is set to 0, regularization isn't in play. As you set λ to larger and larger values, parameters with larger norms will be heavily penalized. The choice of norm varies case by case, but parameters are typically measured by their L1 or L2 norm. Simply put, regularization reduces some of the flexibility of the otherwise easily tangled model.

To figure out which value of the regularization parameter λ performs best, you must split your dataset into two disjointed sets. About 70% of the randomly chosen input/output pairs will consist of the training dataset. The remaining 30% will be used for testing. You'll use the function provided in the following listing for splitting the dataset.

> **Listing 3.4 Splitting the dataset into testing and training sets**

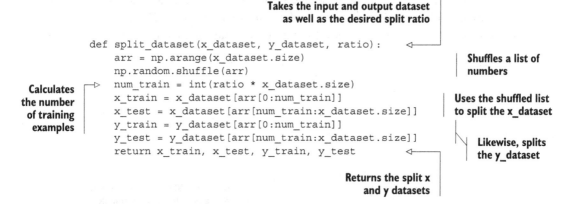

```
def split_dataset(x_dataset, y_dataset, ratio):
    arr = np.arange(x_dataset.size)
    np.random.shuffle(arr)
    num_train = int(ratio * x_dataset.size)
    x_train = x_dataset[arr[0:num_train]]
    x_test = x_dataset[arr[num_train:x_dataset.size]]
    y_train = y_dataset[arr[0:num_train]]
    y_test = y_dataset[arr[num_train:x_dataset.size]]
    return x_train, x_test, y_train, y_test
```

Takes the input and output dataset as well as the desired split ratio

Shuffles a list of numbers

Calculates the number of training examples

Uses the shuffled list to split the x_dataset

Likewise, splits the y_dataset

Returns the split x and y datasets

EXERCISE 3.3

A Python library called *scikit-learn* supports many useful data-preprocessing algorithms. You can call a function in scikit-learn to do exactly what listing 3.4 achieves. Can you find this function on the library's documentation? Hint: http://scikit-learn.org/stable/modules/classes.html#module-sklearn.model_selection.

ANSWER

It's called `sklearn.model_selection.train_test_split`.

With this handy tool, you can begin testing which value of λ performs best on your data. Open a new Python file, and follow along with this listing.

Listing 3.5 Evaluating regularization parameters

```
import tensorflow as tf
import numpy as np
import matplotlib.pyplot as plt          Imports the
                                         relevant libraries
                                         and initializes the
learning_rate = 0.001                    hyperparameters
training_epochs = 1000
reg_lambda = 0.

x_dataset = np.linspace(-1, 1, 100)

num_coeffs = 9
y_dataset_params = [0.] * num_coeffs
y_dataset_params[2] = 1                              Creates a fake
y_dataset = 0                                        dataset, y = x²
for i in range(num_coeffs):
    y_dataset += y_dataset_params[i] * np.power(x_dataset, i)
y_dataset += np.random.randn(*x_dataset.shape) * 0.3
```

Splits the dataset into 70% training and 30% testing using listing 3.4
```
(x_train, x_test, y_train, y_test) = split_dataset(x_dataset, y_dataset, 0.7)

X = tf.placeholder(tf.float32)        Sets up the input/output
Y = tf.placeholder(tf.float32)        placeholders

def model(X, w):
    terms = []
    for i in range(num_coeffs):        Defines
        term = tf.multiply(w[i], tf.pow(X, i))   your
        terms.append(term)             model
    return tf.add_n(terms)
```

Defines the regularized cost function
```
w = tf.Variable([0.] * num_coeffs, name="parameters")
y_model = model(X, w)
cost = tf.div(tf.add(tf.reduce_sum(tf.square(Y-y_model)),
              tf.multiply(reg_lambda, tf.reduce_sum(tf.square(w)))),
        2*x_train.size)
train_op = tf.train.GradientDescentOptimizer(learning_rate).minimize(cost)

sess = tf.Session()                          Sets up the
init = tf.global_variables_initializer()     session
sess.run(init)

for reg_lambda in np.linspace(0,1,100):
    for epoch in range(training_epochs):        Tries various
        sess.run(train_op, feed_dict={X: x_train, Y: y_train})   regularization
    final_cost = sess.run(cost, feed_dict={X: x_test, Y:y_test}) parameters
    print('reg lambda', reg_lambda)
    print('final cost', final_cost)

sess.close()                  ◁──────  Closes the session
```

If you plot the corresponding output per each regularization parameter from listing 3.5, you can see how the curve changes as λ increases. When λ is 0, the algorithm favors using the higher-order terms to fit the data. As you start penalizing parameters with a high L2 norm, the cost decreases, indicating that you're recovering from over-fitting, as shown in figure 3.13.

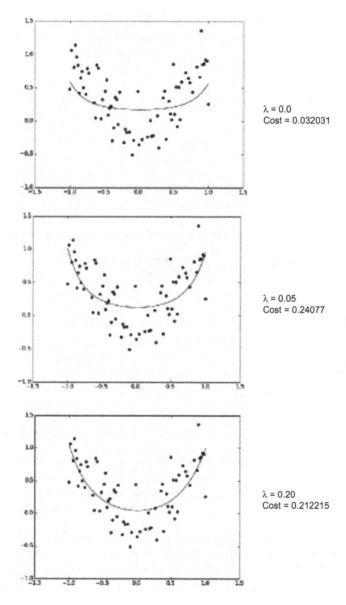

λ = 0.0
Cost = 0.032031

λ = 0.05
Cost = 0.24077

λ = 0.20
Cost = 0.212215

Figure 3.13   As you increase the regularization parameter to some extent, the cost decreases. This implies that the model was originally overfitting the data, and regularization helped add structure.

3.5 *Application of linear regression*

Running linear regression on fake data is like buying a new car and never driving it. This awesome machinery begs to manifest itself in the real world! Fortunately, many datasets are available online to test your newfound knowledge of regression:

- The University of Massachusetts Amherst supplies small datasets of various types: www.umass.edu/statdata/statdata.
- Kaggle contains all types of large-scale data for machine-learning competitions: www.kaggle.com/datasets.
- Data.gov is an open data initiative by the US government that contains many interesting and practical datasets: https://catalog.data.gov.

A good number of datasets contain dates. For example, there's a dataset of all phone calls to the 3-1-1 non-emergency line in Los Angeles, California. You can obtain it at http://mng.bz/6vHx. A good feature to track could be the frequency of calls per day, week, or month. For convenience, the following listing allows you to obtain a weekly frequency count of data items.

Listing 3.6 Parsing raw CSV datasets

```
import csv          ◁── For easily
import time              reading CSV files
                    ◁──  For using useful
                         date functions

def read(filename, date_idx, date_parse, year, bucket=7):

    days_in_year = 365
                        ◁── Sets up initial
                            frequency map
    freq = {}
    for period in range(0, int(days_in_year / bucket)):
        freq[period] = 0

    with open(filename, 'rb') as csvfile:     ◁─┐ Reads data and
        csvreader = csv.reader(csvfile)         │ aggregates count
        csvreader.next()                        │ per period
        for row in csvreader:
            if row[date_idx] == '':
                continue
            t = time.strptime(row[date_idx], date_parse)
            if t.tm_year == year and t.tm_yday < (days_in_year-1):
                freq[int(t.tm_yday / bucket)] += 1

    return freq
                            Obtains a weekly frequency
                            count of 3-1-1 phone calls
freq = read('311.csv', 0, '%m/%d/%Y', 2014)   ◁── in 2014
```

This code gives you the training data for linear regression. The `freq` variable is a dictionary that maps a period (such as a week) to a frequency count. A year has 52 weeks, so you'll have 52 data points, if you leave `bucket=7` as is.

Now that you have data points, you have exactly the input and output necessary to fit a regression model by using the techniques covered in this chapter. More practically, the learned model can be used to interpolate or extrapolate frequency counts.

3.6 *Summary*

- Regression is a type of supervised machine learning for predicting continuous-valued output.
- By defining a set of models, you greatly reduce the search space of possible functions. Moreover, TensorFlow takes advantage of the differentiable property of the functions by running its efficient gradient-descent optimizers to learn the parameters.
- You can easily modify linear regression to learn polynomials or other more complicated curves.
- To avoid overfitting your data, you regularize the cost function by penalizing larger-valued parameters.
- If the output of the function isn't continuous, a classification algorithm should be used instead (see the next chapter).
- TensorFlow enables you to solve linear-regression machine-learning problems effectively and efficiently, and hence make useful predictions about important matters, such as agricultural production, heart conditions, housing prices, and more.

A gentle introduction to classification

This chapter covers

- Writing formal notation
- Using logistic regression
- Working with a confusion matrix
- Understanding multiclass classification

Imagine an advertisement agency collecting information about user interactions to decide what type of ad to show. That's not uncommon. Google, Twitter, Facebook, and other big tech giants that rely on ads have creepy-good personal profiles of their users to help deliver personalized ads. A user who's recently searched for gaming keyboards or graphics cards is probably more likely to click ads about the latest and greatest video games.

Delivering a specially crafted advertisement to each individual may be difficult, so grouping users into categories is a common technique. For example, a user may be categorized as a "gamer" to receive relevant video game–related ads.

Machine learning is the go-to tool to accomplish such a task. At the most fundamental level, machine-learning practitioners want to build a tool to help them understand data. Labeling data items as belonging in separate categories is an excellent way to characterize data for specific needs.

The previous chapter dealt with regression, which was about fitting a curve to data. As you recall, the best-fit curve is a function that takes as input a data item and assigns it a number. Creating a machine-learning model that instead assigns discrete labels to its inputs is called *classification*. It's a supervised-learning algorithm for dealing with discrete output. (Each discrete value is called a *class*.) The input is typically a feature vector, and the output is a class. If there are only two class labels (for example, True/False, On/Off, Yes/No), we call this learning algorithm a *binary classifier*. Otherwise, it's called a *multiclass classifier*.

There are many types of classifiers, but this chapter focuses on the ones outlined in table 4.1. Each has its advantages and disadvantages, which we'll delve into deeper after we start implementing each one in TensorFlow.

Linear regression is the easiest to implement because we already did most of the hard work in chapter 3, but as you'll see, it's a terrible classifier. A much better classifier is the logistic regression algorithm. As the name suggests, it uses logarithmic properties to define a better cost function. And lastly, softmax regression is a direct approach to solving multiclass classification. It's a natural generalization of logistic regression. It's called softmax regression because a function called `softmax` is applied as the last step.

Table 4.1 Classifiers

Type	Pros	Cons
Linear regression	Simple to implement	Not guaranteed to work Supports only binary labels
Logistic regression	Highly accurate Flexible ways to regularize model for custom adjustment Model responses are measures of probability Easy-to-update model with new data	Supports only binary labels
Softmax regression	Supports multiclass classification Model responses are measures of probability	More complicated to implement

4.1 Formal notation

In mathematical notation, a classifier is a function $y = f(x)$, where x is the input data item and y is the output category (figure 4.1). Adopting from traditional scientific literature, we often refer to the input vector x as the *independent variable*, and the output y as the *dependent variable*.

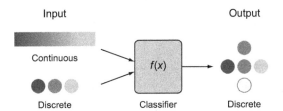

Figure 4.1 A classifier produces discrete outputs but may take either continuous or discrete inputs.

Formally, a category label is restricted to a range of possible values. You can think of two-valued labels as being like Boolean variables in Python. When the input features have only a fixed set of possible values, you need to ensure that your model can understand how to handle them. Because the set of functions in a model typically deal with continuous real numbers, you need to preprocess the dataset to account for discrete variables, which fall into one of two types: ordinal or nominal (figure 4.2).

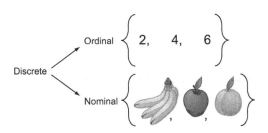

Figure 4.2 There are two types of discrete sets: those with values that can be ordered (ordinal) and those with values that can't (nominal).

Values of an ordinal type, as the name suggests, can be ordered. For example, the values in a set of even numbers from 1 to 10 are ordinal because integers can be compared with each other. On the other hand, an element from a set of fruits {banana, apple, orange} might not come with a natural ordering. We call values from such a set nominal, because they can be described by only their names.

A simple approach to representing nominal variables in a dataset is to assign a number to each label. Our set {banana, apple, orange} could instead be processed as {0, 1, 2}. But some classification models may have a strong bias about how the data behaves. For example, linear regression would interpret our apple as midway between a banana and an orange, which makes no natural sense.

A simple workaround to represent nominal categories of a dependent variable is by adding *dummy variables* for each value of the nominal variable. In this example, the fruit variable would be removed, and replaced by three separate variables: banana, apple, and orange. Each variable holds a value of 0 or 1 (figure 4.3), depending on whether the category for that fruit holds true. This process is often referred to as *one-hot encoding*.

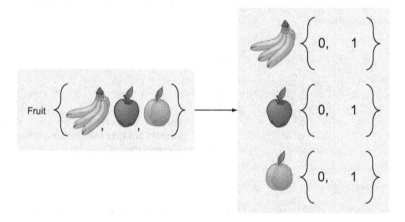

Figure 4.3 If the values of a variable are nominal, they might need to be preprocessed. One solution is to treat each nominal value as a Boolean variable, as shown on the right: banana, apple, and orange are three newly added variables, each having a value of 0 or 1. The original fruit variable is removed.

Just as in linear regression from chapter 3, the learning algorithm must traverse the possible functions supported by the underlying model, called *M*. In linear regression, the model was parameterized by *w*. The function $y = M(w)$ can then be tried out to measure its cost. In the end, we choose a value of *w* with the least cost. The only difference between regression and classification is that the output is no longer a continuous spectrum, but instead a discrete set of class labels.

> **EXERCISE 4.1**
> Is it a better idea to treat each of the following as a regression or classification task?
> (a) Predicting stock prices; (b) Deciding which stocks you should buy, sell, or hold;
> (c) Rating the quality of a computer on a 1–10 scale
>
> **ANSWER**
> (a) Regression, (b) Classification, (c) Either

Because the input/output types for regression are even more general than those of classification, nothing prevents you from running a linear regression algorithm on a classification task. In fact, that's exactly what you'll do in section 4.3. Before you begin implementing TensorFlow code, it's important to gauge the strength of a classifier. The next section covers state-of-the-art approaches to measuring a classifier's success.

4.2 *Measuring performance*

Before you begin writing classification algorithms, you should be able to check the success of your results. This section covers essential techniques to measure performance in classification problems.

4.2.1 *Accuracy*

Do you remember those multiple-choice exams in high school or college? Classification problems in machine learning are similar. Given a statement, your job is to classify it as one of the given multiple-choice "answers." If you have only two choices, as in a true-or-false exam, we call it a *binary classifier*. If this were a graded exam in school, the typical way to measure your score would be to count the number of correct answers and divide that by the total number of questions.

Machine learning adopts this same scoring strategy and calls it *accuracy*. Accuracy is measured by the following formula:

$$accuracy = \frac{\#\,correct}{\#\,total}$$

This formula gives a crude summary of the performance, which may be sufficient if you're worried only about the overall correctness of the algorithm. But the accuracy measure doesn't reveal a breakdown of correct and incorrect results for each label.

To account for this limitation, a *confusion matrix* is a more detailed report of a classifier's success. A useful way to describe how well a classifier performs is by inspecting the way it performs on each of the classes.

For instance, consider a binary classifier with "positive" and "negative" labels. As shown in figure 4.4, a confusion matrix is a table that compares how the predicted responses compare with actual ones. Data items that are correctly predicted as positive are called *true positives* (TP). Those that are incorrectly predicted as positive are called *false positives* (FP). If the algorithm accidentally predicts an element to be negative when in reality it is positive, we call this situation a *false negative* (FN). Lastly, when the prediction and reality both agree that a data item is a negative label, it's called a *true negative* (TN). As you can see, it's called a *confusion matrix* because it enables you to easily see how often a model confuses two classes that it's trying to differentiate.

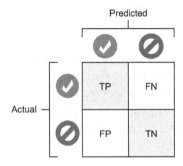

Figure 4.4   **You can compare predicted results to actual results by using a matrix of positive (green check mark) and negative (red forbidden) labels.**

NOTE TO PRINT BOOK READERS   Many graphics in this book include color, which can be viewed in the eBook versions. To get your free eBook in PDF, ePub, or Kindle format, go to www.manning.com/books/machine-learning-with-tensorflow to register your print book.

4.2.2   *Precision and recall*

Although the definitions of true positives (TP), false positives (FP), true negatives (TN), and false negatives (FN) are all useful individually, the true power comes in the interplay between them.

The ratio of true positives to total positive examples is called *precision*. It's a score of how likely a positive prediction is to be correct. The left column in figure 4.4 is the total number of positive predictions (TP + FP), so the equation for precision is the following:

$$precision = \frac{TP}{TP + FP}$$

The ratio of true positives to all possible positives is called *recall*. It measures the ratio of true positives found. It's is a score of how many true positives were successfully predicted (that is, recalled). The top row in figure 4.4 is the total number of all positives (TP + FN), so the equation for recall is the following:

$$recall = \frac{TP}{TP + FN}$$

Simply put, precision is a measure of the predictions the algorithm got right, and recall is a measure of the right things the algorithm identified in the final set. If the precision is higher than the recall, the model is better at successfully identifying correct items than not identifying some wrong items, and vice versa.

Let's do a quick example. Let's say you're trying to identify cats in a set of 100 pictures; 40 of the pictures are cats, and 60 are dogs. When you run your classifier, 10 of the cats are identified as dogs, and 20 of the dogs are identified as cats. Your confusion matrix looks like figure 4.5.

Confusion matrix		Predicted	
		Cat	Dog
Actual	Cat	30 True positives	20 False positives
	Dog	10 False negatives	40 True negatives

Figure 4.5 An example of a confusion matrix for evaluating the performance of a classification algorithm

You can see the total number of cats on the left side of the prediction column: 30 identified correctly, and 10 not, totaling 40.

EXERCISE 4.2
What are the precision and recall for cats? What's the accuracy of the system?

ANSWER
For cats, the precision is 30 / (30 + 20) or 3/5. The recall is 30 / (30 + 10), or 3/4. The accuracy is (30 + 40) / 100, or 70%.

4.2.3 *Receiver operating characteristic curve*

Because binary classifiers are among the most popular tools, many mature techniques exist for measuring their performance, such as the receiver operating characteristic (ROC) curve. The ROC curve is a plot that lets you compare the trade-offs between false positives and true positives. The x-axis is the measure of false-positive values, and the y-axis is the measure of true-positive values.

A binary classifier reduces its input feature vector into a number and then decides the class based on whether the number is greater than or less than a specified threshold. As you adjust a threshold of the machine-learning classifier, you plot the various values of false-positive and true-positive rates.

A robust way to compare various classifiers is by comparing their ROC curves. When two curves don't intersect, one method is certainly better than the other. Good algorithms are far above the baseline. A quantitative way to compare classifiers is by measuring the area under the ROC curve. If a model has an area-under-curve (AUC) value higher than 0.9, it's an excellent classifier. A model that randomly guesses the output will have an AUC value of about 0.5. See figure 4.6 for an example.

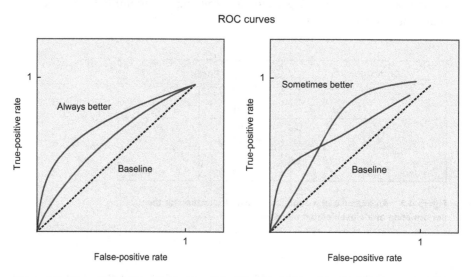

Figure 4.6   **The principled way to compare algorithms is by examining their ROC curves. When the true-positive rate is greater than the false-positive rate in every situation, it's straightforward to declare that one algorithm is dominant in terms of its performance. If the true-positive rate is less than the false-positive rate, the plot dips below the baseline shown by the dotted line.**

EXERCISE 4.3
How would a 100% correct rate (all true positives, no false positives) look as a point on an ROC curve?

ANSWER
The point for a 100% correct rate would be located on the positive y-axis of the ROC curve.

4.3   *Using linear regression for classification*

One of the simplest ways to implement a classifier is to tweak a linear regression algorithm, like the ones in chapter 3. As a reminder, the linear regression model is a set of functions that look linear, $f(x) = wx$. The function $f(x)$ takes continuous real numbers as input and produces continuous real numbers as output. Remember, classification is all about discrete outputs. So, one way to force the regression model to produce a two-valued (binary) output is by setting values above a certain threshold to a number (such as 1) and values below that threshold to a different number (such as 0).

We'll proceed with the following motivating example. Imagine that Alice is an avid chess player, and you have records of her win/loss history. Moreover, each game has a time limit ranging from 1 to 10 minutes. You can plot the outcome of each game as shown in figure 4.7. The x-axis represents the time limit of the game, and the y-axis signifies whether she won ($y = 1$) or lost ($y = 0$).

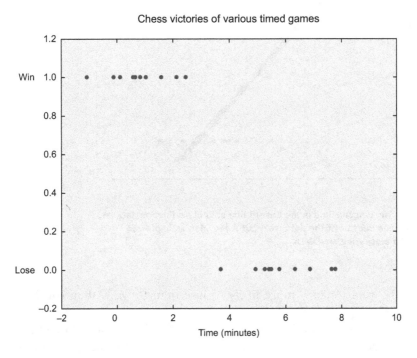

Figure 4.7 A visualization of a binary classification training dataset. The values are divided into two classes: all points where $y = 1$, and all points where $y = 0$.

As you see from the data, Alice is a quick thinker: she always wins short games. But she usually loses games that have longer time limits. From the plot, you'd like to predict the critical game time-limit that decides whether she'll win.

You want to challenge her to a game that you're sure of winning. If you choose an obviously long game, such as one that takes 10 minutes, she'll refuse to play. So, let's set up the game time to be as short as possible so she'll be willing to play against you, while tilting the balance to your advantage.

A linear fit on the data gives you something to work with. Figure 4.8 shows the best-fit line computed using linear regression from listing 4.1 (appearing shortly). The value of the line is closer to 1 than it is to 0 for games that Alice will likely win. It appears that if you pick a time corresponding to when the value of the line is less than

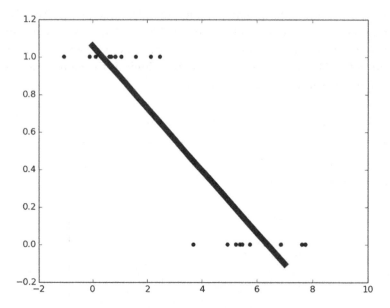

Figure 4.8   The diagonal line is the best-fit line on a classification dataset. Clearly, the line doesn't fit the data well, but it provides an imprecise approach for classifying new data.

0.5 (that is, when Alice is more likely to lose than to win), then you have a good chance of winning.

The line is trying to fit the data as best possible. Due to the nature of the training data, the model will respond with values near 1 for positive examples and values near 0 for negative examples. Because you're modeling this data with a line, some input may produce values between 0 and 1. As you may imagine, values too far into one category will result in values greater than 1 or less than 0. You need a way to decide when an item belongs to one category more than another. Typically, you choose the midpoint, 0.5, as a deciding boundary (also called the *threshold*). Are you've seen, this procedure uses linear regression to perform classification.

EXERCISE 4.4
What are the disadvantages of using linear regression as a tool for classification? (See listing 4.4 for a hint.)

ANSWER
Linear regression is sensitive to outliers in your data, so it isn't an accurate classifier.

Let's write your first classifier! Open a new Python source file, and call it linear.py. Use the following listing to write the code. In the TensorFlow code, you'll need to first define placeholder nodes and then inject values into them from the `session.run()` statement.

Listing 4.1 Using linear regression for classification

```
import tensorflow as tf                          Imports TensorFlow for the core learning
import numpy as np                                algorithm, NumPy for manipulating data,
import matplotlib.pyplot as plt                   and matplotlib for visualizing

x_label0 = np.random.normal(5, 1, 10)
x_label1 = np.random.normal(2, 1, 10)             Initializes fake data, 10
xs = np.append(x_label0, x_label1)                instances of each label
labels = [0.] * len(x_label0) + [1.] * len(x_label1)    Initializes the
                                                         corresponding
plt.scatter(xs, labels)                                  labels

learning_rate = 0.001              Declares the        Plots the data
training_epochs = 1000             hyperparameters

X = tf.placeholder("float")        Sets up the placeholder nodes
Y = tf.placeholder("float")        for the input/output pairs

def model(X, w):                                   Defines a linear
    return tf.add(tf.multiply(w[1], tf.pow(X, 1)),  y = w1 * x + w0 model
                  tf.multiply(w[0], tf.pow(X, 0)))

w = tf.Variable([0., 0.], name="parameters")       Defines a helper variable,
y_model = model(X, w)                              because you'll refer to
cost = tf.reduce_sum(tf.square(Y-y_model))         this multiple times

train_op = tf.train.GradientDescentOptimizer(learning_rate).minimize(cost)

                                                   Defines the rule to
                                                   learn the parameters
```

Sets up the parameter variables → `w = tf.Variable([0., 0.], name="parameters")`

Defines the cost function → `cost = tf.reduce_sum(tf.square(Y-y_model))`

After designing the TensorFlow graph, you'll see in the following listing how to open a new session and execute the graph. `train_op` updates the model's parameters to better and better guesses. You run `train_op` multiple times in a loop because each step iteratively improves the parameter estimate. The following listing generates a plot similar to figure 4.8.

Listing 4.2 Executing the graph

Records the cost computed with the current parameters

```
sess = tf.Session()                               Opens a new session, and
init = tf.global_variables_initializer()          initializes the variables
sess.run(init)
                                                                    Runs the
                                                                    learning
for epoch in range(training_epochs):                                operation
    sess.run(train_op, feed_dict={X: xs, Y: labels})                multiple
    current_cost = sess.run(cost, feed_dict={X: xs, Y: labels})     times
```

```
    if epoch % 100 == 0:
        print(epoch, current_cost)
```
Prints out log info
while the code runs

```
w_val = sess.run(w)
print('learned parameters', w_val)
```
Prints the learned
parameters

```
sess.close()
```
Closes the session when
no longer in use

```
all_xs = np.linspace(0, 10, 100)
plt.plot(all_xs, all_xs*w_val[1] + w_val[0])
plt.show()
```
Shows the
best-fit line

To measure success, you can count the number of correct predictions and compute a
success rate. In the next listing, you'll add two more nodes to the previous code in lin-
ear.py, called correct_prediction and accuracy. You can then print the value of
accuracy to see the success rate. The code can be executed right before closing the
session.

Listing 4.3   Measuring accuracy

When the model's response is greater than 0.5,
it should be a positive label, and vice versa.

```
correct_prediction = tf.equal(Y, tf.to_float(tf.greater(y_model, 0.5)))
accuracy = tf.reduce_mean(tf.to_float(correct_prediction))

print('accuracy', sess.run(accuracy, feed_dict={X: xs, Y: labels}))
```

Computes the
percent of success

Prints the success measure
from provided input

The preceding code produces the following output:

```
('learned parameters', array([ 1.2816, -0.2171], dtype=float32))
('accuracy', 0.95)
```

If classification were that easy, this chapter would be over by now. Unfortunately, the
linear regression approach fails miserably if you train on more-extreme data, also
called *outliers*.

    For example, let's say Alice lost a game that took 20 minutes. You train the classi-
fier on a dataset that includes this new outlier data point. The following listing
replaces one of the game times with the value of 20. Let's see how introducing an outlier affects the classifier's performance.

Listing 4.4   Linear regression failing miserably for classification

```
x_label0 = np.append(np.random.normal(5, 1, 9), 20)
```

When you rerun the code with these changes, you'll see a result similar to figure 4.9.

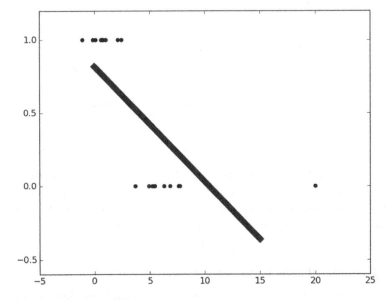

Figure 4.9 A new training element of value 20 greatly influences the best-fit line. The line is too sensitive to outlying data, and therefore linear regression is a sloppy classifier.

The original classifier suggested that you could beat Alice in a three-minute game. She'd probably agree to play such a short game. But the revised classifier, if you stick with the same 0.5 threshold, is now suggesting that the shortest game she'll lose is a five-minute game. She'll likely refuse to play such a long game!

4.4   *Using logistic regression*

Logistic regression provides you with an analytic function with theoretical guarantees on accuracy and performance. It's just like linear regression, except you use a different cost function and slightly transform the model response function.

Let's revisit the linear function shown here:

$$y(x) = wx$$

In linear regression, a line with a nonzero slope may range from negative infinity to infinity. If the only sensible results for classification are 0 or 1, it would be intuitive to instead fit a function with that property. Fortunately, the sigmoid function depicted in figure 4.10 works well because it converges to 0 or 1 quickly.

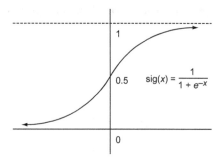

Figure 4.10   A visualization of the sigmoid function

When *x* is 0, the sigmoid function results in 0.5. As *x* increases, the function converges to 1. And as *x* decreases to negative infinity, the function converges to 0.

In logistic regression, our model is sig(linear(*x*)). As it turns out, the best-fit parameters of this function imply a linear separation between the two classes. This separating line is also called a *linear decision boundary*.

4.4.1   *Solving one-dimensional logistic regression*

The cost function used in logistic regression is a bit different from the one you used in linear regression. Although you could use the same cost function as before, it won't be as fast or guarantee an optimal solution. The sigmoid function is the culprit here, because it causes the cost function to have many "bumps." TensorFlow and most other machine-learning libraries work best with simple cost functions. Scholars have found a neat way to modify the cost function to use sigmoids for logistic regression.

The new cost function between the actual value *y* and model response *h* will be a two-part equation as follows:

$$Cost(y, h) = \begin{cases} -\log(h), & \text{if } y = 1 \\ -\log(1 - h), & \text{if } y = 0 \end{cases}$$

You can condense the two equations into one long equation:

$$Cost(y, h) = -y \log(h) - (1 - y)\log(1 - h)$$

This function has exactly the qualities needed for efficient and optimal learning. Specifically, it's convex, but don't worry too much about what that means. You're trying to minimize the cost: think of cost as an altitude and the cost function as a terrain. You're trying to find the lowest point in the terrain. It's a lot easier to find the lowest point in the terrain if there's no place you can ever go uphill. Such a place is called *convex*. There are no hills.

You can think of it as a ball rolling down a hill. Eventually, the ball will settle to the bottom, which is the *optimal point*. A nonconvex function might have a rugged terrain, making it difficult to predict where a ball will roll. It might not even end up at the lowest point. Your function is convex, so the algorithm will easily figure out how to minimize this cost and "roll the ball downhill."

Convexity is nice, but correctness is also an important criterion when picking a cost function. How do you know this cost function does exactly what you intended it to do? To answer that question most intuitively, take a look at figure 4.11. You use $-\log(x)$ to compute the cost when you want your desired value to be 1 (notice: $-\log(1) = 0$). The algorithm strays away from setting the value to 0, because the cost approaches infinity. Adding these functions together gives a curve that approaches infinity at both 0 and 1, with the negative parts cancelling out.

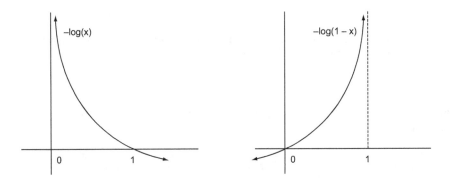

Figure 4.11 Here's a visualization of how the two cost functions penalize values at 0 and 1. Notice that the left function heavily penalizes 0 but has no cost at 1. The right cost function displays the opposite phenomena.

Sure, figures are an informal way to convince you, but the technical discussion about why the cost function is optimal is beyond the scope of this book. If you're interested in the mathematics behind it, you'll be interested to learn that the cost function is derived from the principle of maximum entropy, which you can look up anywhere online.

See figure 4.12 for a best-fit result from logistic regression on a one-dimensional dataset. The sigmoid curve that you'll generate will provide a better linear decision boundary than that from linear regression.

You'll start to notice a pattern in the code listings. In a simple/typical usage of TensorFlow, you generate a fake dataset, define placeholders, define variables, define a model, define a cost function on that model (which is often mean squared error or mean squared log error), create a train_op by using gradient descent, iteratively feed it example data (possibly with a label or output), and, finally, collect the optimized

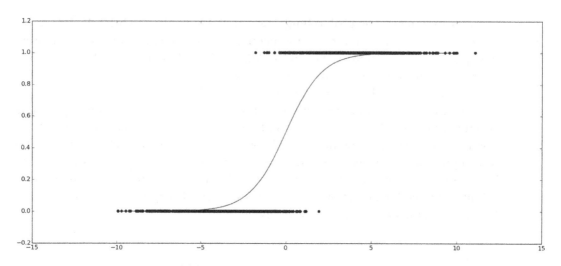

Figure 4.12 Here's a best-fit sigmoid curve for a binary classification dataset. Notice that the curve resides within $y = 0$ and $y = 1$. That way, this curve isn't that sensitive to outliers.

values. Create a new source file called logistic_1d.py and copy into it listing 4.5, which will generate figure 4.12.

Listing 4.5   Using one-dimensional logistic regression

```
import numpy as np
import tensorflow as tf                      Imports relevant
import matplotlib.pyplot as plt              libraries
learning_rate = 0.01                           Sets the
training_epochs = 1000                         hyperparameters

def sigmoid(x):                                Defines a helper function to
    return 1. / (1. + np.exp(-x))             calculate the sigmoid function

x1 = np.random.normal(-4, 2, 1000)
x2 = np.random.normal(4, 2, 1000)             Initializes
xs = np.append(x1, x2)                        fake data
ys = np.asarray([0.] * len(x1) + [1.] * len(x2))
                                                         Visualizes
                                                         the data
plt.scatter(xs, ys)

X = tf.placeholder(tf.float32, shape=(None,), name="x")    Defines the input/
Y = tf.placeholder(tf.float32, shape=(None,), name="y")    output placeholders
w = tf.Variable([0., 0.], name="parameter", trainable=True)
y_model = tf.sigmoid(w[1] * X + w[0])
cost = tf.reduce_mean(-Y * tf.log(y_model) - (1 - Y) * tf.log(1 - y_model))
```

Defines the parameter node

Defines the model using TensorFlow's sigmoid function

Defines the cross-entropy loss function

```
        train_op = tf.train.GradientDescentOptimizer(learning_rate).minimize(cost)

        with tf.Session() as sess:                              Opens a session, and
            sess.run(tf.global_variables_initializer())        defines all variables
            prev_err = 0
            for epoch in range(training_epochs):
                err, _ = sess.run([cost, train_op], {X: xs, Y: ys})
                print(epoch, err)
                if abs(prev_err - err) < 0.0001:               Checks for convergence—if
                    break                                      you're changing by < .01%
                prev_err = err                                 per iteration, you're done
            w_val = sess.run(w, {X: xs, Y: ys})

        all_xs = np.linspace(-10, 10, 100)
        plt.plot(all_xs, sigmoid((all_xs * w_val[1] + w_val[0])))    Plots the learned
        plt.show()                                                   sigmoid function
```

Defines the minimizer to use

Obtains the learned parameter value

Updates the previous error value

Computes the cost, and updates the learning parameters

Iterates until convergence or until the maximum number of epochs is reached

Defines a variable to keep track of the previous error

Cross-entropy loss in TensorFlow

As shown in listing 4.5, the cross-entropy loss is averaged over each input/output pair by using the `tf.reduce_mean` op. Another handy and more general function is provided by the TensorFlow library, called `tf.nn.softmax_cross_entropy_with_logits`. You can find more about it in the official documentation: http://mng.bz/8mEk.

And there you have it! If you were playing chess against Alice, you'd now have a binary classifier to decide the threshold indicating when a chess match might result in a win or loss.

4.4.2 Solving two-dimensional logistic regression

Now we'll explore how to use logistic regression with multiple independent variables. The number of independent variables corresponds to the number of dimensions. In our case, a two-dimensional logistic regression problem will try to label a pair of independent variables. The concepts you learn in this section extrapolate to arbitrary dimensions.

NOTE   Let's say you're thinking about buying a new phone. The only attributes you care about are (1) operating system, (2) size, and (3) cost. The goal is to decide whether a phone is a worthwhile purchase. In this case, there are three independent variables (the attributes of the phone) and one dependent variable (whether it's worth buying). So we regard this as a classification problem in which the input vector is three-dimensional.

Consider the dataset shown in figure 4.13. It represents crime activity of two gangs in a city. The first dimension is the x-axis, which can be thought of as the latitude, and the second dimension is the y-axis, representing longitude. There's one cluster around (3, 2) and another around (7, 6). Your job is to decide which gang is most likely responsible for a new crime that occurred at location (6, 4).

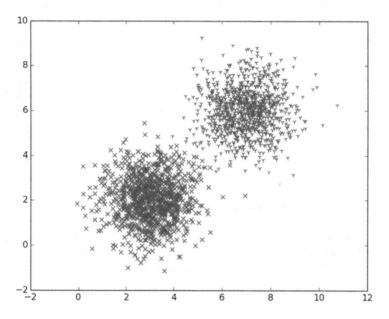

Figure 4.13   The x-axis and y-axis represent the two independent variables. The dependent variable holds two possible labels, represented by the shape and color of the plotted points.

Create a new source file called logistic_2d.py, and follow along with listing 4.6.

Listing 4.6   Setting up data for two-dimensional logistic regression

```
import numpy as np                        Imports
import tensorflow as tf                   relevant
import matplotlib.pyplot as plt           libraries

learning_rate = 0.1                       Sets the
training_epochs = 2000                    hyperparameters
```

```
def sigmoid(x):
    return 1. / (1. + np.exp(-x))
```
Defines a helper sigmoid function

```
x1_label1 = np.random.normal(3, 1, 1000)
x2_label1 = np.random.normal(2, 1, 1000)
x1_label2 = np.random.normal(7, 1, 1000)
x2_label2 = np.random.normal(6, 1, 1000)
x1s = np.append(x1_label1, x1_label2)
x2s = np.append(x2_label1, x2_label2)
ys = np.asarray([0.] * len(x1_label1) + [1.] * len(x1_label2))
```
Initializes fake data

You have two independent variables (*x1* and *x2*). A simple way to model the mapping between the input *x*'s and output $M(x)$ is the following equation, where w is the parameter to be found using TensorFlow:

$$M(x; w) = sig(w_2 x_2 + w_1 x_1 + w_0)$$

In the following listing, you'll implement the equation and its corresponding cost function to learn the parameters.

Listing 4.7 Using TensorFlow for multidimensional logistic regression

Defines the sigmoid model using both input variables

```
X1 = tf.placeholder(tf.float32, shape=(None,), name="x1")
X2 = tf.placeholder(tf.float32, shape=(None,), name="x2")
Y = tf.placeholder(tf.float32, shape=(None,), name="y")
w = tf.Variable([0., 0., 0.], name="w", trainable=True)

y_model = tf.sigmoid(w[2] * X2 + w[1] * X1 + w[0])
cost = tf.reduce_mean(-tf.log(y_model * Y + (1 - y_model) * (1 - Y)))
train_op = tf.train.GradientDescentOptimizer(learning_rate).minimize(cost)

with tf.Session() as sess:
    sess.run(tf.global_variables_initializer())
    prev_err = 0
    for epoch in range(training_epochs):
        err, _ = sess.run([cost, train_op], {X1: x1s, X2: x2s, Y: ys})
        print(epoch, err)
        if abs(prev_err - err) < 0.0001:
            break
        prev_err = err
    w_val = sess.run(w, {X1: x1s, X2: x2s, Y: ys})

x1_boundary, x2_boundary = [], []
for x1_test in np.linspace(0, 10, 100):
    for x2_test in np.linspace(0, 10, 100):
```

Defines the input/output placeholder nodes

Defines the parameter node

Defines the learning step

Creates a new session, initializes variables, and learns parameters until convergence

Defines arrays to hold boundary points

Loops through a window of points

Obtains the learned parameter value before closing the session

If the model response is close the 0.5, updates the boundary points

```
z = sigmoid(-x2_test*w_val[2] - x1_test*w_val[1] - w_val[0])
if abs(z - 0.5) < 0.01:
    x1_boundary.append(x1_test)
    x2_boundary.append(x2_test)
```

```
plt.scatter(x1_boundary, x2_boundary, c='b', marker='o', s=20)
plt.scatter(x1_label1, x2_label1, c='r', marker='x', s=20)
plt.scatter(x1_label2, x2_label2, c='g', marker='1', s=20)

plt.show()
```

Shows the boundary line along with the data

Figure 4.14 depicts the linear boundary line learned from the training data. A crime that occurs on this line has an equal chance of being committed by either gang.

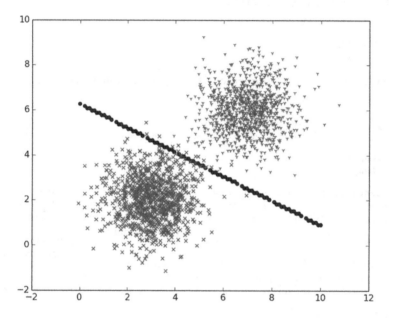

Figure 4.14   The diagonal dotted line represents when the probability between the two decisions is split equally. The confidence of making a decision increases as data lies farther away from the line.

4.5   *Multiclass classifier*

So far, you've dealt with multidimensional input, but not multivariate output, as shown in figure 4.15. For example, instead of binary labels on the data, what if you have 3, or 4, or 100 classes? Logistic regression requires two labels, no more.

Image classification, for example, is a popular multivariate classification problem because the goal is to decide the class of an image from a collection of candidates. A photograph may be bucketed into one of hundreds of categories.

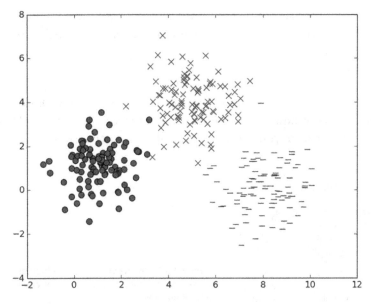

Figure 4.15 The independent variable is two-dimensional, indicated by the x-axis and y-axis. The dependent variable can be one of three labels, shown by the color and shape of the data points.

To handle more than two labels, you may reuse logistic regression in a clever way (using a one-versus-all or one-versus-one approach) or develop a new approach (softmax regression). Let's look at each of the approaches in the next sections. The logistic regression approaches require a decent amount of ad hoc engineering, so let's focus on softmax regression.

4.5.1 One-versus-all

First, you train a classifier for each of the labels, as shown in figure 4.16. If there are three labels, you have three classifiers available to use: f1, f2, and f3. To test on new

One-versus-all

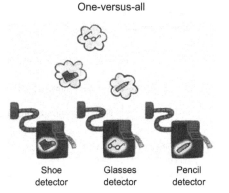

Shoe   Glasses   Pencil
detector   detector   detector

Figure 4.16 One-versus-all is a multiclass classifier approach that requires a detector for each class.

data, you run each of the classifiers to see which one produced the most confident response. Intuitively, you label the new point by the label of the classifier that responded most confidently.

4.5.2   *One-versus-one*

Then you train a classifier for each pair of labels (see figure 4.17). If there are three labels, that's just three unique pairs. But for *k* number of labels, that's $k(k - 1)/2$ pairs of labels. On new data, you run all the classifiers and choose the class with the most wins.

One-versus-one

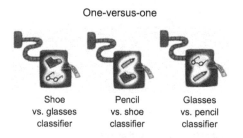

| Shoe vs. glasses classifier | Pencil vs. shoe classifier | Glasses vs. pencil classifier |

Figure 4.17   In one-versus-one multiclass classification, there's a detector for each pair of classes.

4.5.3   *Softmax regression*

Softmax regression is named after the traditional max function, which takes a vector and returns the max value; but softmax isn't exactly the max function, because it has the added benefit of being continuous and differentiable. As a result, it has the helpful properties for stochastic gradient descent to work efficiently.

In this type of multiclass classification setup, each class has a confidence (or probability) score for each input vector. The softmax step picks the highest-scoring output.

Open a new file called softmax.py, and follow along with the next listing. First, you'll visualize fake data to reproduce figure 4.15 (also reproduced in figure 4.18).

Listing 4.8   Visualizing multiclass data

```
import numpy as np                                      Imports NumPy
import matplotlib.pyplot as plt                         and matplotlib

x1_label0 = np.random.normal(1, 1, (100, 1))            Generates points near (1, 1)
x2_label0 = np.random.normal(1, 1, (100, 1))
x1_label1 = np.random.normal(5, 1, (100, 1))            Generates points near (5, 4)
x2_label1 = np.random.normal(4, 1, (100, 1))
x1_label2 = np.random.normal(8, 1, (100, 1))            Generates points near (8, 0)
x2_label2 = np.random.normal(0, 1, (100, 1))

plt.scatter(x1_label0, x2_label0, c='r', marker='o', s=60)     Visualizes the
plt.scatter(x1_label1, x2_label1, c='g', marker='x', s=60)     three labels on
plt.scatter(x1_label2, x2_label2, c='b', marker='_', s=60)     a scatter plot
plt.show()
```

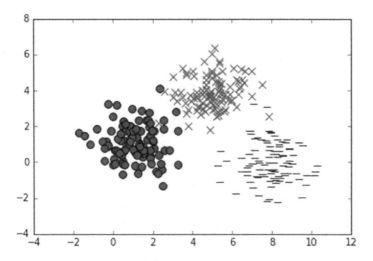

Figure 4.18 2D training data for multi-output classification

Next, in listing 4.9, you'll set up the training and test data to prepare for the softmax regression step. The labels must be represented as a vector in which only one element is 1 and the rest are 0s. This representation is called *one-hot encoding*. For instance, if there are three labels, they'd be represented as the following vectors: [1, 0, 0], [0, 1, 0], and [0, 0, 1].

EXERCISE 4.5
One-hot encoding might appear to be an unnecessary step. Why not just have a one-dimensional output with values of 1, 2, and 3 representing the three classes?

ANSWER
Regression may induce a semantic structure in the output. If outputs are similar, regression implies that their inputs were also similar. If you use just one dimension, you're implying that labels 2 and 3 are more similar to each other than 1 and 3. You must be careful about making unnecessary or incorrect assumptions, so it's a safe bet to use one-hot encoding.

Listing 4.9 Setting up training and test data for multiclass classification

```
xs_label0 = np.hstack((x1_label0, x2_label0))
xs_label1 = np.hstack((x1_label1, x2_label1))
xs_label2 = np.hstack((x1_label2, x2_label2))
xs = np.vstack((xs_label0, xs_label1, xs_label2))
```
Combines all input data into one big matrix

```
labels = np.matrix([[1., 0., 0.]] * len(x1_label0) + [[0., 1., 0.]] *
    len(x1_label1) + [[0., 0., 1.]] * len(x1_label2))
```
Creates the corresponding one-hot labels

```
arr = np.arange(xs.shape[0])
np.random.shuffle(arr)
xs = xs[arr, :]
labels = labels[arr, :]
```
Shuffles the dataset

Constructs the test dataset and labels
```
test_x1_label0 = np.random.normal(1, 1, (10, 1))
test_x2_label0 = np.random.normal(1, 1, (10, 1))
test_x1_label1 = np.random.normal(5, 1, (10, 1))
test_x2_label1 = np.random.normal(4, 1, (10, 1))
test_x1_label2 = np.random.normal(8, 1, (10, 1))
test_x2_label2 = np.random.normal(0, 1, (10, 1))
test_xs_label0 = np.hstack((test_x1_label0, test_x2_label0))
test_xs_label1 = np.hstack((test_x1_label1, test_x2_label1))
test_xs_label2 = np.hstack((test_x1_label2, test_x2_label2))

test_xs = np.vstack((test_xs_label0, test_xs_label1, test_xs_label2))
test_labels = np.matrix([[1., 0., 0.]] * 10 + [[0., 1., 0.]] * 10 + [[0., 0.,
    1.]] * 10)
```

```
train_size, num_features = xs.shape
```
The shape of the dataset tells you the number of examples and features per example.

Finally, in listing 4.10, you'll use softmax regression. Unlike the sigmoid function in logistic regression, here you'll use the `softmax` function provided by the TensorFlow library. The `softmax` function is similar to the `max` function, which outputs the maximum value from a list of numbers. It's called softmax because it's a "soft" or "smooth" approximation of the `max` function, which is not smooth or continuous (and that's bad). Continuous and smooth functions facilitate learning the correct weights of a neural network by back-propagation.

EXERCISE 4.6

Which of the following functions is continuous?

```
f(x) = x2
f(x) = min(x, 0)
f(x) = tan(x)
```

ANSWER

The first two are continuous. The last one, `tan(x)`, has periodic asymptotes, so there are some values for which there are no valid results.

Listing 4.10 Using softmax regression

```
import tensorflow as tf

learning_rate = 0.01
training_epochs = 1000          Defines
num_labels = 3                  hyperparameters
batch_size = 100

X = tf.placeholder("float", shape=[None, num_features])      Defines the input/output
Y = tf.placeholder("float", shape=[None, num_labels])        placeholder nodes

W = tf.Variable(tf.zeros([num_features, num_labels]))    Defines the model
b = tf.Variable(tf.zeros([num_labels]))                  parameters
y_model = tf.nn.softmax(tf.matmul(X, W) + b)        ◄──  Designs the
                                                         softmax model
cost = -tf.reduce_sum(Y * tf.log(y_model))
train_op = tf.train.GradientDescentOptimizer(learning_rate).minimize(cost)

correct_prediction = tf.equal(tf.argmax(y_model, 1), tf.argmax(Y, 1))
accuracy = tf.reduce_mean(tf.cast(correct_prediction, "float"))
```

Sets up the learning algorithm (annotation for `cost` and `train_op` lines)

Defines an op to measure success rate (annotation for `correct_prediction` and `accuracy` lines)

Now that you've defined the TensorFlow computation graph, execute it from a session. You'll try a new form of iteratively updating the parameters this time, called *batch learning*. Instead of passing in the data one piece at a time, you'll run the optimizer on batches of data. This speeds things up but introduces a risk of converging to a local optimum solution instead of the global best. Use the following listing for running the optimizer in batches.

Listing 4.11 Executing the graph

Retrieves a subset of the dataset corresponding to the current batch

Loops only enough times to complete a single pass through the dataset

```
with tf.Session() as sess:                              Opens a new session and
    tf.global_variables_initializer().run()             initializes all variables

    for step in range(training_epochs * train_size // batch_size):   ◄──
        offset = (step * batch_size) % train_size
        batch_xs = xs[offset:(offset + batch_size), :]
        batch_labels = labels[offset:(offset + batch_size)]
        err, _ = sess.run([cost, train_op], feed_dict={X: batch_xs, Y:
    batch_labels})
        print (step, err)        ◄──
```

Runs the optimizer on this batch

Prints ongoing results

```
W_val = sess.run(W)          Prints the                              Prints the
print('w', W_val)            final learned                          success rate
b_val = sess.run(b)          parameters
print('b', b_val)
print("accuracy", accuracy.eval(feed_dict={X: test_xs, Y: test_labels}))  ◁—┘
```

The final output of running the softmax regression algorithm on the dataset is the
following:

```
('w', array([[-2.101,  -0.021,   2.122],
             [-0.371,   2.229,  -1.858]], dtype=float32))
('b', array([10.305, -2.612, -7.693], dtype=float32))
Accuracy 1.0
```

You've learned the weights and biases of the model. You can reuse these learned
parameters to infer on test data. A simple way to do so is by saving and loading the
variables using TensorFlow's `Saver` object (see www.tensorflow.org/programmers_
guide/saved_model). You can run the model (called `y_model` in our code) to obtain
the model responses on your test input data.

4.6   *Application of classification*

Emotion is a difficult concept to operationalize. Happiness, sadness, anger, excite-
ment, and fear are examples of emotions that are subjective. What comes across as
exciting to someone might appear sarcastic to another. Text that appears to convey
anger to some might convey fear to others. If humans have so much trouble, what luck
can computers have?

At the very least, machine-learning researchers have figured out ways to classify
positive and negative sentiments within text. For example, let's say you're building an
Amazon-like website in which each item has user reviews. You want your intelligent
search engine to prefer items with positive reviews. Perhaps the best metric you have
available is the average star rating or number of thumbs-ups. But what if you have a lot
of heavy-text reviews without explicit ratings?

Sentiment analysis can be considered a binary classification problem. The input
is natural language text, and the output is a binary decision that infers positive or
negative sentiment. The following are datasets you can find online to solve this
exact problem:

- Large Movie Review Dataset: http://mng.bz/60nj
- Sentiment Labelled Sentences Data Set: http://mng.bz/CzSM
- Twitter Sentiment Analysis Dataset: http://mng.bz/2M4d

The biggest hurdle is to figure out how to represent raw text as an input to a classification algorithm. Throughout this chapter, the input to classification has always been a
feature vector. One of the oldest methods of converting raw text into a feature vector

is called *bag-of-words*. You can find a nice tutorial and code implementation for it here: http://mng.bz/K8yz.

4.7 Summary

- There are many ways to solve classification problems, but logistic regression and softmax regression are two of the most robust in terms of accuracy and performance.
- It's important to preprocess data before running classification. For example, discrete independent variables can be readjusted into binary variables.
- So far, you've approached classification from the point of view of regression. In later chapters, you'll revisit classification using neural networks.
- There are various ways to approach multiclass classification. There's no clear answer to which one you should try first among one-versus-one, one-versus-all, and softmax regression. But the softmax approach is a little more hands-free and allows you to fiddle with more hyperparameters.

5 Automatically clustering data

This chapter covers

- Basic clustering with k-means
- Representing audio
- Audio segmentation
- Clustering with a self-organizing map

Suppose you have a collection of not-pirated, totally legal MP3s on your hard drive. All your songs are crowded in one massive folder. Perhaps automatically grouping similar songs into categories such as Country, Rap, and Rock would help organize them. This act of assigning an item to a group (such as an MP3 to a playlist) in an unsupervised fashion is called *clustering*.

The previous chapter on classification assumes you're given a training dataset of correctly labeled data. Unfortunately, you don't always have that luxury when you collect data in the real world. For example, suppose you want to divide a large amount of music into interesting playlists. How could you possibly group songs if you don't have direct access to their metadata?

Spotify, SoundCloud, Google Music, Pandora, and many other music-streaming services try to solve this problem in order to recommend similar songs to customers. Their approach includes a mixture of various machine-learning techniques, but clustering is often at the heart of the solution.

Clustering is the process of intelligently categorizing the items in your dataset. The overall idea is that two items in the same cluster are "closer" to each other than items that belong to separate clusters. That's the general definition, leaving the interpretation of *closeness* open. For example, perhaps cheetahs and leopards belong in the same cluster, whereas elephants belong to another, when closeness is measured by the similarity of two species in the hierarchy of biological classification (family, genus, and species).

You can imagine that many clustering algorithms are out there. This chapter focuses on two types: *k-means* and *self-organizing map*. These approaches are completely *unsupervised*, meaning they fit a model without ground-truth examples.

First, you'll learn how to load audio files into TensorFlow and represent them as feature vectors. Then, you'll implement various clustering techniques to solve real-world problems.

5.1 Traversing files in TensorFlow

Some common input types in machine-learning algorithms are audio and image files. This shouldn't come as a surprise, because sound recordings and photographs are raw, redundant, and often noisy representations of semantic concepts. Machine learning is a tool to help handle these complications.

These data files have various implementations: for example, an image can be encoded as a PNG or JPEG file, and an audio file can be an MP3 or a WAV. In this chapter, you'll investigate how to read audio files as input to your clustering algorithm so you automatically group music that sounds similar.

EXERCISE 5.1

What are the pros and cons of MP3 and WAV? How about PNG versus JPEG?

ANSWER

MP3 and JPEG significantly compress the data, so such files are easy to store or transmit. But because these are lossy, WAV and PNG are closer to the original content.

Reading files from disk isn't exactly a machine-learning-specific ability. You can use a variety of Python libraries to load files into memory, such as NumPy or SciPy. Some developers like to treat the data-preprocessing step separately from the machine-learning step. There's no absolute right or wrong way to manage the pipeline, but we'll try TensorFlow for both data preprocessing and learning.

TensorFlow provides an operator called `tf.train.match_filenames_once(...)` to list files in a directory. You can then pass this information along to the queue operator `tf.train.string_input_producer(...)`. That way, you can access filenames one at a time, without loading everything at once. Given a filename, you can decode the file to retrieve usable data. Figure 5.1 outlines the whole process of using the queue.

The following listing shows an implementation of reading files from disk in TensorFlow.

Listing 5.1 Traversing a directory for data

Stores filenames that match a pattern

Sets up a pipeline for retrieving filenames randomly

```
import tensorflow as tf

filenames = tf.train.match_filenames_once('./audio_dataset/*.wav')
count_num_files = tf.size(filenames)
filename_queue = tf.train.string_input_producer(filenames)
reader = tf.WholeFileReader()
filename, file_contents = reader.read(filename_queue)

with tf.Session() as sess:
    sess.run(tf.global_variables_initializer())
    num_files = sess.run(count_num_files)

    coord = tf.train.Coordinator()
    threads = tf.train.start_queue_runners(coord=coord)

    for i in range(num_files):
        audio_file = sess.run(filename)
        print(audio_file)
```

Runs the reader to extract file data

Natively reads a file in TensorFlow

Counts the number of files

Initializes threads for the filename queue

Loops through the data one by one

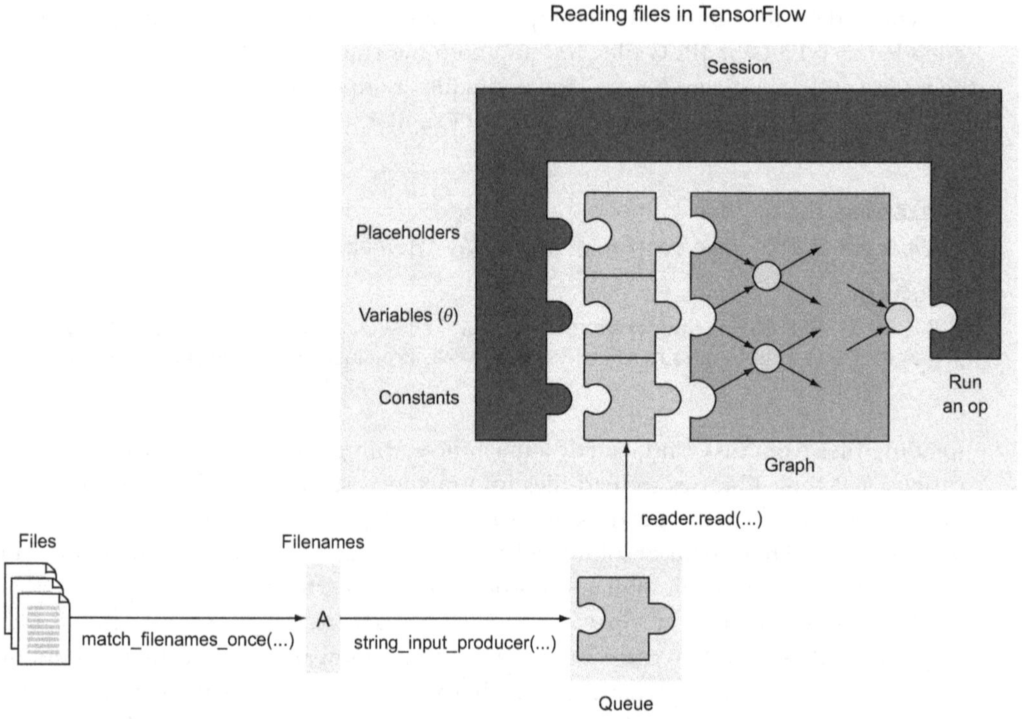

Reading files in TensorFlow

Figure 5.1   **You can use a queue in TensorFlow to read files. The queue is built into the TensorFlow framework, and you can use the `reader.read(...)` function to access (and dequeue) it.**

TIP   If you couldn't get listing 5.1 to work, you may want to try the advice posted on this book's official forum: http://mng.bz/Q9aD.

5.2   *Extracting features from audio*

Machine-learning algorithms are typically designed to use feature vectors as input; but sound files use a different format. You need a way to extract features from sound files to create feature vectors.

It helps to understand how these files are represented. If you've ever seen a vinyl record, you've probably noticed the representation of audio as grooves indented in the disk. Our ears interpret audio from a series of vibrations through air. By recording the vibration properties, an algorithm can store sound in a data format.

The real world is continuous, but computers store data in discrete values. The sound is digitalized into a discrete representation through an analog-to-digital converter (ADC). You can think about sound as fluctuation of a wave over time. But that data is too noisy and difficult to comprehend.

An equivalent way to represent a wave is by examining its frequencies at each time interval. This perspective is called the *frequency domain*. It's easy to convert between time domains and frequency domains by using a mathematical operation called a *discrete Fourier transform* (commonly implemented using an algorithm known as the *fast Fourier transform*). You'll use this technique to extract a feature vector out of a sound.

A handy Python library can help you view audio in this frequency domain. Download it from https://github.com/BinRoot/BregmanToolkit/archive/master.zip. Extract it, and then run the following command to set it up:

```
$ python setup.py install
```

> **Python 2 required**
>
> The BregmanToolkit is officially supported on Python 2. If you're using Jupyter Note-book, you can have access to both versions of Python by following the directions out-lined in the official Jupyter docs: http://mng.bz/ebvw.
>
> In particular, you can include Python 2 with the following commands:
>
> ```
> $ python2 -m pip install ipykernel
> $ python2 -m -ipykernel install --user
> ```

A sound may produce 12 kinds of pitches. In music terminology, the 12 pitches are C, C#, D, D#, E, F, F#, G, G#, A, A#, and B. Listing 5.2 shows how to retrieve the contribution of each pitch in a 0.1-second interval, resulting in a matrix with 12 rows. The number of columns grows as the length of the audio file increases. Specifically, there will be $10 \times t$ columns for a t-second audio. This matrix is also called a *chromagram* of the audio.

Listing 5.2   Representing audio in Python

```
from bregman.suite import *

def get_chromagram(audio_file):
    F = Chromagram(audio_file, nfft=16384, wfft=8192, nhop=2205)
    return F.X
```

Passes in the filename

Uses these parameters to describe 12 pitches every 0.1 second

Represents the values of a 12-dimensional vector 10 times per second

The chromagram output is a matrix, shown in figure 5.2. A sound clip can be read as a chromagram, and chromagram is a recipe for generating a sound clip. Now you have a way to convert between audio and matrices. And as you've learned, most machine-learning algorithms accept feature vectors as a valid form of data. That said, the first machine-learning algorithm you'll look at is k-means clustering.

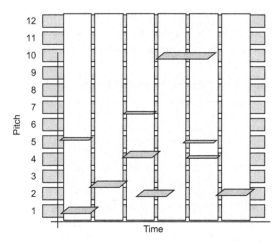

Figure 5.2 The chromagram matrix, where the x-axis represents time, and the y-axis represents pitch class. The green parallelograms indicate the presence of that pitch at that time.

To run machine-learning algorithms on your chromagram, you first need to decide how you're going to represent a feature vector. One idea is to simplify the audio by looking only at the most significant pitch class per time interval, as shown in figure 5.3.

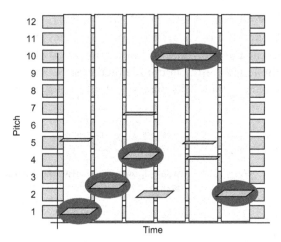

Figure 5.3 The most influential pitch at every time interval is highlighted. You can think of it as the loudest pitch at each time interval.

Then you count the number of times each pitch shows up in the audio file. Figure 5.4 shows this data as a histogram, forming a 12-dimensional vector. If you normalize the vector so that all the counts add up to 1, you can easily compare audio of different lengths.

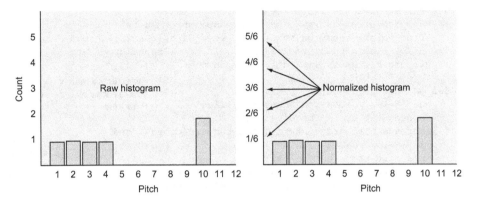

Figure 5.4 You count the frequency of loudest pitches heard at each interval to generate this histogram, which acts as your feature vector.

EXERCISE 5.2
What are some other ways to represent an audio clip as a feature vector?

ANSWER
You can visualize the audio clip as an image (such as a spectrogram), and use image-analysis techniques to extract image features.

Take a look at the following listing to generate the histogram from figure 5.4, which is your feature vector.

Listing 5.3   Obtaining a dataset for k-means

```
import tensorflow as tf
import numpy as np
from bregman.suite import *


filenames = tf.train.match_filenames_once('./audio_dataset/*.wav')
count_num_files = tf.size(filenames)
filename_queue = tf.train.string_input_producer(filenames)
reader = tf.WholeFileReader()
filename, file_contents = reader.read(filename_queue)

chroma = tf.placeholder(tf.float32)
max_freqs = tf.argmax(chroma, 0)

def get_next_chromagram(sess):
    audio_file = sess.run(filename)
    F = Chromagram(audio_file, nfft=16384, wfft=8192, nhop=2205)
    return F.X
```

Creates an op to identify the pitch with the biggest contribution

```
def extract_feature_vector(sess, chroma_data):
    num_features, num_samples = np.shape(chroma_data)
    freq_vals = sess.run(max_freqs, feed_dict={chroma: chroma_data})
    hist, bins = np.histogram(freq_vals, bins=range(num_features + 1))
    return hist.astype(float) / num_samples

def get_dataset(sess):
    num_files = sess.run(count_num_files)
    coord = tf.train.Coordinator()
    threads = tf.train.start_queue_runners(coord=coord)
    xs = []
    for _ in range(num_files):
        chroma_data = get_next_chromagram(sess)
        x = [extract_feature_vector(sess, chroma_data)]
        x = np.matrix(x)
        if len(xs) == 0:
            xs = x
        else:
            xs = np.vstack((xs, x))
    return xs
```

**Constructs a matrix
where each row is a
data item**

**Converts a
chromagram
into a feature
vector**

NOTE   All code listings are available from this book's website at www.manning
.com/books/machine-learning-with-tensorflow and on GitHub at https://
github.com/BinRoot/TensorFlow-Book/tree/master/ch05_clustering.

5.3   *K-means clustering*

The *k-means algorithm* is one of the oldest yet most robust ways to cluster data. The k
in k-means is a variable representing a natural number. So, you can imagine there's
3-means clustering, or 4-means clustering, or any other value for k. Thus, the first step
of k-means clustering is to choose a value for k. Just to be more concrete, let's pick
$k = 3$. With that in mind, the goal of 3-means clustering is to divide the dataset into
three categories (also called *clusters*).

> ### Choosing the number of clusters
> Choosing the right number of clusters often depends on the task. For example, sup-
> pose you're planning an event for hundreds of people, both young and old. If you have
> the budget for only two entertainment options, you can use k-means clustering with
> $k = 2$ to separate the guests into two age groups. Other times, determining the value
> of k isn't as obvious. Automatically figuring out the value of k is a bit more compli-
> cated, so we won't touch on that much in this section. In simplified terms, a straight-
> forward way of determining the best value of k is to iterate over a range of k-means
> simulations and apply a cost function to determine which value of k caused the best
> differentiation between clusters at the lowest value of k.

The k-means algorithm treats data points as points in space. If your dataset is a collection of guests at an event, you can represent each one by their age. Thus, your dataset is
a collection of feature vectors. In this case, each feature vector is only one-dimensional,
because you're considering only the age of the person.

For clustering music by the audio data, the data points are feature vectors from the audio files. If two points are close together, their audio features are similar. You want to discover which audio files belong in the same "neighborhood," because those clusters will probably be a good way to organize your music files.

The midpoint of all the points in a cluster is called its *centroid*. Depending on the audio features you choose to extract, a centroid could capture concepts such as loud sound, high-pitched sound, or saxophone-like sound. It's important to note that the k-means algorithm assigns nondescript labels, such as cluster 1, cluster 2, and cluster 3. Figure 5.5 shows examples of the sound data.

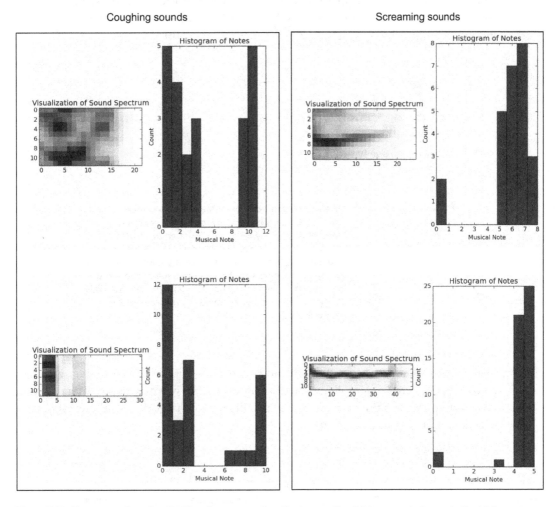

Figure 5.5 Four examples of audio files. As you can see, the two on the right appear to have similar histograms. The two on the left also have similar histograms. Your clustering algorithms will be able to group these sounds together.

The k-means algorithm assigns a feature vector to one of the k clusters by choosing the cluster whose centroid is closest to it. The k-means algorithm starts by guessing the cluster location. It iteratively improves its guess over time. The algorithm either converges when it no longer improves the guesses, or stops after a maximum number of attempts.

The heart of the algorithm consists of two tasks, assignment and recentering:

1   In the assignment step, you assign each data item (feature vector) to a category of the closest centroid.

2   In the recentering step, you calculate the midpoints of the newly updated clusters.

These two steps repeat to provide increasingly better clustering results, and the algorithm stops either when it has repeated a desired number of times or when the assignments no longer change. Figure 5.6 illustrates the algorithm.

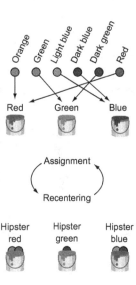

Figure 5.6   One iteration of the k-means algorithm. Let's say you're clustering colors into three buckets (an informal way to say *category*). You can start with an initial guess of red, green, and blue and begin the assignment step. Then you update the bucket colors by averaging the colors that belong to each bucket. You keep repeating until the buckets no longer substantially change color, arriving at the color representing the centroid of each cluster.

Listing 5.4 shows how to implement the k-means algorithm using the dataset generated by listing 5.3. For simplicity, you'll choose $k = 2$, so you can easily verify that your algorithm partitions the audio files into two dissimilar categories. You'll use the first k vectors as initial guesses for centroids.

Listing 5.4   Implementing k-means

```
k = 2
max_iterations = 100

def initial_cluster_centroids(X, k):
    return X[0:k, :]
```

Chooses the initial guesses of cluster centroids

Declares the maximum number of iterations to run k-means

Decides the number of clusters

```
def assign_cluster(X, centroids):
    expanded_vectors = tf.expand_dims(X, 0)
    expanded_centroids = tf.expand_dims(centroids, 1)
    distances = tf.reduce_sum(tf.square(tf.subtract(expanded_vectors,
     expanded_centroids)), 2)
    mins = tf.argmin(distances, 0)
    return mins

def recompute_centroids(X, Y):
    sums = tf.unsorted_segment_sum(X, Y, k)
    counts = tf.unsorted_segment_sum(tf.ones_like(X), Y, k)
    return sums / counts

with tf.Session() as sess:
    sess.run(tf.global_variables_initializer())
    X = get_dataset(sess)
    centroids = initial_cluster_centroids(X, k)
    i, converged = 0, False
    while not converged and i < max_iterations:
        i += 1
        Y = assign_cluster(X, centroids)
        centroids = sess.run(recompute_centroids(X, Y))
    print(centroids)
```

Assigns each data item to its nearest cluster

Updates the cluster centroids to their midpoint

Iterates to find the best cluster locations

And that's it! If you know the number of clusters and the feature vector representation, you can use listing 5.4 to cluster anything! In the next section, you'll apply clustering to audio snippets within an audio file.

5.4 Audio segmentation

In the preceding section, you clustered various audio files to automatically group them. This section is about using clustering algorithms within just one audio file. Whereas the former is called *clustering*, the latter is referred to as *segmentation*. Segmentation is another word for clustering, but we often say *segment* instead of *cluster* when dividing a single image or audio file into separate components. It's similar to the way dividing a sentence into words is different from dividing a word into letters. Though they both share the general idea of breaking bigger pieces into smaller components, words are different from letters.

Let's say you have a long audio file, maybe of a podcast or talk show. Imagine writing a machine-learning algorithm to identify which of two people is speaking in an audio interview. The goal of segmenting an audio file is to associate which parts of the audio clip belong to the same category. In this case, you'd have a category for each person, and the utterances made by each person should converge to their appropriate categories, as shown in figure 5.7.

Open a new source file, and follow along with listing 5.5, which will get you started by organizing the audio data for segmentation. It splits an audio file into multiple

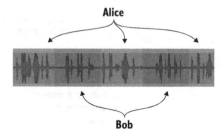

Figure 5.7   Audio segmentation is the process of automatically labeling segments.

segments of size `segment_size`. A long audio file would contain hundreds, if not thousands, of segments.

Listing 5.5   Organizing data for segmentation

```
import tensorflow as tf
import numpy as np
from bregman.suite import *


k = 2
segment_size = 50
max_iterations = 100


chroma = tf.placeholder(tf.float32)
max_freqs = tf.argmax(chroma, 0)

def get_chromagram(audio_file):
    F = Chromagram(audio_file, nfft=16384, wfft=8192, nhop=2205)
    return F.X


def get_dataset(sess, audio_file):
    chroma_data = get_chromagram(audio_file)
    print('chroma_data', np.shape(chroma_data))
    chroma_length = np.shape(chroma_data)[1]
    xs = []
    for i in range(chroma_length / segment_size):
        chroma_segment = chroma_data[:, i*segment_size:(i+1)*segment_size]
        x = extract_feature_vector(sess, chroma_segment)
        if len(xs) == 0:
            xs = x
        else:
            xs = np.vstack((xs, x))
    return xs
```

- **Decides the number of clusters**
- **The smaller the segment size, the better the results (but slower performance).**
- **Decides when to stop the iterations**
- **Obtains a dataset by extracting segments of the audio as separate data items**

Now run k-means clustering on this dataset to identify when segments are similar. The intention is that k-means will categorize similar-sounding segments with the same label. If two people have significantly different-sounding voices, their sound snippets will belong to different labels.

Listing 5.6 Segmenting an audio clip

```
with tf.Session() as sess:
    X = get_dataset(sess, 'TalkingMachinesPodcast.wav')
    print(np.shape(X))
    centroids = initial_cluster_centroids(X, k)
    i, converged = 0, False
    while not converged and i < max_iterations:          Runs the k-means
        i += 1                                           algorithm
        Y = assign_cluster(X, centroids)
        centroids = sess.run(recompute_centroids(X, Y))
        if i % 50 == 0:
            print('iteration', i)                        Prints the labels
    segments = sess.run(Y)                               for each time
    for i in range(len(segments)):                       interval
        seconds = (i * segment_size) / float(10)
        min, sec = divmod(seconds, 60)
        time_str = '{}m {}s'.format(min, sec)
        print(time_str, segments[i])
```

The output of running listing 5.6 is a list of timestamps and cluster IDs that correspond to who is talking during the podcast:

```
('0.0m 0.0s', 0)
('0.0m 2.5s', 1)
('0.0m 5.0s', 0)
('0.0m 7.5s', 1)
('0.0m 10.0s', 1)
('0.0m 12.5s', 1)
('0.0m 15.0s', 1)
('0.0m 17.5s', 0)
('0.0m 20.0s', 1)
('0.0m 22.5s', 1)
('0.0m 25.0s', 0)
('0.0m 27.5s', 0)
```

EXERCISE 5.3

How can you detect whether the clustering algorithm has converged (so that you can stop the algorithm early)?

ANSWER

One way is to monitor how the cluster centroids change, and declare convergence once no more updates are necessary (for example, when the difference in the size of the error isn't changing significantly between iterations). To do this, you'd need to calculate the size of the error and decide what constitutes "significantly."

5.5   *Clustering using a self-organizing map*

A *self-organizing map* (SOM) is a model for representing data into a lower-dimensional space. In doing so, it automatically shifts similar data items closer together. For example, suppose you're ordering pizza for a large gathering of people. You don't want to order the same type of pizza for every single person—because one might happen to fancy pineapple with mushrooms and peppers for their toppings, and you may prefer anchovies with arugula and onions.

Each person's preference of toppings can be represented as a three-dimensional vector. An SOM lets you embed these three-dimensional vectors in two dimensions (as long as you define a distance metric between pizzas). Then, a visualization of the two-dimensional plot reveals good candidates for the number of clusters.

Although it may take longer to converge than the k-means algorithm, the SOM approach has no assumptions about the number of clusters. In the real world, it's hard to select a value for the number of clusters. Consider a gathering of people, as shown in figure 5.8, in which the clusters change over time.

Figure 5.8   In the real world, we see groups of people in clusters all the time. Applying k-means requires knowing the number of clusters ahead of time. A more flexible tool is a self-organizing map, which has no preconceptions about the number of clusters.

The SOM merely reinterprets the data into a structure conducive to clustering. The algorithm works as follows. First, you design a grid of nodes; each node holds a weight vector of the same dimension as a data item. The weights of each node are initialized to random numbers, typically from a standard normal distribution.

Next, you show data items to the network one by one. For each data item, the network identifies the node whose weight vector most closely matches it. This node is called the *best matching unit* (BMU).

After the network identifies the BMU, all neighbors of the BMU are updated so their weight vectors move closer to the BMU's value. The closer nodes are affected more strongly than nodes farther away. Moreover, the number of neighbors around a BMU shrinks over time at a rate determined usually by trial and error. Figure 5.9 illustrates the algorithm.

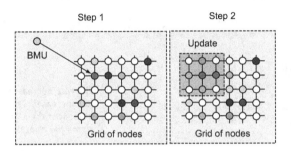

Figure 5.9 One iteration of the SOM algorithm. The first step is to identify the best matching unit (BMU), and the second step is to update the neighboring nodes. You keep iterating these two steps with training data until certain convergence criteria are reached.

The following listing shows how to start implementing a SOM in TensorFlow. Follow along by opening a new source file.

Listing 5.7 Setting up the SOM algorithm

```
import tensorflow as tf
import numpy as np


class SOM:
    def __init__(self, width, height, dim):
        self.num_iters = 100
        self.width = width
        self.height = height
        self.dim = dim
        self.node_locs = self.get_locs()

        nodes = tf.Variable(tf.random_normal([width*height, dim]))
        self.nodes = nodes

        x = tf.placeholder(tf.float32, [dim])
        iter = tf.placeholder(tf.float32)

        self.x = x
        self.iter = iter
```

Each node is a vector of dimension dim. For a 2D grid, there are width × height nodes; get_locs is defined in listing 5.10.

These two ops are inputs at each iteration.

You'll need to access them from another method.

```
   ┌──▷   bmu_loc = self.get_bmu_loc(x)
   │
   │      self.propagate_nodes = self.get_propagation(bmu_loc, x, iter)   ◁──────┐
   │                                                                            │
```

Finds the node that most closely   **Updates the values of the**
matches the input (in listing 5.9)   **neighbors (in listing 5.8)**

In the next listing, you define how to update neighboring weights, given the current time interval and BMU location. As time goes by, the BMU's neighboring weights are less influenced to change. That way, over time the weights gradually settle.

Listing 5.8   Defining how to update the values of neighbors

Expands bmu_loc, so you can
efficiently compare it pairwise with
each element of node_locs
                                                          The rate decreases as
                                                          iter increases. This value
```
      def get_propagation(self, bmu_loc, x, iter):         influences the alpha and
          num_nodes = self.width * self.height             sigma parameters.
          rate = 1.0 - tf.div(iter, self.num_iters)   ◁──┘
          alpha = rate * 0.5
          sigma = rate * tf.to_float(tf.maximum(self.width, self.height)) / 2.
   ┌───▷  expanded_bmu_loc = tf.expand_dims(tf.to_float(bmu_loc), 0)
   │      sqr_dists_from_bmu = tf.reduce_sum(
   │        tf.square(tf.subtract(expanded_bmu_loc, self.node_locs)), 1)
   ┌──▷  neigh_factor =
   │        tf.exp(-tf.div(sqr_dists_from_bmu, 2 * tf.square(sigma)))
   │      rate = tf.multiply(alpha, neigh_factor)
   │      rate_factor =
   │        tf.stack([[tf.tile(tf.slice(rate, [i], [1]),
   │                  [self.dim]) for i in range(num_nodes)])
   │      nodes_diff = tf.multiply(
   │        rate_factor,
   │        tf.subtract(tf.stack([[x for i in range(num_nodes)]]), self.nodes))
   │      update_nodes = tf.add(self.nodes, nodes_diff)   ◁─────┐
   │      return tf.assign(self.nodes, update_nodes)   ◁──────┐  │  Defines the
   │                                                          │  │  updates
```
Ensures that nodes closer to the   **Returns an op to**
BMU change more dramatically   **perform the updates**

The following listing shows how to find the BMU location, given an input data item. It searches through the grid of nodes to find the one with the closest match. This is similar to the assignment step in k-means clustering, where each node in the grid is a potential cluster centroid.

Listing 5.9   Getting the node location of the closest match

```
      def get_bmu_loc(self, x):
          expanded_x = tf.expand_dims(x, 0)
          sqr_diff = tf.square(tf.subtract(expanded_x, self.nodes))
```

```
dists = tf.reduce_sum(sqr_diff, 1)
bmu_idx = tf.argmin(dists, 0)
bmu_loc = tf.stack([tf.mod(bmu_idx, self.width), tf.div(bmu_idx,
➥ self.width)])
return bmu_loc
```

In the next listing, you create a helper method to generate a list of (x, y) locations on all the nodes in the grid.

Listing 5.10 Generating a matrix of points

```
def get_locs(self):
    locs = [[x, y]
                for y in range(self.height)
                for x in range(self.width)]
    return tf.to_float(locs)
```

Finally, let's define a method called `train` to run the algorithm, as shown in listing 5.11. First, you must set up the session and run the global_variables_initializer op. Next, you loop num_iters a certain number of times to update weights using the input data one by one. After the loop ends, you record the final node weights and their locations.

Listing 5.11 Running the SOM algorithm

```
def train(self, data):
    with tf.Session() as sess:
        sess.run(tf.global_variables_initializer())
        for i in range(self.num_iters):
            for data_x in data:
                sess.run(self.propagate_nodes, feed_dict={self.x: data_x,
                ➥ self.iter: i})
        centroid_grid = [[] for i in range(self.width)]
        self.nodes_val = list(sess.run(self.nodes))
        self.locs_val = list(sess.run(self.node_locs))
        for i, l in enumerate(self.locs_val):
            centroid_grid[int(l[0])].append(self.nodes_val[i])
        self.centroid_grid = centroid_grid
```

That's it! Now let's see it in action. Test the implementation by showing the SOM some input. In listing 5.12, the input is a list of three-dimensional feature vectors. By training the SOM, you'll discover clusters within the data. You'll use a 4 × 4 grid, but it's best to try various values to cross-validate the best grid size. Figure 5.10 shows the output of running the code.

Listing 5.12   Testing the implementation and visualizing the results

```python
from matplotlib import pyplot as plt
import numpy as np
from som import SOM

colors = np.array(
    [[0., 0., 1.],
     [0., 0., 0.95],
     [0., 0.05, 1.],
     [0., 1., 0.],
     [0., 0.95, 0.],
     [0., 1, 0.05],
     [1., 0., 0.],
     [1., 0.05, 0.],
     [1., 0., 0.05],
     [1., 1., 0.]])

som = SOM(4, 4, 3)       ◁——  The grid size is 4 × 4,
som.train(colors)              and the input
                               dimension is 3.

plt.imshow(som.centroid_grid)
plt.show()
```

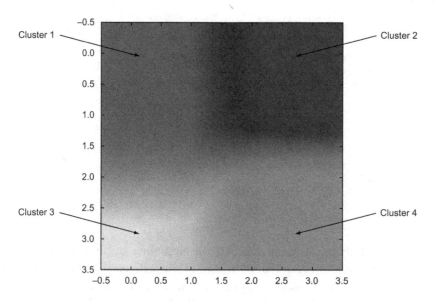

Figure 5.10   The SOM places all three-dimensional data points into a two-dimensional grid. From it, you can pick the cluster centroids (automatically or manually) and achieve clustering in an intuitive lower-dimensional space.

The SOM embeds higher-dimensional data into 2D to make clustering easy. This acts as a handy preprocessing step. You can manually go in and indicate the cluster centroids by observing the SOM's output, but it's also possible to automatically find good centroid candidates by observing the gradient of the weights. For the adventurous, we suggest reading the famous paper "Clustering of the Self-Organizing Map," by Juha Vesanto and Esa Alhoniemi: http://mng.bz/XzyS.

5.6 *Application of clustering*

You've already seen two practical applications of clustering: organizing music and segmenting an audio clip to label similar sounds. Clustering is especially helpful when the training dataset doesn't contain corresponding labels. As you know, such a situation characterizes unsupervised learning. Sometimes, data is just too inconvenient to annotate.

For example, suppose you want to understand sensor data from the accelerometer of a phone or smartwatch. At each time step, the accelerometer provides a three-dimensional vector, but you have no idea whether the human is walking, standing, sitting, dancing, jogging, or so on. You can obtain such a dataset at http://mng.bz/rTMe.

To cluster the time-series data, you'll need to summarize the list of accelerometer vectors into a concise feature vector. One way is to generate a histogram of differences between consecutive magnitudes of the acceleration. The derivative of acceleration is called *jerk*, and you can apply the same operation to obtain a histogram outlining differences in jerk magnitudes.

This process of generating a histogram out of data is exactly like the preprocessing steps on audio data explained in this chapter. After you've transformed the histograms into feature vectors, you can use the same code listings taught earlier (such as k-means in TensorFlow).

> **NOTE** Whereas previous chapters discussed supervised learning, this chapter focused on unsupervised learning. In the next chapter, you'll see a machine-learning algorithm that is neither of the two. It's a modeling framework that doesn't get much attention by programmers nowadays but is the essential tool for statisticians for unveiling hidden factors in data.

5.7 *Summary*

- Clustering is an unsupervised machine-learning algorithm for discovering structure in data.
- K-means clustering is one of the easiest algorithms to implement and understand, and it also performs well in terms of speed and accuracy.
- If the number of clusters isn't specified, you can use the self-organizing map (SOM) algorithm to view the data in a simplified perspective.

Hidden Markov models

This chapter covers

- Defining interpretive models
- Using Markov chains to model data
- Inferring hidden state using a hidden Markov model

If a rocket blows up, someone's probably going to get fired, so rocket scientists and engineers must be able to make confident decisions about all components and configurations. They do so by physical simulations and mathematical deduction from first principles. You, too, have solved science problems with pure logical thinking. Consider Boyle's law: pressure and volume of a gas are inversely related under a fixed temperature. You can make insightful inferences from these simple laws that have been discovered about the world. Recently, machine learning has started to play the role of an important sidekick to deductive reasoning.

Rocket science and *machine learning* aren't phrases that usually appear together. But nowadays, modeling real-world sensor readings by using intelligent data-driven algorithms is more approachable in the aerospace industry. Also, the use of machine-learning techniques is flourishing in the healthcare and automotive industries. But why?

This influx can be partly attributed to better understanding of *interpretable* models, which are machine-learning models in which the learned parameters have clear interpretations. If a rocket blows up, for example, an interpretable model might help trace the root cause.

EXERCISE 6.1

What makes a model interpretable may be slightly subjective. What's your criteria for an interpretable model?

ANSWER

We like to refer to mathematical proofs as the de facto explanation technique. If one were to convince another about the truth of a mathematical theorem, then a proof that irrefutably traces the steps of reasoning is sufficient.

This chapter is about exposing the hidden explanations behind observations. Consider a puppet master pulling strings to make a puppet appear alive. Analyzing only the motions of the puppet might lead to overly complicated conclusions about how it's possible for an inanimate object to move. After you notice the attached strings, you'll realize that a puppet master is the best explanation for the lifelike motions.

On that note, this chapter introduces *hidden Markov models* (HMMs), which reveal intuitive properties about the problem under study. The HMM is the "puppet master," which explains the observations. You model observations by using Markov chains, which are described in section 6.2.

Before going into detail about Markov chains and HMMs, let's consider alternative models. In the next section, you'll see models that may not be interpretable.

6.1 *Example of a not-so-interpretable model*

One classic example of a black-box machine-learning algorithm that's difficult to interpret is image classification. In an image-classification task, the goal is to assign a label to each input image. More simply, image classification is often posed as a multiple-choice question: which one of the listed categories best describes the image? Machine-learning practitioners have made tremendous advancements in solving this problem, to the point where today's best image classifiers match human-level performance on certain datasets.

You'll learn how to solve the problem of classifying images in chapter 9—convolutional neural networks (CNNs), which are a class of machine-learning models that end up learning a lot of parameters. But those parameters are the problem with CNNs: what do each of the thousands, if not millions, of parameters mean? It's difficult to ask an image classifier why it made the decision that it did. All we have available are the learned parameters, which may not easily explain the reasoning behind the classification.

Machine learning sometimes gets the notoriety of being a black-box tool that solves a specific problem without revealing how it arrives at its conclusion. The purpose of this chapter is to unveil an area of machine learning with an interpretable model. Specifically, you'll learn about the HMM and use TensorFlow to implement it.

6.2 *Markov model*

Andrey Markov was a Russian mathematician who studied the ways systems change over time in the presence of randomness. Imagine gas particles bouncing around in the air. Tracking the position of each particle by Newtonian physics can get way too complicated, so introducing randomness helps simplify the physical model a little.

Markov realized that what helps simplify a random system even further is considering only a limited area around the gas particle to model it. For example, maybe a gas particle in Europe has barely any effect on a particle in the United States. So why not ignore it? The mathematics is simplified when you look only at a nearby neighborhood instead of the entire system. This notion is now referred to as the *Markov property*.

Consider modeling the weather. A meteorologist evaluates various conditions with thermometers, barometers, and anemometers to help predict the weather. They draw on brilliant insight and years of experience to do their job.

Let's use the Markov property to help us get started with a simple model. First, you identify the possible situations, or *states*, that you care to study. Figure 6.1 shows three weather states as nodes in a graph: Cloudy, Rainy, and Sunny.

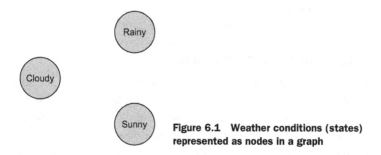

Figure 6.1   Weather conditions (states) represented as nodes in a graph

Now that you have the states, you want to also define how one state transforms into another. Modeling weather as a deterministic system is difficult. It's not an obvious conclusion that if it's sunny today, it'll certainly be sunny again tomorrow. Instead, you can introduce randomness and say that if it's sunny today, there's a 90% chance it'll be sunny again tomorrow, and a 10% chance it'll be cloudy. The Markov property comes into play when you use only today's weather condition to predict tomorrow's (instead of using all previous history).

EXERCISE 6.2

A robot that decides which action to perform based on only its current state is said to follow the Markov property. What are the advantages and disadvantages of such a decision-making process?

ANSWER

The Markov property is computationally easy to work with. But these models aren't able to generalize to situations that require accumulating a history of knowledge. Examples of these are models in which a trend over time is important, or in which knowledge of more than one past state gives a better idea of what to expect next.

Figure 6.2 demonstrates the transitions as directed edges drawn between nodes, with the arrow pointing toward the next future state. Each edge has a weight representing the probability (for example, there's a 30% chance that if today is rainy, tomorrow will be cloudy). The lack of an edge between two nodes is an elegant way of showing that the probability of that transformation is near zero. The transition probabilities can be learned from historical data, but for now, let's assume they're given to us.

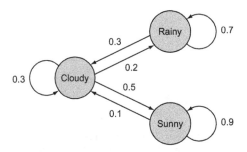

Figure 6.2 Transition probabilities between weather conditions are represented as directed edges.

If you have three states, you can represent the transitions as a 3 × 3 matrix. Each element of the matrix (at row i and column j) corresponds to the probability associated with the edge from node i to node j. In general, if you have N states, the *transition matrix* will be $N \times N$ in size (see figure 6.4 for an example).

We call this system a *Markov model.* Over time, a state changes using the transition probabilities defined in figure 6.2. In our example, Sunny has a 90% chance of Sunny again tomorrow, so we show an edge of probability 0.9, looping back to itself. There's a 10% chance of a sunny day being followed by a cloudy day, shown in the diagram as the edge 0.1, pointing from Sunny to Cloudy.

Figure 6.3 is another way to visualize how the states change, given the transition probabilities. It's often called a *trellis diagram*, which turns out to be an essential tool, as you'll see later when we implement the TensorFlow algorithms.

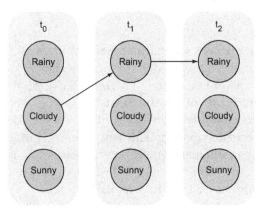

Figure 6.3 A trellis representation of the Markov system changing states over time

You've seen in previous chapters how TensorFlow code builds a graph to represent computation. It might be tempting to treat each node in a Markov model as a node in TensorFlow. But even though figures 6.2 and 6.3 nicely illustrate state transitions, there's a more efficient way to implement them in code, as shown in figure 6.4.

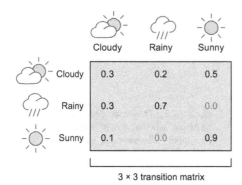

Figure 6.4   **A transition matrix conveys the probabilities of a state from the left (rows) transitioning to a state at the top (columns).**

Remember, nodes in a TensorFlow graph are tensors, so you can represent a transition matrix (let's call it *T*) as a node in TensorFlow. Then, you can apply mathematical operations on the TensorFlow node to achieve interesting results.

For example, suppose you prefer sunny days over rainy ones, so you have a score associated with each day. You represent your scores for each state in a 3 × 1 matrix called *s*. Then, multiplying the two matrices in TensorFlow using `tf.matmul(T*s)` gives the expected preference of transitioning from each state.

Representing a scenario in a Markov model allows you to greatly simplify how you view the world. But it's frequently difficult to measure the state of the world directly. Often, you have to use evidence from multiple observations to figure out the hidden meaning. And that's what the next section aims to solve!

6.3   *Hidden Markov model*

The Markov model defined in the previous section is convenient when all the states are observable, but that's not always the case. Consider having access to only temperature readings of a town. Temperature isn't weather, but it's related to it. How then can you infer the weather from this indirect set of measurements?

Rainy weather most likely causes a lower temperature reading, whereas a sunny day most likely causes a higher temperature reading. With temperature knowledge and transition probabilities alone, you can still make intelligent inferences about the most likely weather. Problems like this are common in the real world. A state might leave traces of hints behind, and those hints are all you have available to you.

Models like these are HMMs because the true states of the world (such as whether it's raining or sunny) aren't directly observable. These hidden states follow a Markov model, and each state emits a measurable observation with a certain likelihood. For example, the hidden state of Sunny might emit high temperature readings, but occasionally also low readings for one reason or another.

In an HMM, you have to define the emission probability, which is usually represented as a matrix called the *emission matrix*. The number of rows in the matrix is the number of states (Sunny, Cloudy, Rainy), and the number of columns is the number of observation types (Hot, Mild, Cold). Each element of the matrix is the probability associated with the emission.

The canonical way of visualizing an HMM is by appending the trellis with observations, as shown in figure 6.5.

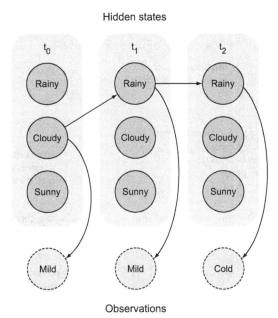

Figure 6.5 A hidden Markov model trellis showing how weather conditions might produce temperature readings

So that's *almost* it. The HMM is a description of transition probabilities, emission probabilities, and one more thing: *initial probabilities.* The initial probability is the probability of each state happening with no prior knowledge. If you're modeling the weather in Los Angeles, perhaps the initial probability of Sunny would be much greater. Or let's say you're modeling the weather in Seattle; well, you know you can set the initial probability of Rainy to something higher.

An HMM lets you understand a sequence of observations. In this weather-modeling scenario, one question you may ask is, what's the probability of observing a certain sequence of temperature readings? We'll answer this question by using the *forward algorithm.*

6.4   *Forward algorithm*

The *forward algorithm* computes the probability of an observation. Many permutations may cause a particular observation, so enumerating all possibilities the naïve way will take an exponentially long time to compute.

Instead, you can solve the problem by using *dynamic programming,* which is a strategy of breaking a complex problem into simple little ones and using a lookup table to cache the results. In your code, you'll save the lookup table as a NumPy array and feed it to a TensorFlow op to keep updating it.

As shown in the following listing, create an HMM class to capture the hidden Markov model parameters, which include the initial probability vector, transition probability matrix, and emission probability matrix.

Listing 6.1   Defining the HMM class

```
import numpy as np                          Imports the
import tensorflow as tf                     required libraries


class HMM(object):
    def __init__(self, initial_prob, trans_prob, obs_prob):
        self.N = np.size(initial_prob)
        self.initial_prob = initial_prob                    Stores the
        self.trans_prob = trans_prob                        parameters as
        self.emission = tf.constant(obs_prob)               method variables

        assert self.initial_prob.shape == (self.N, 1)       Double-checks that
        assert self.trans_prob.shape == (self.N, self.N)    the shapes of all the
        assert obs_prob.shape[0] == self.N                  matrices make sense

        self.obs_idx = tf.placeholder(tf.int32)       Defines the placeholders used
        self.fwd = tf.placeholder(tf.float64)         for the forward algorithm
```

Next, you'll define a quick helper function to access a row from the emission matrix. The code in the following listing is a helper function to efficiently obtain data from an arbitrary matrix. The slice function extracts a fraction of the original tensor. This function requires as input the relevant tensor, the starting location specified by a tensor, and the size of the slice specified by a tensor.

Listing 6.2   Creating a helper function to access emission probability of an observation

```
                                            The location of
                                            where to slice
                                            the emission
    def get_emission(self, obs_idx):        matrix                The shape
        slice_location = [0, obs_idx]    ◄──┘                     of the slice
        num_rows = tf.shape(self.emission)[0]
        slice_shape = [num_rows, 1]                        ◄──┘
        return tf.slice(self.emission, slice_location, slice_shape)  ◄──┐

                                                           Performs the
                                                           slicing operation
```

You need to define two TensorFlow ops. The first one, in the following listing, will be run only once to initialize the forward algorithm's cache.

Listing 6.3 Initializing the cache

```
def forward_init_op(self):
    obs_prob = self.get_emission(self.obs_idx)
    fwd = tf.multiply(self.initial_prob, obs_prob)
    return fwd
```

And the next op will update the cache at each observation, as shown in listing 6.4. Running this code is often called *executing a forward step*. Although it looks like this forward_op function takes no input, it depends on placeholder variables that need to be fed to the session. Specifically, self.fwd and self.obs_idx are the inputs to this function.

Listing 6.4 Updating the cache

```
def forward_op(self):
    transitions = tf.matmul(self.fwd,
  tf.transpose(self.get_emission(self.obs_idx)))
    weighted_transitions = transitions * self.trans_prob
    fwd = tf.reduce_sum(weighted_transitions, 0)
    return tf.reshape(fwd, tf.shape(self.fwd))
```

Outside the HMM class, let's define a function to run the forward algorithm, as shown in the following listing. The forward algorithm runs the forward step for each observation. In the end, it finally outputs a probability of observations.

Listing 6.5 Defining the forward algorithm given an HMM

```
def forward_algorithm(sess, hmm, observations):
    fwd = sess.run(hmm.forward_init_op(), feed_dict={hmm.obs_idx:
    observations[0]})
    for t in range(1, len(observations)):
        fwd = sess.run(hmm.forward_op(), feed_dict={hmm.obs_idx:
    observations[t], hmm.fwd: fwd})
    prob = sess.run(tf.reduce_sum(fwd))
    return prob
```

In the main function, let's set up the HMM class by feeding it the initial probability vector, transition probability matrix, and emission probability matrix. For consistency, the example in listing 6.6 is lifted directly from the Wikipedia article on HMMs: http://mng.bz/8ztL, as shown in figure 6.6.

In general, the three concepts are defined as follows:

- *Initial probability vector*—Starting probability of the states
- *Transition probability matrix*—Probabilities associated with landing on the next states, given the current state
- *Emission probability matrix*—Likelihood of an observed state implying the state you're interested in has occurred

Given these matrices, you'll call the forward algorithm that you just defined.

```
states = ('Rainy', 'Sunny')

observations = ('walk', 'shop', 'clean')

start_probability = {'Rainy': 0.6, 'Sunny': 0.4}

transition_probability = {
   'Rainy  : {'Rainy': 0.7, 'Sunny': 0.3},
   'Sunny' : {'Rainy': 0.4, 'Sunny': 0.6},
}

emission_probability = {
   'Rainy  : {'walk': 0.1, 'shop': 0.4, 'clean': 0.5},
   'Sunny' : {'walk': 0.6, 'shop': 0.3, 'clean': 0.1},
}
```

Figure 6.6   Screenshot of HMM example scenario from Wikipedia

---

Listing 6.6   Defining the HMM and calling the forward algorithm

```
if __name__ == '__main__':
    initial_prob = np.array([[0.6],
                             [0.4]])

    trans_prob = np.array([[0.7, 0.3],
                           [0.4, 0.6]])

    obs_prob = np.array([[0.1, 0.4, 0.5],
                         [0.6, 0.3, 0.1]])

    hmm = HMM(initial_prob=initial_prob, trans_prob=trans_prob,
     obs_prob=obs_prob)

    observations = [0, 1, 1, 2, 1]
    with tf.Session() as sess:
        prob = forward_algorithm(sess, hmm, observations)
        print('Probability of observing {} is {}'.format(observations, prob))
```

When you run listing 6.6, the algorithm outputs the following:

```
Probability of observing [0, 1, 1, 2, 1] is 0.0045403
```

6.5   *Viterbi decoding*

The *Viterbi decoding algorithm* finds the most likely sequence of hidden states, given a sequence of observations. It requires a caching scheme similar to the forward algorithm. You'll name the cache viterbi. In the HMM constructor, append the line shown in the following listing.

Listing 6.7   Adding the Viterbi cache as a member variable

```
def __init__(self, initial_prob, trans_prob, obs_prob):
  ...
  ...
  ...
  self.viterbi = tf.placeholder(tf.float64)
```

In the next listing, you'll define a TensorFlow op to update the viterbi cache. This will be a method in the HMM class.

Listing 6.8   Defining an op to update the forward cache

```
def decode_op(self):
        transitions = tf.matmul(self.viterbi,
     tf.transpose(self.get_emission(self.obs_idx)))
        weighted_transitions = transitions * self.trans_prob
        viterbi = tf.reduce_max(weighted_transitions, 0)
        return tf.reshape(viterbi, tf.shape(self.viterbi))
```

You'll also need an op to update the back pointers.

Listing 6.9   Defining an op to update the back pointers

```
def backpt_op(self):
    back_transitions = tf.matmul(self.viterbi, np.ones((1, self.N)))
    weighted_back_transitions = back_transitions * self.trans_prob
    return tf.argmax(weighted_back_transitions, 0)
```

Lastly, in the following listing, define the Viterbi decoding function outside the HMM.

Listing 6.10   Defining the Viterbi decoding algorithm

```
def viterbi_decode(sess, hmm, observations):
    viterbi = sess.run(hmm.forward_init_op(), feed_dict={hmm.obs:
     observations[0]})
    backpts = np.ones((hmm.N, len(observations)), 'int32') * -1
    for t in range(1, len(observations)):
        viterbi, backpt = sess.run([hmm.decode_op(), hmm.backpt_op()],
                                   feed_dict={hmm.obs: observations[t],
                                              hmm.viterbi: viterbi})
        backpts[:, t] = backpt
    tokens = [viterbi[:, -1].argmax()]
    for i in range(len(observations) - 1, 0, -1):
        tokens.append(backpts[tokens[-1], i])
    return tokens[::-1]
```

You can run the code in the next listing in the main function to evaluate the Viterbi decoding of an observation.

> **Listing 6.11   Running the Viterbi decode**

```
seq = viterbi_decode(sess, hmm, observations)
print('Most likely hidden states are {}'.format(seq))
```

6.6   Uses of hidden Markov models

Now that you've implemented the forward algorithm and Viterbi algorithm, let's take a look at interesting uses for your newfound power.

6.6.1   Modeling a video

Imagine being able to recognize a person based solely (no pun intended) on how they walk. Identifying people based on their gait is a pretty cool idea, but first you need a model to recognize the gait. Consider an HMM in which the sequence of hidden states for a gait are (1) rest position, (2) right foot forward, (3) rest position, (4) left foot forward, and finally (5) rest position. The observed states are silhouettes of a person walking/jogging/running taken from a video clip (a dataset of such examples is available at http://mng.bz/Tqfx).

6.6.2   Modeling DNA

DNA is a sequence of nucleotides, and we're gradually learning more about its structure. One clever way to understand a long DNA string is by modeling the regions, if we know some probability about the order in which they appear. Just as cloudy days are common after a rainy day, maybe a certain region on the DNA sequence (*start codon*) is more common before another region (*stop codon*).

6.6.3   Modeling an image

In handwriting recognition, we aim to retrieve the plaintext from an image of handwritten words. One approach is to resolve characters one at a time and then concatenate the results. You can use the insight that characters are written in sequences—words—to build an HMM. Knowing the previous character could probably help you rule out possibilities of the next character. The hidden states are the plaintext, and the observations are cropped images containing individual characters.

6.7   Application of hidden Markov models

Hidden Markov models work best when you have an idea about what the hidden states are and how they change over time. Luckily, in the field of natural language processing, tagging a sentence's parts of speech can be solved using HMMs:

- A sequence of words in a sentence corresponds to the observations of the HMM. For example, the sentence "Open the pod bay doors, HAL" has six observed words.

- The hidden states are the parts of speech, such as verb, noun, adjective, and so on. The observed word *open* in the previous example should correspond to the hidden state *verb*.
- The transition probabilities can be designed by the programmer or obtained through data. These probabilities represent the rules of the parts of speech. For example, the probability of two verbs occurring one after another should be low. By setting up a transition probability, you avoid having the algorithm brute-forcing all possibilities.
- The emitting probabilities of each word can be obtained from data. A traditional part-of-speech tagging dataset is called Moby; you can find it at www.gutenberg.org/ebooks/3203.

NOTE You now have what it takes to design your own experiments using hidden Markov models! It's a powerful tool, and we urge you to try it on your own data. Predefine some transitions and emissions, and see if you can recover hidden states. Hopefully, this chapter can help get you started.

6.8 Summary

- A complicated, entangled system can be simplified using a Markov model.
- The hidden Markov model is particularly useful in real-world applications because most observations are measurements of hidden states.
- The forward and Viterbi algorithms are among the most common algorithms used on HMMs.

Part 3

The neural network paradigm

W**e're** seeing a huge push from industries to place neural networks on a pedestal. Deep-learning research has become a corporate status symbol, with the theory behind it obfuscated by smoke and mirrors. Massive amounts of money have been thrown at marketing this technology by companies including NVIDIA, Facebook, Amazon, Microsoft, and, let's not forget, Google. Regardless, deep learning works exceptionally well for solving some problems, and using Tensor-Flow is how we'll implement it.

The chapters in this part of the book introduce neural networks from the basics and apply these architectures to real-world practical applications. In order, the chapters are about autoencoders, reinforcement learning, convolutional neural networks, recurrent neural networks, sequence-to-sequence models, and ranking. Full speed ahead!

A peek into autoencoders

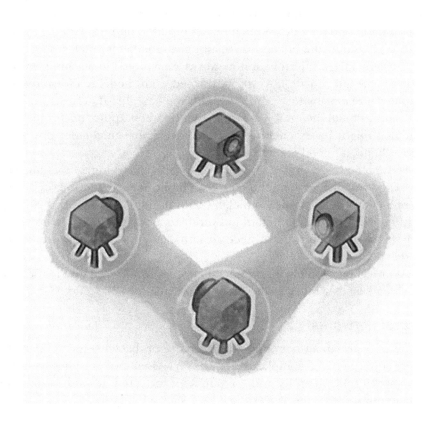

This chapter covers

- Getting to know neural networks
- Designing autoencoders
- Representing images by using an autoencoder

Have you ever heard a person humming a melody, and identified the song? It might be easy for you, but I'm comically tone-deaf when it comes to music. Humming, of itself, is an approximation of a song. An even better approximation could be singing. Include some instrumentals, and sometimes a cover of a song sounds indistinguishable from the original.

Instead of songs, in this chapter, you'll approximate functions. Functions are a general notion of relations between inputs and outputs. In machine learning, you typically want to find the function that relates inputs to outputs. Finding the best possible function fit is difficult, but approximating the function is much easier.

Conveniently, artificial neural networks are a model in machine learning that can approximate any function. As you've learned, your model is a function that gives the output you're looking for, given the inputs you have. In ML terms, given training data, you want to build a neural network model that best approximates the implicit function that might have generated the data—one that might not give you the exact answer but that's good enough to be useful.

So far, you've generated models by explicitly designing a function, whether it be linear, polynomial, or something more complicated. Neural networks enable a little bit of leeway when it comes to picking out the right function, and consequently the right model. In theory, a neural network can model general-purpose types of transformation—where you don't need to know much at all about the function being modeled!

After section 7.1 introduces neural networks, you'll learn how to use autoencoders, which encode data into smaller, faster representations, in section 7.2.

7.1   *Neural networks*

If you've heard about neural networks, you've probably seen diagrams of nodes and edges connected in a complicated mesh. That visualization is mostly inspired by biology—specifically, neurons in the brain. As it turns out, it's also a convenient way to visualize functions, such as $f(x) = w \times x + b$, shown in figure 7.1.

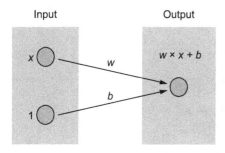

Input   Output

w × *x* + *b*

x

w

b

1

Figure 7.1 A graphical representation of the linear equation $f(x) = w \times x + b$**. The nodes are represented as circles, and edges are represented as arrows. The values on the edges are often called** *weights*, **and they act as a multiplication on the input. When two arrows lead to the same node, they act as a summation of the inputs.**

As a reminder, a *linear model* is set of linear functions; for example, $f(x) = w \times x + b$, where (w, b) is the vector of parameters. The learning algorithm drifts around the values of w and b until it finds a combination that best matches the data. After the algorithm successfully converges, it'll find the best possible linear function to describe the data.

Linear is a good place to start, but the real world isn't always that pretty. And thus, we dive into the type of machine learning responsible for TensorFlow's inception; this chapter is your introduction to a type of model called an *artificial neural network*, which can approximate arbitrary functions (not just linear ones).

EXERCISE 7.1
Is $f(x) = |x|$ a linear function?

ANSWER
No. It's two linear functions stitched together at zero, and that's not a single straight line.

To incorporate the concept of nonlinearity, it's effective to apply a nonlinear function, called the *activation function*, to each neuron's output. Three of the most commonly used activation functions are *sigmoid* (sig), *hyperbolic tangent* (tan), and a type of *ramp* function called a *Rectifying Linear Unit* (ReLU), plotted in figure 7.2.

You don't have to worry too much about which activation function is better under what circumstances. That's still an active research topic. Feel free to experiment with the three shown in figure 7.2. Usually, the best one is chosen by using cross-validation to determine which one gives the best model, given the dataset you're working with. Remember our confusion matrix in chapter 4? You test which model gives the fewest false-positives or false-negatives, or whatever other criteria best suits your needs.

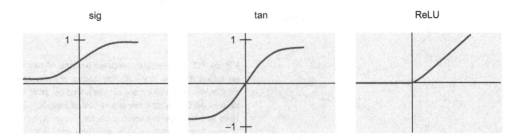

Figure 7.2 Use nonlinear functions such as sig, tan, and ReLU to introduce nonlinearity to your models.

The sigmoid function isn't new to you. As you may recall, the logistic regression classifier in chapter 4 applied this sigmoid function to the linear function $w \times x + b$. The neural network model in figure 7.3 represents the function $f(x) = \text{sig}(w \times x + b)$. It's a one-input, one-output network, where w and b are the parameters of this model.

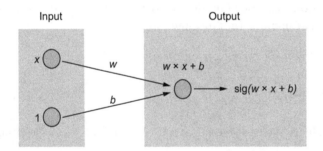

Figure 7.3 A nonlinear function, such as sigmoid, is applied to the output of a node.

If you have two inputs ($x1$ and $x2$), you can modify your neural network to look like the one in figure 7.4. Given training data and a cost function, the parameters to be learned are $w1$, $w2$, and b. When trying to model data, having multiple inputs to a function is common. For example, image classification takes the entire image (pixel by pixel) as the input.

Naturally, you can generalize to an arbitrary number of inputs ($x1, x2, ..., xn$). The corresponding neural network represents the function $f(x1, ..., xn) = \text{sig}(wn \times xn + ... + w1 \times x1 + b)$, as shown in figure 7.5.

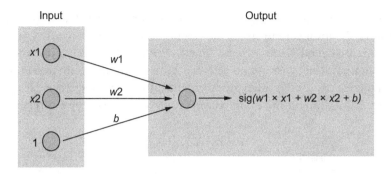

Figure 7.4 A two-input network will have three parameters ($w1$, $w2$, and b). Remember, multiple lines leading to the same node indicate summation.

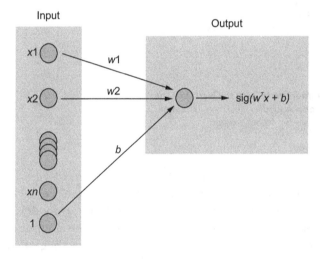

Figure 7.5 The input dimension can be arbitrarily long. For example, each pixel in a grayscale image can have a corresponding input xi. This neural network uses all inputs to generate a single output number, which you might use for regression or classification. The notation w^T means you're transposing w, which is an $n \times 1$ vector, into a $1 \times n$ vector. That way, you can properly multiply it with x (which has the dimensions $n \times 1$). Such a matrix multiplication is also called a *dot product*, and it yields a scalar (one-dimensional) value.

So far, you've dealt with only an input layer and an output layer. Nothing's stopping you from arbitrarily adding neurons in between. Neurons that are used as neither input nor output are called *hidden neurons*. They're hidden from the input and output interfaces of the neural network, so no one can directly influence their values. A *hidden layer* is any collection of hidden neurons that don't connect to each other, as shown in figure 7.6. Adding more hidden layers greatly improves the expressive power of the network.

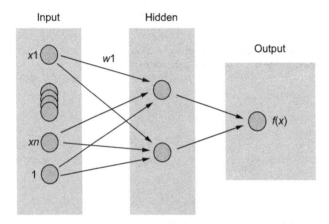

Figure 7.6 Nodes that don't interface to both the input and the output are called *hidden neurons*. A hidden layer is a collection of hidden units that aren't connected to each other.

As long as the activation function is something nonlinear, a neural network with at least one hidden layer can approximate arbitrary functions. In linear models, no matter what parameters are learned, the function remains linear. The nonlinear neural network model with a hidden layer, on the other hand, is flexible enough to approximately represent any function! What a time to be alive!

TensorFlow comes with many helper functions to help you obtain the parameters of a neural network in an efficient way. You'll see how to invoke those tools in this chapter when you start using your first neural network architecture: an autoencoder.

7.2 *Autoencoders*

An *autoencoder* is a type of neural network that tries to learn parameters that make the output as close to the input as possible. An obvious way to do so is to return the input directly, as shown in figure 7.7.

But an autoencoder is more interesting than that. It contains a small hidden layer! If that hidden layer has a smaller dimension than the input, the hidden layer is a compression of your data, called *encoding*.

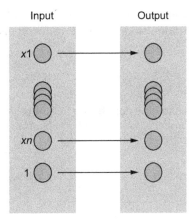

Figure 7.7 If you want to create a network where the input equals the output, you can connect the corresponding nodes and set each parameter's weight to 1.

Encoding data in the real world

A couple of audio formats are out there, but the most popular may be MP3 because of its relatively small file size. You may have already guessed that such efficient storage comes with a trade-off. The algorithm to generate an MP3 file takes original uncompressed audio and shrinks it into a much smaller file that sounds approximately the same to your ears. But it's lossy, meaning that you won't be able to completely recover the original uncompressed audio from the encoded version. Similarly, in this chapter, we want to reduce the dimensionality of the data to make it more workable, but not necessarily create a perfect reproduction.

The process of reconstructing the input from the hidden layer is called *decoding*. Figure 7.8 shows an exaggerated example of an autoencoder.

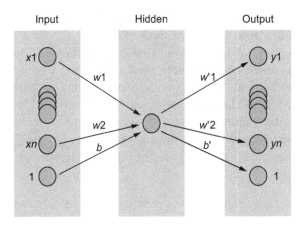

Figure 7.8 Here, you introduce a restriction to a network that tries to reconstruct its input. Data will pass through a narrow channel, as illustrated by the hidden layer. In this example, there's only one node in the hidden layer. This network is trying to encode (and decode) an *n*-dimensional input signal into just one dimension, which will likely be difficult in practice.

Encoding is a great way to reduce the dimensions of the input. For example, if you can represent a 256×256 image in just 100 hidden nodes, you've reduced each data item by a factor of thousands!

EXERCISE 7.2

Let x denote the input vector $(x1, x2, ..., xn)$, and let y denote the output vector $(y1, y2, ..., yn)$. Lastly, let w and w' denote the encoder and decoder weights, respectively. What's a possible cost function to train this neural network?

ANSWER

See the loss function in listing 7.3.

It makes sense to use an object-oriented programming style to implement an autoencoder. That way, you can later reuse the class in other applications without worrying about tightly coupled code. Creating your code as outlined in listing 7.1 helps build deeper architectures, such as a *stacked autoencoder*, which has been known to perform better empirically.

TIP   Generally, with neural networks, adding more hidden layers seems to improve performance if you have enough data to not overfit the model.

Listing 7.1   Python class schema

```
class Autoencoder:
    def __init__(self, input_dim, hidden_dim):        Initializes
                                                      variables

    def train(self, data):        Trains on a
                                  dataset

    def test(self, data):        Tests on some
                                 new data
```

Open a new Python source file, and call it autoencoder.py. This file will define the autoencoder class that you'll use from a separate piece of code.

The constructor will set up all the TensorFlow variables, placeholders, optimizers, and operators. Anything that doesn't immediately need a session can go in the constructor. Because you're dealing with two sets of weights and biases (one for the encoding step and the other for the decoding step), you can use TensorFlow's name scopes to disambiguate a variable's name.

For instance, the following listing shows an example of defining a variable within a named scope. Now you can seamlessly save and restore this variable without worrying about name collisions.

Listing 7.2　Using name scopes

```
with tf.name_scope('encode'):
    weights = tf.Variable(tf.random_normal([input_dim, hidden_dim],
     dtype=tf.float32), name='weights')
    biases = tf.Variable(tf.zeros([hidden_dim]), name='biases')
```

Moving on, let's implement the constructor, as shown in the following listing.

Listing 7.3　Autoencoder class

```
import tensorflow as tf
import numpy as np

class Autoencoder:
    def __init__(self, input_dim, hidden_dim, epoch=250,
     learning_rate=0.001):
        self.epoch = epoch
        self.learning_rate = learning_rate

        x = tf.placeholder(dtype=tf.float32, shape=[None, input_dim])

        with tf.name_scope('encode'):
            weights = tf.Variable(tf.random_normal([input_dim, hidden_dim],
     dtype=tf.float32), name='weights')
            biases = tf.Variable(tf.zeros([hidden_dim]), name='biases')
            encoded = tf.nn.tanh(tf.matmul(x, weights) + biases)
        with tf.name_scope('decode'):
            weights = tf.Variable(tf.random_normal([hidden_dim, input_dim],
     dtype=tf.float32), name='weights')
            biases = tf.Variable(tf.zeros([input_dim]), name='biases')
            decoded = tf.matmul(encoded, weights) + biases

        self.x = x
        self.encoded = encoded
        self.decoded = decoded

        self.loss = tf.sqrt(tf.reduce_mean(tf.square(tf.subtract(self.x,
     self.decoded))))
        self.train_op =
     tf.train.RMSPropOptimizer(self.learning_rate).minimize(self.loss)
        self.saver = tf.train.Saver()
```

Number of learning cycles

Hyperparameter of the optimizer

Defines the input layer dataset

Defines the weights and biases under a name scope so you can tell them apart from the decoder's weights and biases

The decoder's weights and biases are defined under this name scope.

These will be method variables.

Defines the reconstruction cost

Sets up a saver to save model parameters as they're being learned

Chooses the optimizer

Now, in the next listing, you'll define a class method called train that will receive a dataset and learn parameters to minimize its loss.

Listing 7.4   Training the autoencoder

One sample at a time, trains the neural network on a data item

Starts a TensorFlow session, and initializes all variables

Iterates through the number of cycles defined in the constructor

Prints the reconstruction error once every 10 cycles

Saves the learned parameters to file

```
def train(self, data):
    num_samples = len(data)
    with tf.Session() as sess:
        sess.run(tf.global_variables_initializer())
        for i in range(self.epoch):
            for j in range(num_samples):
                l, _ = sess.run([self.loss, self.train_op],
                    feed_dict={self.x: [data[j]]})
            if i % 10 == 0:
                print('epoch {0}: loss = {1}'.format(i, l))
                self.saver.save(sess, './model.ckpt')
        self.saver.save(sess, './model.ckpt')
```

You now have enough code to design an algorithm that learns an autoencoder from arbitrary data. Before you start using this class, let's create one more method. As shown in the next listing, the test method will let you evaluate the autoencoder on new data.

Listing 7.5   Testing the model on data

Loads the learned parameters

Reconstructs the input

```
def test(self, data):
    with tf.Session() as sess:
        self.saver.restore(sess, './model.ckpt')
        hidden, reconstructed = sess.run([self.encoded, self.decoded],
    feed_dict={self.x: data})
        print('input', data)
        print('compressed', hidden)
        print('reconstructed', reconstructed)
        return reconstructed
```

Finally, create a new Python source file called main.py, and use your Autoencoder class, as shown in the following listing.

Listing 7.6   Using your Autoencoder class

```
from autoencoder import Autoencoder
from sklearn import datasets

hidden_dim = 1
data = datasets.load_iris().data
input_dim = len(data[0])
ae = Autoencoder(input_dim, hidden_dim)
ae.train(data)
ae.test([[8, 4, 6, 2]])
```

Running the `train` function will output debug info about how the loss decreases over the epochs. The `test` function shows info about the encoding and decoding process:

```
('input', [[8, 4, 6, 2]])
('compressed', array([[ 0.78238308]], dtype=float32))
('reconstructed', array([[ 6.87756062,  2.79838109,  6.25144577,
    2.23120356]], dtype=float32))
```

Notice that you're able to compress a four-dimensional vector into just one dimension and then decode it back into a four-dimensional vector with some loss in data.

7.3 Batch training

Training a network one sample at a time is the safest bet if you're not pressured by time. But if your network training is taking longer than desired, one solution is to train it with multiple data inputs at a time, called *batch training*.

Typically, as the batch size increases, the algorithm speeds up but has a lower likelihood of successfully converging. It's a double-edged sword. Go wield it in the following listing. You'll use that helper function later.

> **Listing 7.7 Batch helper function**

```
def get_batch(X, size):
    a = np.random.choice(len(X), size, replace=False)
    return X[a]
```

To use batch learning, you'll need to modify the `train` method from listing 7.4. The batch version is shown in the following listing. It inserts an additional inner loop for each batch of data. Typically, the number of batch iterations should be enough so that all data is covered in the same epoch.

> **Listing 7.8 Batch learning**

```
def train(self, data, batch_size=10):
    with tf.Session() as sess:
        sess.run(tf.global_variables_initializer())
        for i in range(self.epoch):
            for j in range(500):
                batch_data = get_batch(data, self.batch_size)
                l, _ = sess.run([self.loss, self.train_op],
    feed_dict={self.x: batch_data})
            if i % 10 == 0:
                print('epoch {0}: loss = {1}'.format(i, l))
                self.saver.save(sess, './model.ckpt')
        self.saver.save(sess, './model.ckpt')
```

Loops through various batch selections

Runs the optimizer on a randomly selected batch

7.4   *Working with images*

Most neural networks, like your autoencoder, accept only one-dimensional input. Pixels of an image, on the other hand, are indexed by both rows and columns. Moreover, if a pixel is in color, it has a value for its red, green, and blue concentration, as shown in figure 7.9.

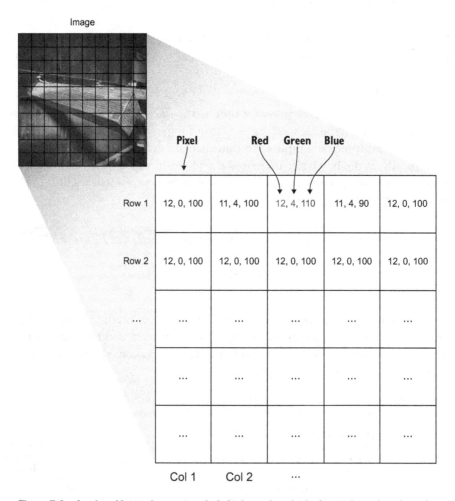

Figure 7.9   A colored image is composed of pixels, and each pixel contains values for red, green, and blue.

A convenient way to manage the higher dimensions of an image involves two steps:

1 Convert the image to grayscale: merge the values of red, green, and blue into the *pixel intensity*, which is a weighted average of the color values.

2 Rearrange the image into row-major order. *Row-major order* stores an array as a longer, single-dimension set; you put all the dimensions of an array on the end of the first dimension. This allows you to index the image by one number instead of two. If an image is 3 × 3 pixels in size, you rearrange it into the structure shown in figure 7.10.

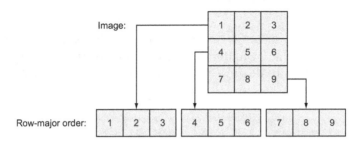

Figure 7.10   An image can be represented in row-major order. That way, you can represent a two-dimensional structure as a one-dimensional structure.

You can use images in TensorFlow in many ways. If you have pictures lying around on your hard drive, you can load them using SciPy, which comes with TensorFlow. The following listing shows you how to load an image in grayscale, resize it, and represent it in row-major order.

Listing 7.9   Loading images

```
from scipy.misc import imread, imresize

gray_image = imread(filepath, True)
small_gray_image = imresize(gray_image, 1. / 8.)
x = small_gray_image.flatten()
```

Loads an image as grayscale

Resizes it to something smaller

Converts it to a one-dimensional structure

Image processing is a lively field of research, so datasets are readily available for you to use, instead of using your own limited images. For instance, a dataset called CIFAR-10 contains 60,000 labeled images, each 32 × 32 in size.

EXERCISE 7.3

Can you name other online image datasets? Search online and look around for more!

ANSWER

Perhaps the most used in the deep-learning community is ImageNet (www.image-net.org). A great list can also be found online at http://deeplearning.net/datasets.

Download the Python dataset from www.cs.toronto.edu/~kriz/cifar.html. Place the extracted cifar-10-batches-py folder in your working directory. The following listing is provided from the CIFAR-10 web page; add the code to a new file called main_imgs.py.

Listing 7.10   Reading from the extracted CIFAR-10 dataset

```
import pickle


def unpickle(file):                                    ◄─┐ Reads the CIFAR-10 file,
    fo = open(file, 'rb')                                │ returning the loaded
    dict = pickle.load(fo, encoding='latin1')            │ dictionary
    fo.close()
    return dict
```

Let's read each of the dataset files by using the unpickle function you just created. The CIFA-10 dataset contains six files, each prefixed with data_batch_ and followed by a number. Each file contains information about the image data and corresponding label. The following listing shows how to loop through all the files and append the datasets to memory.

Listing 7.11   Reading all CIFAR-10 files to memory

```
import numpy as np

names = unpickle('./cifar-10-batches-py/batches.meta')['label_names']
data, labels = [], []
for i in range(1, 6):
    filename = './cifar-10-batches-py/data_batch_' + str(i)     ◄─┐ Loops through
    batch_data = unpickle(filename)                               │ the six files
    if len(data) > 0:
        data = np.vstack((data, batch_data['data']))       ◄─┐ The rows of a
        labels = np.hstack((labels, batch_data['labels'])) ◄─┐ │ data sample
    else:                                                    │ │ represent each
        data = batch_data['data']                            │ │ sample, so you
        labels = batch_data['labels']                        │ │ stack it vertically.
```

Loads the file to obtain a Python dictionary

Labels are one-dimensional, so you stack them horizontally.

Each image is represented as a series of red pixels, followed by green pixels, and then blue pixels. Listing 7.12 creates a helper function to convert the image into grayscale by averaging the red, green, and blue values.

> **NOTE** You can achieve more-realistic grayscale in other ways, but this approach of averaging the three values gets the job done. Human perception is more sensitive to green light, so in some other versions of grayscaling, green values might have a higher weight in the averaging.

Listing 7.12 Converting CIFAR-10 image to grayscale

```
def grayscale(a):
    return a.reshape(a.shape[0], 3, 32, 32).mean(1).reshape(a.shape[0], -1)

data = grayscale(data)
```

Lastly, let's collect all images of a certain class, such as horse. You'll run your autoencoder on all pictures of horses, as shown in the following listing.

Listing 7.13 Setting up the autoencoder

```
from autoencoder import Autoencoder

x = np.matrix(data)
y = np.array(labels)

horse_indices = np.where(y == 7)[0]

horse_x = x[horse_indices]

print(np.shape(horse_x))  # (5000, 3072)

input_dim = np.shape(horse_x)[1]
hidden_dim = 100
ae = Autoencoder(input_dim, hidden_dim)
ae.train(horse_x)
```

You can now encode images similar to your training dataset into just 100 numbers. This autoencoder model is one of the simplest, so clearly it'll be a lossy encoding. Beware: running this code may take up to 10 minutes. The output will trace loss values of every 10 epochs:

```
epoch 0: loss = 99.8635025024
epoch 10: loss = 35.3869667053
epoch 20: loss = 15.9411172867
epoch 30: loss = 7.66391372681
epoch 40: loss = 1.39575612545
epoch 50: loss = 0.00389165547676
```

```
epoch 60: loss = 0.00203850422986
epoch 70: loss = 0.00186171964742
epoch 80: loss = 0.00231492402963
epoch 90: loss = 0.00166488380637
epoch 100: loss = 0.00172081717756
epoch 110: loss = 0.0018497039564
epoch 120: loss = 0.00220602494664
epoch 130: loss = 0.00179589167237
epoch 140: loss = 0.00122790911701
epoch 150: loss = 0.0027100709267
epoch 160: loss = 0.00213225837797
epoch 170: loss = 0.00215123943053
epoch 180: loss = 0.00148373935372
epoch 190: loss = 0.00171591725666
```

See the book's website or GitHub repo for a full example of the output: https://www.manning.com/books/machine-learning-with-tensorflow or http://mng.bz/D0Na.

7.5 *Application of autoencoders*

This chapter introduced the most straightforward type of autoencoder, but other variants have been studied, each with their benefits and applications. Let's take a look at a few:

- A *stacked autoencoder* starts the same way a normal autoencoder does. It learns the encoding for an input into a smaller hidden layer by minimizing the reconstruction error. The hidden layer is now treated as the input to a new autoencoder that tries to encode the first layer of hidden neurons to an even smaller layer (the second layer of hidden neurons). This continues as desired. Often, the learned encoding weights are used as initial values for solving regression or classification problems in a deep neural network architecture.

- A *denoising autoencoder* receives a noised-up input instead of the original input, and it tries to "denoise" it. The cost function is no longer used to minimize the reconstruction error. Now, you're trying to minimize the error between the denoised image and the original image. The intuition is that our human minds can still comprehend a photograph even after scratches or markings on it. If a machine can also see through the noised input to recover the original data, maybe it has a better understanding of the data. Denoising models have been shown to better capture salient features of an image.

- A *variational autoencoder* can generate new natural images, given the hidden variables directly. Let's say you encode a picture of a man as a 100-dimensional vector, and then a picture of a woman as another 100-dimensional vector. You can take the average of the two vectors, run it through the decoder, and produce a reasonable image that represents visually a person who's between a man and a woman. This generative power of the variational autoencoder is derived from a type of probabilistic models called *Bayesian networks*.

7.6 *Summary*

- A neural network is useful when a linear model is ineffective for describing the dataset.
- Autoencoders are unsupervised learning algorithms that try to reproduce their inputs, and in doing so reveal interesting structure about the data.
- Images can easily be fed as input to a neural network by flattening and gray-scaling.

Reinforcement learning 8

Humans learn from past experiences (or, at least they *should*). You didn't get so charming by accident. Years of positive compliments as well as negative criticism have all helped shape who you are today. This chapter is about designing a machine-learning system driven by criticisms and rewards.

You learn what makes people happy, for example, by interacting with friends, family, or even strangers, and you figure out how to ride a bike by trying out various muscle movements until riding just clicks. When you perform actions, you're sometimes rewarded immediately. For example, finding a good restaurant nearby might yield instant gratification. Other times, the reward doesn't appear right away, such as traveling a long distance to find an exceptional place to eat. Reinforcement learning is about making the right actions, given any state—such as in figure 8.1, which shows a person making decisions to arrive at their destination.

Moreover, suppose on your drive from home to work, you always choose the same route. But one day your curiosity takes over, and you decide to try a different path in

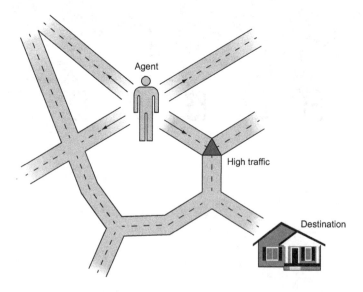

Figure 8.1   A person navigating to reach a destination in the midst of traffic and unexpected situations is a problem setup for reinforcement learning.

hopes of a shorter commute. This dilemma of trying out new routes or sticking to the best-known route is an example of *exploration versus exploitation*.

> **NOTE** Why is the trade-off between trying new things and sticking with old ones called exploration versus exploitation? Exploration makes sense, but you can think of exploitation as exploiting your knowledge of the status quo by sticking with what you know.

All these examples can be unified under a general formulation: performing an action in a scenario can yield a reward. A more technical term for scenario is *state*. And we call the collection of all possible states a *state space*. Performing an action causes the state to change. But the question is, what series of actions yields the highest expected rewards?

8.1 Formal notions

Whereas supervised and unsupervised learning appear at opposite ends of the spectrum, *reinforcement learning* (RL) exists somewhere in the middle. It's not supervised learning, because the training data comes from the algorithm deciding between exploration and exploitation. And it's not unsupervised, because the algorithm receives feedback from the environment. As long as you're in a situation where performing an action in a state produces a reward, you can use reinforcement learning to discover a good sequence of actions to take that maximize expected rewards.

You may notice that reinforcement-learning lingo involves anthropomorphizing the algorithm into taking *actions* in *situations* to *receive rewards*. The algorithm is often referred to as an *agent* that *acts with* the environment. It shouldn't be a surprise that much of reinforcement-learning theory is applied in robotics. Figure 8.2 demonstrates the interplay between states, actions, and rewards.

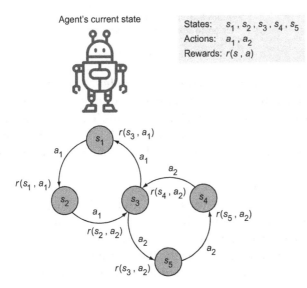

Figure 8.2 Actions are represented by arrows, and states are represented by circles. Performing an action on a state produces a reward. If you start at state s1, you can perform action a1 to obtain a reward $r(s1, a1)$.

A robot performs actions to change states. But how does it decide which action to take? The next section introduces a new concept, called a *policy*, to answer this question.

Do humans use reinforcement learning?

Reinforcement learning seems like the best way to explain how to perform the next action based on the current situation. Perhaps humans behave the same way biologically. But let's not get ahead of ourselves; consider the following example.

Sometimes, humans act without thinking. If I'm thirsty, I might instinctively grab a cup of water to quench my thirst. I don't iterate through all possible joint motions in my head and choose the optimal one after thorough calculations.

Most important, the actions we make aren't characterized solely by our observations at each moment. Otherwise, we're no smarter than bacteria, which act deterministically given their environment. There seems to be a lot more going on, and a simple RL model might not fully explain human behavior.

8.1.1   Policy

Everyone cleans their room differently. Some people start by making their bed. I prefer cleaning my room clockwise so I don't miss a corner. Have you ever seen a robotic vacuum cleaner, such as a Roomba? Someone programmed a strategy it can follow to clean any room. In reinforcement-learning lingo, the way an agent decides which action to take is called a *policy*: it's the set of actions that determines the next state (see figure 8.3).

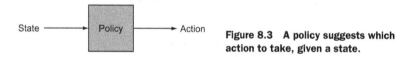

Figure 8.3   **A policy suggests which action to take, given a state.**

The goal of reinforcement learning is to discover a good policy. A common way to create that policy is by observing the long-term consequences of actions at each state. The *reward* is the measure of the outcome of taking an action. The best possible policy is called the *optimal policy*, and it's often the Holy Grail of reinforcement learning. The optimal policy tells you the optimal action, given any state—but it may not provide the highest reward at the moment.

If you measure the reward by looking at the immediate consequence—the state of things after taking the action—it's easy to calculate. This is called the *greedy strategy*— but it's not always a good idea to "greedily" choose the action with the best *immediate* reward. For example, when cleaning your room, you might make your bed first, because the room looks neater with the bed made. But if another goal is to wash your sheets, making the bed first may not be the best overall strategy. You need to look at the results of the next few actions, and the eventual end state, to come up with the optimal approach. Similarly, in chess, grabbing your opponent's queen may maximize the points for the pieces on the board—but if it puts you in checkmate five moves later, it isn't the best possible move.

You can also arbitrarily choose an action: this is a *random policy*. If you come up with a policy to solve a reinforcement-learning problem, it's often a good idea to double-check that your learned policy performs better than both the random and greedy policies.

Limitations of (Markovian) reinforcement learning

Most RL formulations assume that the best action to take can be figured out from knowing the current state, instead of considering the longer-term history of states and actions that got you there. This approach of making decisions based on the current state is called *Markovian*, and the general framework is often referred to as the *Markov decision process* (MDP).

Such situations in which the state sufficiently captures what to do next can be modeled with RL algorithms discussed in this chapter. But most real-world situations aren't Markovian and therefore need a more realistic approach, such as a hierarchical representation of states and actions. In a grossly oversimplified sense, hierarchical models are like context-free grammars, whereas MDPs are like finite-state machines. The expressive leap of modeling a problem as an MDP to something more hierarchical can dramatically improve the effectiveness of the planning algorithm.

8.1.2 Utility

The long-term reward is called a *utility*. If you know the utility of performing an action at a state, learning the policy is easy using reinforcement learning. For example, to decide which action to take, you select the action that produces the highest utility. The hard part, as you might have guessed, is uncovering these utility values.

The utility of performing an action a at a state s is written as a function $Q(s, a)$, called the *utility function*, shown in figure 8.4.

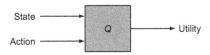

Figure 8.4 Given a state and the action taken, applying a utility function Q predicts the expected and the total rewards: the immediate reward (next state) plus rewards gained later by following an optimal policy.

EXERCISE 8.1

If you were given the utility function $Q(s, a)$, how could you use it to derive a policy function?

ANSWER

Policy(s) = argmax_a $Q(s, a)$

An elegant way to calculate the utility of a particular state-action pair (s, a) is by recursively considering the utilities of future actions. The utility of your current action is influenced not only by the immediate reward but also by the next best action, as shown in the next formula. In the formula, s' denotes the next state, and a' denotes the next action. The reward of taking action a in state s is denoted by $r(s, a)$:

$$Q(s, a) = r(s, a) + \gamma \max Q(s', a')$$

Here, γ is a hyperparameter that you get to choose, called the *discount factor*. If γ is 0, the agent chooses the action that maximizes the immediate reward. Higher values of γ will make the agent put more importance on considering long-term consequences. You can read the formula as "the value of this action is the immediate reward provided by taking this action, added to the discount factor times the best thing that can happen after that."

Looking ahead at future rewards is one type of hyperparameter you can play with, but there's also another. In some applications of reinforcement learning, newly available information might be more important than historical records, or vice versa. For example, if a robot is expected to learn to solve tasks quickly but not necessarily optimally, you might want to set a faster learning rate. Or if a robot is allowed more time to explore and exploit, you might tune down the learning rate. Let's call the learning rate α, and change the utility function as follows (notice that when $\alpha = 1$, both equations are identical).

$$Q(s, a) \leftarrow Q(s, a) + \alpha(r(s, a) + \gamma \max Q(s', a') - Q(s, a))$$

Reinforcement learning can be solved if you know the Q-function: $Q(s, a)$. Conveniently for us, *neural networks* (chapter 7) are a way to approximate functions, given enough training data. TensorFlow is the perfect tool to deal with neural networks because it comes with many essential algorithms to simplify neural network implementation.

8.2   *Applying reinforcement learning*

Application of reinforcement learning requires defining a way to retrieve rewards after an action is taken from a state. A stock-market trader fits these requirements easily, because buying and selling a stock changes the state of the trader (cash on hand), and each action generates a reward (or loss).

The states in this situation are a vector containing information about the current budget, the current number of stocks, and a recent history of stock prices (the last 200 stock prices). Each state is a 202-dimensional vector.

EXERCISE 8.2

What are some possible disadvantages of using reinforcement learning for buying and selling stocks?

ANSWER

By performing actions on the market, such as buying or selling shares, you could end up influencing the market, causing it to change dramatically from your training data.

For simplicity, there are only three actions—buy, sell, and hold:

- Buying a stock at the current stock price decreases the budget while incrementing the current stock count.
- Selling a stock trades it in for money at the current share price.
- Holding does neither. This action waits a single time period and yields no reward.

Figure 8.5 demonstrates one possible policy, given stock market data.

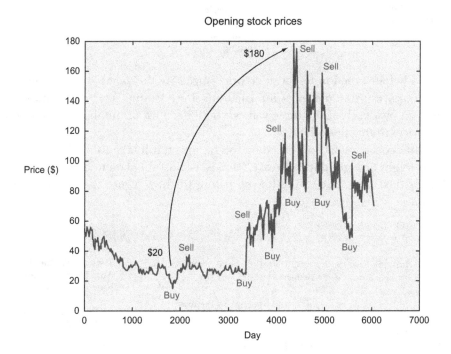

Figure 8.5 **Ideally, our algorithm should buy low and sell high. Doing so just once, as shown here, might yield a reward of around $160. But the real profit rolls in when you buy and sell more frequently. Ever heard the term** *high-frequency trading***? It's about buying low and selling high as frequently as possible to maximize profits within a period of time.**

The goal is to learn a policy that gains the maximum net worth from trading in a stock market. Wouldn't that be cool? Let's do it!

8.3   *Implementing reinforcement learning*

To gather stock prices, you'll use the `yahoo_finance` library in Python. You can install it using `pip` or follow the official guide (https://pypi.python.org/pypi/yahoo-finance). The command to install it using `pip` is as follows:

```
$ pip install yahoo-finance
```

With that installed, let's import all the relevant libraries.

Listing 8.1   Importing relevant libraries

```
from yahoo_finance import Share      ◁── For obtaining stock-price raw data
from matplotlib import pyplot as plt  ◁──
import numpy as np
import tensorflow as tf
import random
```

For numeric manipulation and machine learning

For plotting stock prices

Create a helper function to get stock prices by using the `yahoo_finance` library. The library requires three pieces of information: share symbol, start date, and end date. When you pick each of the three values, you'll get a list of numbers representing the share prices in that period by day.

If you choose a start and end date too far apart, it'll take some time to fetch that data. It might be a good idea to save (that is, cache) the data to disk so you can load it locally next time. See the following listing for how to use the library and cache the data.

Listing 8.2   Helper function to get prices

```
def get_prices(share_symbol, start_date, end_date,
               cache_filename='stock_prices.npy'):
    try:
        stock_prices = np.load(cache_filename)
    except IOError:
        share = Share(share_symbol)
        stock_hist = share.get_historical(start_date, end_date)
        stock_prices = [stock_price['Open'] for stock_price in stock_hist]
        np.save(cache_filename, stock_prices)

    return stock_prices.astype(float)
```

Tries to load the data from file if it has already been computed

Retrieves stock prices from the library

Caches the result

Extracts only relevant info from the raw data

Just for a sanity check, it's a good idea to visualize the stock-price data. Create a plot, and save it to disk.

Listing 8.3　Helper function to plot the stock prices

```
def plot_prices(prices):
    plt.title('Opening stock prices')
    plt.xlabel('day')
    plt.ylabel('price ($)')
    plt.plot(prices)
    plt.savefig('prices.png')
    plt.show()
```

You can grab some data and visualize it by using the following listing.

Listing 8.4　Get data and visualize it

```
if __name__ == '__main__':
    prices = get_prices('MSFT', '1992-07-22', '2016-07-22')
    plot_prices(prices)
```

Figure 8.6 shows the chart produced from running listing 8.4.

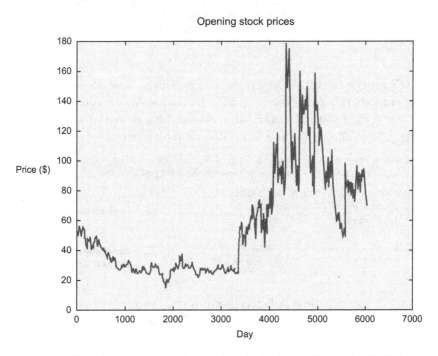

Figure 8.6　This chart summarizes the opening stock prices of Microsoft (MSFT) from 7/22/1992 to 7/22/2016. Wouldn't it have been nice to buy around day 3000 and sell around day 5000? Let's see if our code can learn to buy, sell, and hold to make optimal gain.

Most reinforcement-learning algorithms follow similar implementation patterns. As a result, it's a good idea to create a class with the relevant methods to reference later, such as an abstract class or interface. See the following listing for an example and figure 8.7 for an illustration. Reinforcement learning needs two operations well defined: how to select an action, and how to improve the utility Q-function.

Listing 8.5   Defining a superclass for all decision policies

```
class DecisionPolicy:
    def select_action(self, current_state):       ◁─┐  Given a state, the decision
        pass                                           policy will calculate the
                                                       next action to take.

    def update_q(self, state, action, reward, next_state):   ◁─┐  Improve the
        pass                                                      Q-function from a
                                                                  new experience of
                                                                  taking an action.
```

Infer(s) => a

Do(s, a) => r, s'

Learn(s, r, a, s')

Figure 8.7   Most reinforcement-learning algorithms boil down to just three main steps: infer, do, and learn. During the first step, the algorithm selects the best action (a), given a state (s), using the knowledge it has so far. Next, it does the action to find out the reward (r) as well as the next state (s'). Then it improves its understanding of the world by using the newly acquired knowledge (s, r, a, s').

Next, let's inherit from this superclass to implement a policy where decisions are made at random, otherwise known as a *random decision policy*. You need to define only the select_action method, which will randomly pick an action without even looking at the state. The following listing shows how to implement it.

Listing 8.6   Implementing a random decision policy

```
class RandomDecisionPolicy(DecisionPolicy):      ◁─┐  Inherits from DecisionPolicy to
    def __init__(self, actions):                       implement its functions
        self.actions = actions

    def select_action(self, current_state):      ◁─┐  Randomly chooses
        action = random.choice(self.actions)          the next action
        return action
```

In listing 8.7, you assume a policy is given to you (such as the one from listing 8.6) and run it on the real-world stock-price data. This function takes care of exploration and exploitation at each interval of time. Figure 8.8 illustrates the algorithm from listing 8.7.

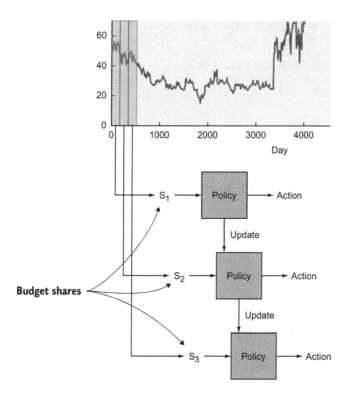

Figure 8.8 A rolling window of a certain size iterates through the stock prices, as shown by the chart segmented to form states S_1, S_2, and S_3. The policy suggests an action to take: you may either choose to exploit it or randomly explore another action. As you get rewards for performing an action, you can update the policy function over time.

Listing 8.7 Using a given policy to make decisions, and returning the performance

```
def run_simulation(policy, initial_budget, initial_num_stocks, prices, hist):
    budget = initial_budget
    num_stocks = initial_num_stocks
    share_value = 0
    transitions = list()
    for i in range(len(prices) - hist - 1):
        if i % 1000 == 0:
            print('progress {:.2f}%'.format(float(100*i) / (len(prices) -
    hist - 1)))
        current_state = np.asmatrix(np.hstack((prices[i:i+hist], budget,
    num_stocks)))
        current_portfolio = budget + num_stocks * share_value
        action = policy.select_action(current_state, i)
        share_value = float(prices[i + hist])
```

Initializes values that depend on computing the net worth of a portfolio

The state is a hist + 2 dimensional vector. You'll force it to be a NumPy matrix.

Calculates the portfolio value

Selects an action from the current policy

Computes a new portfolio value after taking action

Updates portfolio values based on action

```
    if action == 'Buy' and budget >= share_value:
        budget -= share_value
        num_stocks += 1
    elif action == 'Sell' and num_stocks > 0:
        budget += share_value
        num_stocks -= 1
    else:
        action = 'Hold'
    new_portfolio = budget + num_stocks * share_value
    reward = new_portfolio - current_portfolio
    next_state = np.asmatrix(np.hstack((prices[i+1:i+hist+1], budget,
  num_stocks)))
    transitions.append((current_state, action, reward, next_state))
    policy.update_q(current_state, action, reward, next_state)
portfolio = budget + num_stocks * share_value
return portfolio
```

Computes the reward from taking an action at a state

Updates the policy after experiencing a new action

Computes the final portfolio worth

To obtain a more robust measurement of success, let's run the simulation a couple of times and average the results. Doing so may take a while to complete (perhaps 5 minutes), but your results will be more reliable.

Listing 8.8 Running multiple simulations to calculate an average performance

Decides the number of times to rerun the simulations

Stores the portfolio worth of each run in this array

Runs this simulation

```
def run_simulations(policy, budget, num_stocks, prices, hist):
    num_tries = 10
    final_portfolios = list()
    for i in range(num_tries):
        final_portfolio = run_simulation(policy, budget, num_stocks, prices,
  hist)
        final_portfolios.append(final_portfolio)
        print('Final portfolio: ${}'.format(final_portfolio))
    plt.title('Final Portfolio Value')
    plt.xlabel('Simulation #')
    plt.ylabel('Net worth')
    plt.plot(final_portfolios)
    plt.show()
```

In the main function, append the following lines to define the decision policy and run simulations to see how it performs.

Listing 8.9 Defining the decision policy

Defines the list of actions the agent can take

```
if __name__ == '__main__':
    prices = get_prices('MSFT', '1992-07-22', '2016-07-22')
    plot_prices(prices)
    actions = ['Buy', 'Sell', 'Hold']
    hist = 3
```

```
policy = RandomDecisionPolicy(actions)
budget = 100000.0
num_stocks = 0
run_simulations(policy, budget, num_stocks, prices, hist)
```

Sets the initial amount of money available to use

Runs simulations multiple times to compute the expected value of your final net worth

Initializes a random decision policy

Sets the number of stocks already owned

Now that you have a baseline to compare your results, let's implement a neural network approach to learn the Q-function. The decision policy is often called the *Q-learning decision policy*. Listing 8.10 introduces a new hyperparameter, epsilon, to keep the solution from getting "stuck" when applying the same action over and over. The lower its value, the more often it will randomly explore new actions. The Q-function is defined by the function depicted in figure 8.9.

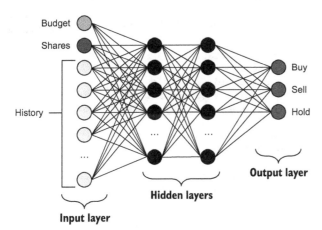

Figure 8.9   The input is the state space vector, with three outputs: one for each output's Q-value.

EXERCISE 8.3

What are other possible factors that your state-space representation ignores that can affect the stock prices? How could you factor them into the simulation?

ANSWER

Stock prices depend on a variety of factors, including general market trends, breaking news, and specific industry trends. Each of these, once quantified, could be applied as additional dimensions to the model.

Listing 8.10   Implementing a more intelligent decision policy

```python
class QLearningDecisionPolicy(DecisionPolicy):
    def __init__(self, actions, input_dim):
        self.epsilon = 0.95
        self.gamma = 0.3
        self.actions = actions
        output_dim = len(actions)
        h1_dim = 20

        self.x = tf.placeholder(tf.float32, [None, input_dim])
        self.y = tf.placeholder(tf.float32, [output_dim])
        W1 = tf.Variable(tf.random_normal([input_dim, h1_dim]))
        b1 = tf.Variable(tf.constant(0.1, shape=[h1_dim]))
        h1 = tf.nn.relu(tf.matmul(self.x, W1) + b1)
        W2 = tf.Variable(tf.random_normal([h1_dim, output_dim]))
        b2 = tf.Variable(tf.constant(0.1, shape=[output_dim]))
        self.q = tf.nn.relu(tf.matmul(h1, W2) + b2)

        loss = tf.square(self.y - self.q)
        self.train_op = tf.train.AdagradOptimizer(0.01).minimize(loss)
        self.sess = tf.Session()
        self.sess.run(tf.global_variables_initializer())

    def select_action(self, current_state, step):
        threshold = min(self.epsilon, step / 1000.)
        if random.random() < threshold:
            # Exploit best option with probability epsilon
            action_q_vals = self.sess.run(self.q, feed_dict={self.x:
    current_state})
            action_idx = np.argmax(action_q_vals)
            action = self.actions[action_idx]
        else:
            # Explore random option with probability 1 - epsilon
            action = self.actions[random.randint(0, len(self.actions) - 1)]
        return action

    def update_q(self, state, action, reward, next_state):
        action_q_vals = self.sess.run(self.q, feed_dict={self.x: state})
        next_action_q_vals = self.sess.run(self.q, feed_dict={self.x:
    next_state})
        next_action_idx = np.argmax(next_action_q_vals)
        current_action_idx = self.actions.index(action)
        action_q_vals[0, current_action_idx] = reward + self.gamma *
    next_action_q_vals[0, next_action_idx]
        action_q_vals = np.squeeze(np.asarray(action_q_vals))
        self.sess.run(self.train_op, feed_dict={self.x: state, self.y:
    action_q_vals})
```

Annotations (left margin, top to bottom):

Sets the hyperparameters from the Q-function

Sets the number of hidden nodes in the neural networks

Defines the input and output tensors

Defines the op to compute the utility

Designs the neural network architecture

Sets the loss as the square error

Sets up the session, and initializes variables

Uses an optimizer to update model parameters to minimize the loss

Explores a random option with probability 1 - epsilon

Exploits the best option with probability epsilon

Updates the Q-function by updating its model parameters

The resulting output when running the entire script is shown in figure 8.10.

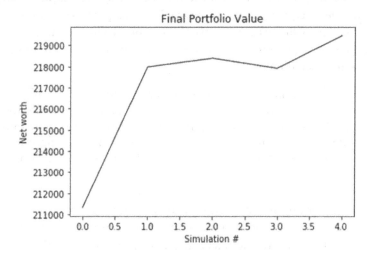

Figure 8.10 The algorithm learns a good policy to trade Microsoft stocks.

8.4 *Exploring other applications of reinforcement learning*

Reinforcement learning is used more often than you might expect. It's too easy to forget that it exists when you've learned supervised- and unsupervised-learning methods. But the following examples will open your eyes to successful uses of RL by Google:

- *Game playing*—In February 2015, Google developed a reinforcement-learning system called Deep RL to learn how to play arcade video games from the Atari 2600 console. Unlike most RL solutions, this algorithm had a high-dimensional input: it perceived the raw frame-by-frame images of the video game. That way, the same algorithm could work with any video game without much reprogramming or reconfiguring.
- *More game playing*—In January 2016, Google released a paper about an AI agent capable of winning the board game Go. The game is known to be unpredictable because of the enormous number of possible configurations (even more than chess!), but this algorithm using RL could beat top human Go players. The latest version, AlphaGo Zero, was released in late 2017 and was able to beat the earlier version consistently—100 games to 0—in only 40 days of training. It will be considerably better than that by the time you read this.
- *Robotics and control*—In March 2016, Google demonstrated a way for a robot to learn by many examples how to grab an object. Google collected more than 800,000 grasp attempts by using multiple robots and developed a model to

grasp arbitrary objects. Impressively, the robots were capable of grasping an object with the help of camera input alone. Learning the simple concept of grasping an object required aggregating the knowledge of many robots spending many days in brute-force attempts until enough patterns were detected. Clearly, there's a long way to go for robots to be able to generalize, but it's an interesting start, nonetheless.

NOTE Now that you've applied reinforcement learning to the stock market, it's time for you to drop out of school or quit your job and start gaming the system. Turns out this is your payoff, dear reader, for making it this far into the book! Just kidding—the actual stock market is a much more complicated beast, but the techniques used in this chapter generalize to many situations.

8.5   Summary

- Reinforcement learning is a natural tool for problems that can be framed by states that change due to actions taken by an agent to discover rewards.
- Implementing the reinforcement-learning algorithm requires three primary steps: infer the best action from the current state, perform the action, and learn from the results.
- Q-learning is an approach to solving reinforcement learning whereby you develop an algorithm to approximate the utility function (Q-function). After a good enough approximation is found, you can start inferring the best actions to take from each state.

Convolutional
neural networks

9

This chapter covers

- Examining the components of a convolutional neural network
- Classifying natural images using deep learning
- Improving neural network performance—tips and tricks

Grocery shopping after an exhausting day is a taxing experience. My eyes get bombarded with too much information. Sales, coupons, colors, toddlers, flashing lights, and crowded aisles are just a few examples of all the signals forwarded to my visual cortex, whether or not I actively try to pay attention. The visual system absorbs an abundance of information.

Ever heard the phrase "a picture is worth a thousand words"? That might be true for you or me, but can a machine find meaning within images as well? The photoreceptor cells in our retinas pick up wavelengths of light, but that information doesn't seem to propagate up to our consciousness. After all, I can't put into words exactly what wavelengths of lights I'm picking up. Similarly, a camera picks up pixels, yet we want to squeeze out some form of higher-level knowledge instead, such as names or locations of objects. How do we get from pixels to human-level perception?

To achieve intelligent meaning from raw sensory input with machine learning, you'll design a neural network model. In the previous chapters, you've seen a few types of neural network models such as fully connected ones (chapter 8) and autoencoders (chapter 7). In this chapter, you'll meet another type of model called a *convolutional neural network* (CNN), which performs exceptionally well on images and other sensory data such as audio. For example, a CNN model can reliably classify what object is being displayed in an image.

The CNN model that you'll implement in this chapter will learn how to classify images to 1 of 10 candidate categories. In effect, "a picture is worth only *one* word" out of just 10 possibilities. It's a tiny step toward human-level perception, but you have to start somewhere, right?

9.1   Drawback of neural networks

Machine learning constitutes an eternal struggle of designing a model that's expressive enough to represent the data, yet not so flexible that it overfits and memorizes the patterns. Neural networks are proposed as a way to improve that expressive power; yet, as you may guess, they often suffer from the pitfalls of overfitting.

NOTE Overfitting occurs when your learned model performs exceptionally well on the training dataset, yet tends to perform poorly on the test dataset. The model is likely too flexible for what little data is available, and it ends up more or less memorizing the training data.

A quick and dirty heuristic you can use to compare the flexibility of two machine-learning models is to count the number of parameters to be learned. As shown in figure 9.1, a fully connected neural network that takes in a 256×256 image and maps it to a layer of 10 neurons will have $256 \times 256 \times 10 = 655,360$ parameters! Compare that to a model with perhaps only 5 parameters. It's likely that the fully connected neural network can represent more-complex data than the model with 5 parameters.

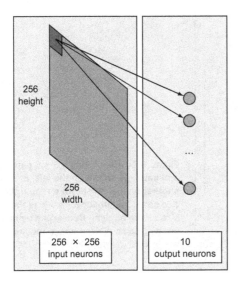

Figure 9.1 In a fully connected network, each pixel of an image is treated as an input. For a grayscale image of size 256×256, that's 256×256 neurons! Connecting each neuron to 10 outputs yields $256 \times 256 \times 10 = 655,360$ weights.

The next section introduces convolutional neural networks, which are a clever way to reduce the number of parameters. Instead of dealing with a fully connected network, the CNN approach reuses the same parameter multiple times.

9.2 *Convolutional neural networks*

The big idea behind convolutional neural networks is that a local understanding of an image is good enough. The practical benefit is that having fewer parameters greatly improves the time it takes to learn as well as reduces the amount of data required to train the model.

Instead of a fully connected network of weights from each pixel, a CNN has just enough weights to look at a small patch of the image. It's like reading a book by using a magnifying glass; eventually, you read the whole page, but you look at only a small patch of the page at any given time.

Consider a 256 × 256 image. Instead of your TensorFlow code processing the whole image at once, it can efficiently scan it chunk by chunk—say, a 5 × 5 window. The 5 × 5 window slides along the image (usually left to right, and top to bottom), as shown in figure 9.2. How "quickly" it slides is called its *stride length*. For example, a stride length of 2 means the 5 × 5 sliding window moves by 2 pixels at a time until it spans the entire image. In TensorFlow, you can easily adjust the stride length and window size by using the built-in library functions, as you'll soon see.

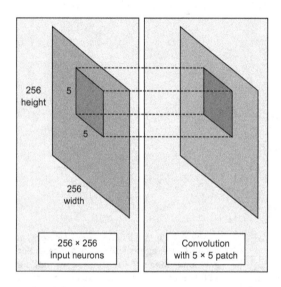

Figure 9.2   Convolving a 5 × 5 patch over an image, as shown on the left, produces another image, as shown on the right. In this case, the produced image is the same size as the original. Converting an original image to a convolved image requires only 5 × 5 = 25 parameters!

This 5 × 5 window has an associated 5 × 5 matrix of weights.

> **DEFINITION**   A *convolution* is a weighted sum of the pixel values of the image, as the window slides across the whole image. Turns out, this convolution process throughout an image with a weight matrix produces another image (of the same size, depending on the convention). *Convolving* is the process of applying a convolution.

The sliding-window shenanigans happen in the *convolution layer* of the neural network. A typical CNN has multiple convolution layers. Each convolutional layer typically generates many alternate convolutions, so the weight matrix is a tensor of 5 × 5 × *n*, where *n* is the number of convolutions.

As an example, let's say an image goes through a convolution layer on a weight matrix of 5 × 5 × 64. It generates 64 convolutions by sliding a 5 × 5 window. Therefore, this model has $5 \times 5 \times 64$ (= 1,600) parameters, which is remarkably fewer parameters than a fully connected network, 256×256 (= 65,536).

The beauty of the CNN is that the number of parameters is independent of the size of the original image. You can run the same CNN on a 300×300 image, and the number of parameters won't change in the convolution layer!

9.3 Preparing the image

To start implementing CNNs in TensorFlow, let's first obtain some images to work with. The code listings in this section will help you set up a training dataset for the remainder of the chapter.

First, download the CIFAR-10 dataset from www.cs.toronto.edu/~kriz/cifar-10-python.tar.gz. This dataset contains 60,000 images, evenly split into 10 categories, which makes it a great resource for classification tasks. Go ahead and extract that file to your working directory. Figure 9.3 shows examples of images from the dataset.

Figure 9.3 Images from the CIFAR-10 dataset. Because they're only 32 × 32 in size, they're a bit difficult to see, but you can generally recognize some of the objects.

You used the CIFAR-10 dataset in the previous chapter about autoencoders, so let's pull up that code again. The following listing comes straight from the CIFAR-10 documentation located at www.cs.toronto.edu/~kriz/cifar.html. Place the code in a file called cifar_tools.py.

Listing 9.1   Loading images from a CIFAR-10 file in Python

```python
import pickle

def unpickle(file):
    fo = open(file, 'rb')
    dict = pickle.load(fo, encoding='latin1')
    fo.close()
    return dict
```

Neural networks are already prone to overfitting, so it's essential that you do as much as you can to minimize that error. For that reason, always remember to clean the data before processing it.

Cleaning data is a core process in the machine-learning pipeline. Listing 9.2 implements the following three steps for cleaning a dataset of images:

1   If you have an image in color, try converting it to grayscale to lower the dimensionality of the input data, and consequently lower the number of parameters.

2   Consider center-cropping the image, because the edges of an image might provide no useful information.

3   Normalize your input by subtracting the mean and dividing by the standard deviation of each data sample so that the gradients during back-propagation don't change too dramatically.

The following listing shows how to clean a dataset of images by using these techniques.

Listing 9.2   Cleaning data

```python
import numpy as np

def clean(data):
    imgs = data.reshape(data.shape[0], 3, 32, 32)
    grayscale_imgs = imgs.mean(1)
    cropped_imgs = grayscale_imgs[:, 4:28, 4:28]
    img_data = cropped_imgs.reshape(data.shape[0], -1)
    img_size = np.shape(img_data)[1]
    means = np.mean(img_data, axis=1)
    meansT = means.reshape(len(means), 1)
    stds = np.std(img_data, axis=1)
    stdsT = stds.reshape(len(stds), 1)
    adj_stds = np.maximum(stdsT, 1.0 / np.sqrt(img_size))
    normalized = (img_data - meansT) / adj_stds
    return normalized
```

Reorganizes the data so it's a 32 × 32 matrix with three channels

Grayscales the image by averaging the color intensities

Crops the 32 × 32 image to a 24 × 24 image

Normalizes the pixels' values by subtracting the mean and dividing by standard deviation

Collect all the images from CIFAR-10 into memory, and run your cleaning function on them. The following listing sets up a convenient method to read, clean, and structure your data for use in TensorFlow. Include this in cifar_tools.py, as well.

```
def read_data(directory):
    names = unpickle('{}/batches.meta'.format(directory))['label_names']
    print('names', names)

    data, labels = [], []
    for i in range(1, 6):
        filename = '{}/data_batch_{}'.format(directory, i)
        batch_data = unpickle(filename)
        if len(data) > 0:
            data = np.vstack((data, batch_data['data']))
            labels = np.hstack((labels, batch_data['labels']))
        else:
            data = batch_data['data']
            labels = batch_data['labels']

    print(np.shape(data), np.shape(labels))

    data = clean(data)
    data = data.astype(np.float32)
    return names, data, labels
```

In another file called using_cifar.py, you can now use the method by importing cifar_tools. Listings 9.4 and 9.5 show how to sample a few images from the dataset and visualize them.

```
import cifar_tools

names, data, labels = \
    cifar_tools.read_data('your/location/to/cifar-10-batches-py')
```

You can randomly select a few images and draw them along their corresponding label. The following listing does exactly that, so you can get a better understanding of the type of data you'll be dealing with.

```
import numpy as np
import matplotlib.pyplot as plt
import random
```

```
def show_some_examples(names, data, labels):
    plt.figure()
    rows, cols = 4, 4
    random_idxs = random.sample(range(len(data)), rows * cols)
    for i in range(rows * cols):
        plt.subplot(rows, cols, i + 1)
        j = random_idxs[i]
        plt.title(names[labels[j]])
        img = np.reshape(data[j, :], (24, 24))
        plt.imshow(img, cmap='Greys_r')
        plt.axis('off')
    plt.tight_layout()
    plt.savefig('cifar_examples.png')

show_some_examples(names, data, labels)
```

Randomly pick images from the dataset to show

Change this to as many rows and columns as you desire.

By running this code, you'll generate a file called cifar_examples.png that will look similar to figure 9.3.

9.3.1   Generating filters

In this section, you'll convolve an image with a couple of random 5 × 5 patches, also called *filters*. This is an important step in a convolutional neural network, so you'll carefully examine how the data transforms. To understand a CNN model for image processing, it's wise to observe the way an image filter transforms an image. Filters are a way to extract useful image features such as edges and shapes. You can train a machine-learning model on these features.

Remember: a feature vector indicates how you represent a data point. When you apply a filter to an image, the corresponding point in the transformed image is a feature—a feature that says, "When you apply this filter to this point, it now has this new value." The more filters you use on an image, the greater the dimensionality of the feature vector.

Open a new file called conv_visuals.py. Let's randomly initialize 32 filters. You'll do so by defining a variable called W of size 5 × 5 × 1 × 32. The first two dimensions correspond to the filter size. The last dimension corresponds to the 32 convolutions. The 1 in the variable's size corresponds to the input dimension, because the conv2d function is capable of convolving images of multiple channels. (In our example, you care about only grayscale images, so the number of input channels is 1.) The following listing provides the code to generate filters, which are shown in figure 9.4.

Listing 9.6   Generating and visualizing random filters

```
W = tf.Variable(tf.random_normal([5, 5, 1, 32]))

def show_weights(W, filename=None):
    plt.figure()
```

Defines the tensor representing the random filters

```
                 rows, cols = 4, 8
Visualizes  ┌─▷  for i in range(np.shape(W)[3]):          ◁─┐  Defines just enough rows
each filter │        img = W[:, :, 0, i]                     │  and columns to show the
   matrix   │        plt.subplot(rows, cols, i + 1)          │  32 figures in figure 9.4
            │        plt.imshow(img, cmap='Greys_r', interpolation='none')
            │        plt.axis('off')
                 if filename:
                     plt.savefig(filename)
                 else:
                     plt.show()
```

Figure 9.4 These are 32 randomly initialized matrices, each of size 5 × 5. They represent the filters you'll use to convolve an input image.

EXERCISE 9.1
Change listing 9.6 to generate 64 filters of size 3 × 3.

ANSWER
```
W = tf.Variable(tf.random_normal([3, 3, 1, 64]))
```

Use a session, as shown in the following listing, and initialize some weights by using the `global_variables_initializer` op. Call the `show_weights` function to visualize random filters, as shown in figure 9.4.

Listing 9.7   Using a session to initialize weights

```
with tf.Session() as sess:
    sess.run(tf.global_variables_initializer())

    W_val = sess.run(W)
    show_weights(W_val, 'step0_weights.png')
```

9.3.2   Convolving using filters

The previous section prepared filters to use. In this section, you'll use TensorFlow's convolve function on your randomly generated filters. The following listing sets up code to visualize the convolution outputs. You'll use it later, just as you used show_ weights.

Listing 9.8   Showing convolution results

```
def show_conv_results(data, filename=None):
    plt.figure()
    rows, cols = 4, 8
    for i in range(np.shape(data)[3]):
        img = data[0, :, :, i]
        plt.subplot(rows, cols, i + 1)
        plt.imshow(img, cmap='Greys_r', interpolation='none')
        plt.axis('off')
    if filename:
        plt.savefig(filename)
    else:
        plt.show()
```

> Unlike in listing 9.6, this time the shape of the tensor is different.

Let's say you have an example input image, such as the one shown in figure 9.5. You can convolve the 24 × 24 image by using 5 × 5 filters to produce many convolved

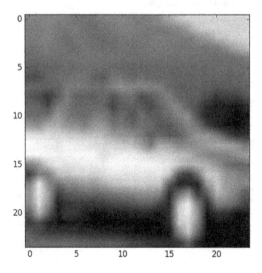

Figure 9.5   An example 24 × 24 image from the CIFAR-10 dataset

images. All these convolutions are unique perspectives of looking at the same image. These different perspectives work together to comprehend the object that exists in the image. The following listing shows how to do this, step by step.

Listing 9.9 Visualizing convolutions

```
raw_data = data[4, :]
raw_img = np.reshape(raw_data, (24, 24))          Gets an image from
plt.figure()                                       the CIFAR dataset,
plt.imshow(raw_img, cmap='Greys_r')                and visualizes it
plt.savefig('input_image.png')
                                                   Defines the input
                                                   tensor for the
                                                   24 × 24 image
x = tf.reshape(raw_data, shape=[-1, 24, 24, 1])  ⟵

b = tf.Variable(tf.random_normal([32]))           Defines the filters
conv = tf.nn.conv2d(x, W, strides=[1, 1, 1, 1], padding='SAME')  and corresponding
conv_with_b = tf.nn.bias_add(conv, b)             parameters
conv_out = tf.nn.relu(conv_with_b)

with tf.Session() as sess:
    sess.run(tf.global_variables_initializer())

    conv_val = sess.run(conv)                     Runs the
    show_conv_results(conv_val, 'step1_convs.png')  convolution on
    print(np.shape(conv_val))                     the selected
                                                   image
conv_out_val = sess.run(conv_out)
    show_conv_results(conv_out_val, 'step2_conv_outs.png')
    print(np.shape(conv_out_val))
```

Finally, by running the conv2d function in TensorFlow, you get the 32 images in figure 9.6. The idea of convolving images is that each of the 32 convolutions captures different features about the image.

With the addition of a bias term and an activation function such as relu (see listing 9.12 for an example), the convolution layer of the network behaves nonlinearly, which improves its expressiveness. Figure 9.7 shows what each of the 32 convolution outputs becomes.

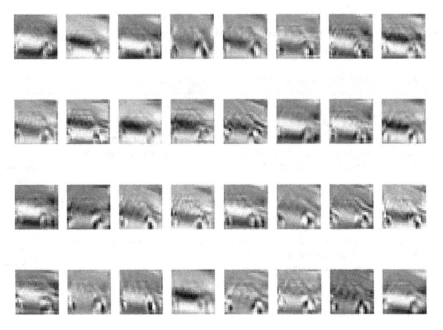

Figure 9.6   Resulting images from convolving the random filters on an image of a car

Figure 9.7   After you add a bias term and an activation function, the resulting convolutions can capture more-powerful patterns within images.

9.3.3 *Max pooling*

After a convolution layer extracts useful features, it's usually a good idea to reduce the size of the convolved outputs. Rescaling or subsampling a convolved output helps reduce the number of parameters, which in turn can help to not overfit the data.

This is the main idea behind a technique called *max pooling*, which sweeps a window across an image and picks the pixel with the maximum value. Depending on the stride length, the resulting image is a fraction of the size of the original. This is useful because it lessens the dimensionality of the data, consequently reducing the number of parameters in future steps.

> **EXERCISE 9.2**
>
> Let's say you want to max pool over a 32 × 32 image. If the window size is 2 × 2 and the stride length is 2, how big will the resulting max-pooled image be?
>
> **ANSWER**
>
> The 2 × 2 window would need to move 16 times in each direction to span the 32 × 32 image, so the image would shrink by half: 16 × 16. Because it shrank by half in both dimensions, the image is one-fourth the size of the original image (½ × ½).

Place the following listing within the Session context.

Listing 9.10 Running the maxpool function to subsample convolved images

```
k = 2
maxpool = tf.nn.max_pool(conv_out,
                         ksize=[1, k, k, 1],
                         strides=[1, k, k, 1],
                         padding='SAME')

with tf.Session() as sess:
    maxpool_val = sess.run(maxpool)
    show_conv_results(maxpool_val, 'step3_maxpool.png')
    print(np.shape(maxpool_val))
```

As a result of running this code, the max-pooling function halves the image size and produces lower-resolution convolved outputs, as shown in figure 9.8.

You have the tools necessary to implement the full convolutional neural network. In the next section, you'll finally train the image classifier.

Figure 9.8   After running `maxpool`, **the convolved outputs are halved in size, making the algorithm computationally faster without losing too much information.**

9.4   *Implementing a convolutional neural network in TensorFlow*

A convolutional neural network has multiple layers of convolutions and max pooling. The convolution layer offers different perspectives on the image, while the max-pooling layer simplifies the computations by reducing the dimensionality without losing too much information.

Consider a full-size 256 × 256 image convolved by a 5 × 5 filter into 64 convolutions. As shown in figure 9.9, each convolution is subsampled by using max pooling to produce 64 smaller convolved images of size 128 × 128.

Now that you know how to make filters and use the convolution op, let's create a new source file. You'll start by defining all your variables. In listing 9.11, import all libraries, load the dataset, and, finally, define all variables.

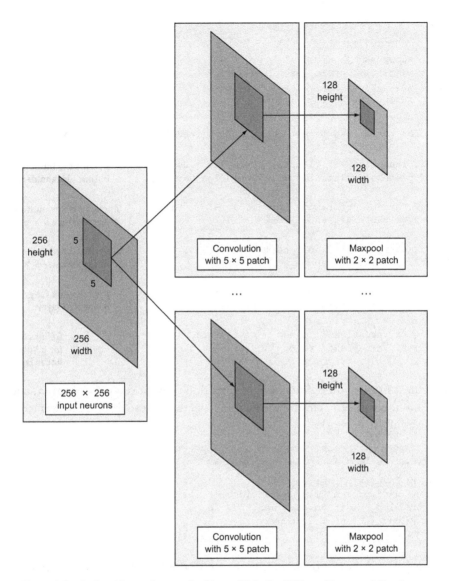

Figure 9.9 **An input image is convolved by multiple 5 × 5 filters. The convolution layer includes an added bias term with an activation function, resulting in 5 × 5 + 5 = 30 parameters. Next, a max-pooling layer reduces the dimensionality of the data (which requires no extra parameters).**

Listing 9.11   Setting up CNN weights

```
import numpy as np
import matplotlib.pyplot as plt
import cifar_tools
import tensorflow as tf

names, data, labels = \                                          Loads the
    cifar_tools.read_data('/home/binroot/res/cifar-10-batches-py')  ◁  dataset

x = tf.placeholder(tf.float32, [None, 24 * 24])        Defines the input and
y = tf.placeholder(tf.float32, [None, len(names)])     output placeholders

W1 = tf.Variable(tf.random_normal([5, 5, 1, 64]))      Applies 64 convolutions
b1 = tf.Variable(tf.random_normal([64]))               of window size 5 × 5

W2 = tf.Variable(tf.random_normal([5, 5, 64, 64]))     Applies 64 more convolutions
b2 = tf.Variable(tf.random_normal([64]))               of window size 5 × 5

W3 = tf.Variable(tf.random_normal([6*6*64, 1024]))     Introduces a fully
b3 = tf.Variable(tf.random_normal([1024]))             connected layer

W_out = tf.Variable(tf.random_normal([1024, len(names)]))   Defines the variables
b_out = tf.Variable(tf.random_normal([len(names)]))         for a fully connected
                                                            linear layer
```

In the next listing, you define a helper function to perform a convolution, add a bias
term, and then add an activation function. Together, these three steps form a convolution layer of the network.

Listing 9.12   Creating a convolution layer

```
def conv_layer(x, W, b):
    conv = tf.nn.conv2d(x, W, strides=[1, 1, 1, 1], padding='SAME')
    conv_with_b = tf.nn.bias_add(conv, b)
    conv_out = tf.nn.relu(conv_with_b)
    return conv_out
```

The next listing shows how to define the max-pool layer by specifying the kernel and
stride size.

Listing 9.13   Creating a max-pool layer

```
def maxpool_layer(conv, k=2):
    return tf.nn.max_pool(conv, ksize=[1, k, k, 1], strides=[1, k, k, 1],
      padding='SAME')
```

You can stack together the convolution and max-pool layers to define the convolutional neural network architecture. The following listing defines a possible CNN

model. The last layer is typically just a fully connected network connected to each of the 10 output neurons.

Listing 9.14 The full CNN model

```
def model():
    x_reshaped = tf.reshape(x, shape=[-1, 24, 24, 1])
```

Constructs the first layer of convolution and max pooling

```
    conv_out1 = conv_layer(x_reshaped, W1, b1)
    maxpool_out1 = maxpool_layer(conv_out1)
    norm1 = tf.nn.lrn(maxpool_out1, 4, bias=1.0, alpha=0.001 / 9.0,
      beta=0.75)
```

Constructs the second layer

```
    conv_out2 = conv_layer(norm1, W2, b2)
    norm2 = tf.nn.lrn(conv_out2, 4, bias=1.0, alpha=0.001 / 9.0, beta=0.75)
    maxpool_out2 = maxpool_layer(norm2)
```

```
    maxpool_reshaped = tf.reshape(maxpool_out2, [-1,
      W3.get_shape().as_list()[0]])
    local = tf.add(tf.matmul(maxpool_reshaped, W3), b3)
    local_out = tf.nn.relu(local)

    out = tf.add(tf.matmul(local_out, W_out), b_out)
    return out
```

Constructs the concluding fully connected layers

9.4.1 *Measuring performance*

With a neural network architecture designed, the next step is to define a cost function that you want to minimize. You'll use TensorFlow's `softmax_cross_entropy_with_logits` function, which is best described by the official documentation (http://mng.bz/8mEk):

> *[The function* `softmax_cross_entropy_with_logits`*] measures the probability error in discrete classification tasks in which the classes are mutually exclusive (each entry is in exactly one class). For example, each CIFAR-10 image is labeled with one and only one label: an image can be a dog or a truck, but not both.*

Because an image can belong to 1 of 10 possible labels, you'll represent that choice as a 10-dimensional vector. All elements of this vector have a value of 0, except the element corresponding to the label will have a value of 1. This representation, as you've seen in earlier chapters, is called *one-hot encoding*.

As shown in listing 9.15, you'll calculate the cost via the cross-entropy loss function we mentioned in chapter 4. This returns the probability error for your classification. Note that this works only for simple classifications—those in which your classes are mutually exclusive (for example, a truck can't also be a dog). You can employ many types of optimizers, but in this example, let's stick with the AdamOptimizer, which is a simple and fast optimizer (described in detail at http://mng.bz/zW98). It may be worth playing around with the arguments to this in real-world applications, but it works well off the shelf.

Listing 9.15 Defining ops to measure the cost and accuracy

```
model_op = model()                                    Defines the classification
                                                      loss function
cost = tf.reduce_mean(                         ←┘
    tf.nn.softmax_cross_entropy_with_logits(logits=model_op, labels=y)
)

train_op = tf.train.AdamOptimizer(learning_rate=0.001).minimize(cost)   ←┐

correct_pred = tf.equal(tf.argmax(model_op, 1), tf.argmax(y, 1))
accuracy = tf.reduce_mean(tf.cast(correct_pred, tf.float32))

                                                  Defines the training op to
                                                  minimize the loss function
```

Finally, in the next section, you'll run the training op to minimize the cost of the neural network. Doing so multiple times throughout the dataset will learn the optimal weights (or parameters).

9.4.2 Training the classifier

In the following listing, you'll loop through the dataset of images in small batches to train the neural network. Over time, the weights will slowly converge to a local optimum to accurately predict the training images.

Listing 9.16 Training the neural network by using the CIFAR-10 dataset

```
with tf.Session() as sess:
    sess.run(tf.global_variables_initializer())
    onehot_labels = tf.one_hot(labels, len(names), on_value=1., off_value=0.,
     axis=-1)
    onehot_vals = sess.run(onehot_labels)
    batch_size = len(data) // 200                     Loops through
    print('batch size', batch_size)                   1,000 epochs
    for j in range(0, 1000):                    ←┘
        print('EPOCH', j)                             Trains the network
        for i in range(0, len(data), batch_size):  ←┘ in batches
            batch_data = data[i:i+batch_size, :]
            batch_onehot_vals = onehot_vals[i:i+batch_size, :]
            _, accuracy_val = sess.run([train_op, accuracy], feed_dict={x:
     batch_data, y: batch_onehot_vals})
            if i % 1000 == 0:
                print(i, accuracy_val)
        print('DONE WITH EPOCH')
```

That's it! You've successfully designed a convolutional neural network to classify images. Beware: it might take more than 10 minutes. If you're running this code on

CPU, it might even take hours! Can you imagine discovering a bug in your code after a day of waiting? That's why deep-learning researchers use powerful computers and GPUs to speed up computations.

9.5　*Tips and tricks to improve performance*

The CNN you developed in this chapter is a simple approach to solve the problem of image classification, but many techniques exist to improve performance after you finish your first working prototype:

- *Augmenting data*—From a single image, you can easily generate new training images. As a start, flip an image horizontally or vertically, and you can quadruple your dataset size. You may also adjust the brightness of the image or the hue to ensure that the neural network generalizes to other fluctuations. You may even want to add random noise to the image to make the classifier robust to small occlusions. Scaling the image up or down can also be helpful; having exactly the same-size items in your training images will almost guarantee overfitting!

- *Early stopping*—Keep track of the training and testing error while you train the neural network. At first, both errors should slowly dwindle, because the network is learning. But sometimes, the test error goes back up. This is a signal that the neural network has started overfitting on the training data and is unable to generalize to previously unseen input. You should stop the training the moment you witness this phenomenon.

- *Regularizing weights*—Another way to combat overfitting is by adding a regularization term to the cost function. You've already seen regularization in previous chapters, and the same concepts apply here.

- *Dropout*—TensorFlow comes with a handy tf.nn.dropout function, which can be applied to any layer of the network to reduce overfitting. It turns off a randomly selected number of neurons in that layer during training so that the network must be redundant and robust to inferring output.

- *Deeper architecture*—A deeper architecture results from adding more hidden layers to the neural network. If you have enough training data, it's been shown that adding more hidden layers improves performance.

EXERCISE 9.3

After the first iteration of this CNN architecture, try applying a couple of tips and tricks mentioned in this chapter.

ANSWER

Fine-tuning is, unfortunately, part of the process. You should begin by adjusting the hyperparameters and retraining the algorithm until you find a setting that works best.

9.6   *Application of convolutional neural networks*

Convolutional neural networks blossom when the input contains sensor data from audio or images. Images, in particular, are of major interest in industry. For example, when you sign up for a social network, you usually upload a profile photo, not an audio recording of yourself saying "hello." It seems that humans are naturally more entertained by photos, so let's see how CNNs can be used to detect faces in images.

The overall CNN architecture can be as simple or as complicated as you desire. You should start simple, and gradually tune your model until satisfied. There's no absolutely correct path, because facial recognition isn't completely solved. Researchers are still publishing papers that one-up previous state-of-the-art solutions.

You should first obtain a dataset of images. One of the largest datasets of arbitrary images is ImageNet (http://image-net.org/). Here, you can find negative examples for your binary classifier. To obtain positive examples of faces, you can find numerous datasets at the following sites that specialize in human faces:

- VGG Face Dataset: www.robots.ox.ac.uk/~vgg/data/vgg_face/
- FDDB: Face Detection Data Set and Benchmark: http://vis-www.cs.umass.edu/fddb/
- Databases for Face Detection and Pose Estimation: http://mng.bz/25N6
- YouTube Faces Database: www.cs.tau.ac.il/~wolf/ytfaces/

9.7   *Summary*

- Convolutional neural networks make assumptions that capturing the local patterns of a signal are sufficient to characterize it, and thus reduce the number of parameters of a neural network.
- Cleaning data is vital to the performance of most machine-learning models. The hour you spend to write code that cleans data is nothing compared to the amount of time it can take for a neural network to learn that cleaning function by itself.

10
Recurrent
neural networks

10.1   Contextual information

Back in school, I remember my sigh of relief when one of my midterm exams consisted of only true-or-false questions. I can't be the only one who assumed that half the answers would be True and the other half would be False.

I figured out answers to most of the questions and left the rest to random guessing. But that guessing was based on something clever, a strategy that you might have employed as well. After counting my number of True answers, I realized that a disproportionate number of False answers were lacking. So, a majority of my guesses were False to balance the distribution.

It worked. I sure felt sly in the moment. What exactly is this feeling of craftiness that makes us feel so confident in our decisions, and how can we give a neural network the same power?

One answer is to use context to answer questions. Contextual cues are important signals that can improve the performance of machine-learning algorithms. For example, imagine you want to examine an English sentence and tag the part of speech of each word.

The naïve approach is to individually classify each word as a noun, an adjective, and so on, without acknowledging its neighboring words. Consider trying that technique on the words in *this* sentence. The word *trying* is used as a verb, but depending on the context, you can also use it as an adjective, making parts-of-speech tagging a *trying* problem.

A better approach considers the context. To bestow neural networks with contextual cues, you'll study an architecture called a *recurrent neural network*. Instead of natural language data, you'll be dealing with continuous time-series data, such as the stock market prices covered in previous chapters. By the end of the chapter, you'll be able to model the patterns in time-series data to predict future values.

10.2   Introduction to recurrent neural networks

To understand recurrent neural networks, let's first look at the simple architecture in figure 10.1. It takes as input a vector $X(t)$ and generates as output a vector $Y(t)$, at some time (t). The circle in the middle represents the hidden layer of the network.

Figure 10.1 A neural network with the input and output layers labeled as $X(t)$ and $Y(t)$, respectively

With enough input/output examples, you can learn the parameters of the network in TensorFlow. For instance, let's refer to the input weights as a matrix W_{in} and the output weights as a matrix W_{out}. Assume there's just one hidden layer, referred to as a vector $Z(t)$.

As shown in figure 10.2, the first half of the neural network is characterized by the function $Z(t) = X(t) \times W_{in}$, and the second half of the neural network takes the form $Y(t) = Z(t) \times W_{out}$. Equivalently, if you prefer, the whole neural network is the function $Y(t) = (X(t) \times W_{in}) \times W_{out}$.

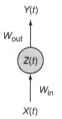

Figure 10.2 The hidden layer of a neural network can be thought of as a hidden representation of the data, which is encoded by the input weights and decoded by the output weights.

After spending nights fine-tuning the network, you probably want to start using your learned model in a real-world scenario. Typically, that implies calling the model multiple times, maybe even repeatedly, as depicted in figure 10.3.

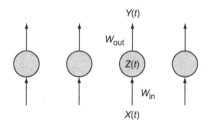

Figure 10.3 Often you end up running the same neural network multiple times, without using knowledge about the hidden states of the previous runs.

At each time *t*, when calling the learned model, this architecture doesn't take into account knowledge about the previous runs. It's like predicting stock market trends by looking only at data from the current day. A better idea is to exploit overarching patterns from a week's worth or a month's worth of data.

A *recurrent neural network* (RNN) is different from a traditional neural network because it introduces a transition weight *W* to transfer information over time. Figure 10.4 shows the three weight matrices that must be learned in an RNN. The introduction of the transition weight means that the next state is now dependent on the previous model, as well as the previous state. This means your model now has a "memory" of what it did!

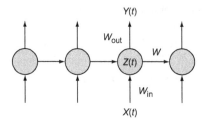

Figure 10.4   A recurrent neural network architecture can use the previous states of the network to its advantage.

Diagrams are nice, but you're here to get your hands dirty. Let's get right to it! The next section shows how to use TensorFlow's built-in RNN models. Then, you'll use an RNN on real-world time-series data to predict the future!

10.3   *Implementing a recurrent neural network*

As you implement the RNN, you'll use TensorFlow to do much of the heavy lifting. You won't need to manually build up a network as shown earlier in figure 10.4, because the TensorFlow library already supports some robust RNN models.

> **NOTE**   For TensorFlow library information on RNNs, see www.tensorflow.org/tutorials/recurrent.

One type of RNN model is called *Long Short-Term Memory* (LSTM). I admit, it's a fun name. It means exactly what it sounds like, too: short-term patterns aren't forgotten in the long term.

The precise implementation details of LSTM are beyond the scope of this book. Trust me, a thorough inspection of the LSTM model would distract from the chapter, because there's no definite standard yet. That's where TensorFlow comes to the rescue. It takes care of how the model is defined so you can use it out of the box. It also means that as TensorFlow is updated in the future, you'll be able to take advantage of improvements to the LSTM model without modifying your code.

TIP To understand how to implement LSTM from scratch, I suggest the following explanation: https://apaszke.github.io/lstm-explained.html. The paper that describes the implementation of regularization used in the following listings is available at http://arxiv.org/abs/1409.2329.

Begin by writing your code in a new file called simple_regression.py. Import the relevant libraries, as shown in the following listing.

Listing 10.1 Importing relevant libraries

```
import numpy as np
import tensorflow as tf
from tensorflow.contrib import rnn
```

Now, define a class called `SeriesPredictor`. The constructor, shown in the following listing, will set up model hyperparameters, weights, and the cost function.

Listing 10.2 Defining a class and its constructor

```
class SeriesPredictor:
    def __init__(self, input_dim, seq_size, hidden_dim=10):

        self.input_dim = input_dim
        self.seq_size = seq_size            Hyperparameters
        self.hidden_dim = hidden_dim

        self.W_out = tf.Variable(tf.random_normal([hidden_dim, 1]),
          name='W_out')
        self.b_out = tf.Variable(tf.random_normal([1]), name='b_out')
        self.x = tf.placeholder(tf.float32, [None, seq_size, input_dim])
        self.y = tf.placeholder(tf.float32, [None, seq_size])

        self.cost = tf.reduce_mean(tf.square(self.model() - self.y))
        self.train_op = tf.train.AdamOptimizer().minimize(self.cost)

        self.saver = tf.train.Saver()          Auxiliary ops
```

Weight variables and input placeholders — labels for the `W_out`, `b_out`, `x`, `y` block.

Cost optimizer — labels for the `cost`, `train_op` block.

Next, let's use TensorFlow's built-in RNN model called `BasicLSTMCell`. The hidden dimension of the cell passed into the `BasicLSTMCell` object is the dimension of the hidden state that gets passed through time. You can run this cell with data by using the `rnn.dynamic_rnn` function, to retrieve the output results. The following listing details how to use TensorFlow to implement a predictive model using LSTM.

Listing 10.3 Defining the RNN model

```
def model(self):
    """
    :param x: inputs of size [T, batch_size, input_size]
    :param W: matrix of fully-connected output layer weights
    :param b: vector of fully-connected output layer biases
    """
```

```
cell = rnn.BasicLSTMCell(self.hidden_dim)
outputs, states = tf.nn.dynamic_rnn(cell, self.x, dtype=tf.float32)
num_examples = tf.shape(self.x)[0]
W_repeated = tf.tile(tf.expand_dims(self.W_out, 0), [num_examples, 1, 1])
out = tf.matmul(outputs, W_repeated) + self.b_out
out = tf.squeeze(out)
return out
```

Computes the output layer as a fully connected linear function

Runs the cell on the input to obtain tensors for outputs and states

Creates an LSTM cell

With a model and cost function defined, you can now implement the training function, which will learn the LSTM weights, given example input/output pairs. As listing 10.4 shows, you open a session and repeatedly run the optimizer on the training data.

> **NOTE** You can use cross-validation to figure out how many iterations you need to train the model. In this case, you assume a fixed number of epochs. Some good insights and answers can be found through online Q&A sites such as ResearchGate: http://mng.bz/lB92.

After training, save the model to a file so you can load it later.

Listing 10.4   Training the model on a dataset

```
def train(self, train_x, train_y):
    with tf.Session() as sess:
        tf.get_variable_scope().reuse_variables()
        sess.run(tf.global_variables_initializer())
        for i in range(1000):
            _, mse = sess.run([self.train_op, self.cost],
    feed_dict={self.x: train_x, self.y: train_y})
            if i % 100 == 0:
                print(i, mse)
        save_path = self.saver.save(sess, 'model.ckpt')
        print('Model saved to {}'.format(save_path))
```

Runs the train op 1,000 times

Let's say all went well, and your model has successfully learned parameters. Next, you'd like to evaluate the predictive model on other data. The following listing loads the saved model and runs the model in a session by feeding in test data. If a learned model doesn't perform well on testing data, you can try tweaking the number of hidden dimensions of the LSTM cell.

Listing 10.5   Testing the learned model

```
def test(self, test_x):
    with tf.Session() as sess:
        tf.get_variable_scope().reuse_variables()
        self.saver.restore(sess, './model.ckpt')
        output = sess.run(self.model(), feed_dict={self.x: test_x})
        print(output)
```

It's done! But just to convince yourself that it works, let's make up some data and try to train the predictive model. In the next listing, you'll create input sequences, `train_x`, and corresponding output sequences, `train_y`.

Listing 10.6   Training and testing on dummy data

```
if __name__ == '__main__':
    predictor = SeriesPredictor(input_dim=1, seq_size=4, hidden_dim=10)
    train_x = [[[1], [2], [5], [6]],
               [[5], [7], [7], [8]],
               [[3], [4], [5], [7]]]
    train_y = [[1, 3, 7, 11],
               [5, 12, 14, 15],
               [3, 7, 9, 12]]
    predictor.train(train_x, train_y)

    test_x = [[[1], [2], [3], [4]],
              [[4], [5], [6], [7]]]
    predictor.test(test_x)
```

Predicted result should be 1, 3, 5, 7

Predicted result should be 4, 9, 11, 13

You can treat this predictive model as a black box and train it using real-world time-series data for prediction. In the next section, you'll get data to work with.

10.4   A predictive model for time-series data

Time-series data is abundantly available online. For this example, you'll use data about international airline passengers for a specific period. You can obtain this data from http://mng.bz/5UWL. Clicking that link will take you to a nice plot of the time-series data, as shown in figure 10.5.

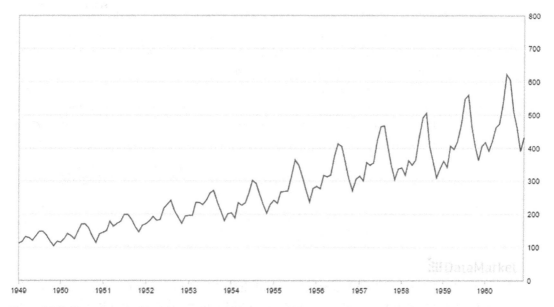

Figure 10.5   Raw data showing the number of international airline passengers throughout the years

You can download the data by clicking the Export tab and then selecting CSV (,) in the Export group. You'll have to manually edit the CSV file to remove the header line as well as the additional footer line.

In a file called data_loader.py, add the following code.

Listing 10.7   Loading data

```
import csv
import numpy as np
import matplotlib.pyplot as plt

def load_series(filename, series_idx=1):
    try:
        with open(filename) as csvfile:
            csvreader = csv.reader(csvfile)

            data = [float(row[series_idx]) for row in csvreader
                                           if len(row) > 0]
            normalized_data = (data - np.mean(data)) / np.std(data)
        return normalized_data
    except IOError:
        return None


def split_data(data, percent_train=0.80):
    num_rows = len(data) * percent_train
    return data[:num_rows], data[num_rows:]
```

> Loops through the lines of the file and converts to a floating-point number

> Calculates training data samples

> Splits the dataset into training and testing

> Preprocesses the data by mean-centering and dividing by standard deviation

Here, you define two functions, load_series and split_data. The first function loads the time-series file on disk and normalizes it, and the other function divides the dataset into two components, for training and testing.

Because you'll be evaluating the model multiple times to predict future values, let's modify the test function from SeriesPredictor. It now takes as an argument the session, instead of initializing the session on every call. See the following listing for this tweak.

Listing 10.8   Modifying the test function to pass in the session

```
def test(self, sess, test_x):
    tf.get_variable_scope().reuse_variables()
    self.saver.restore(sess, './model.ckpt')
    output = sess.run(self.model(), feed_dict={self.x: test_x})
    return output
```

You can now train the predictor by loading the data in the acceptable format. Listing 10.9 shows how to train the network and then use the trained model to predict future values. You'll generate the training data (`train_x` and `train_y`) to look like those shown previously in listing 10.6.

Listing 10.9 Generate training data

```
if __name__ == '__main__':
    seq_size = 5
    predictor = SeriesPredictor(
        input_dim=1,
        seq_size=seq_size,
        hidden_dim=100)

    data = data_loader.load_series('international-airline-passengers.csv')
    train_data, actual_vals = data_loader.split_data(data)

    train_x, train_y = [], []
    for i in range(len(train_data) - seq_size - 1):
        train_x.append(np.expand_dims(train_data[i:i+seq_size],
axis=1).tolist())
        train_y.append(train_data[i+1:i+seq_size+1])

    test_x, test_y = [], []
    for i in range(len(actual_vals) - seq_size - 1):
        test_x.append(np.expand_dims(actual_vals[i:i+seq_size],
axis=1).tolist())
        test_y.append(actual_vals[i+1:i+seq_size+1])

    predictor.train(train_x, train_y, test_x, test_y)

    with tf.Session() as sess:
        predicted_vals = predictor.test(sess, test_x)[:,0]
        print('predicted_vals', np.shape(predicted_vals))
        plot_results(train_data, predicted_vals, actual_vals,
'predictions.png')

        prev_seq = train_x[-1]
        predicted_vals = []
        for i in range(20):
            next_seq = predictor.test(sess, [prev_seq])
            predicted_vals.append(next_seq[-1])
            prev_seq = np.vstack((prev_seq[1:], next_seq[-1]))
        plot_results(train_data, predicted_vals, actual_vals,
'hallucinations.png')
```

The dimension of each element of the sequence is a scalar (one-dimensional).

Size of the RNN hidden dimension

Length of each sequence

Loads the data

Slides a window through the time-series data to construct the training dataset

Uses the same window-sliding strategy to construct the test dataset

Trains a model on the training dataset

Visualizes the model's performance

The predictor generates two graphs. The first is prediction results of the model, given ground-truth values, as shown in figure 10.6.

The other graph shows the prediction results when only the training data is given (blue line) and nothing else (see figure 10.7). This procedure has less information available, but it still did a good job matching trends of the data.

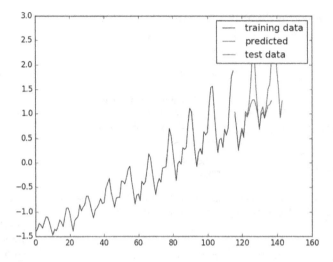

Figure 10.6 The predictions match trends fairly well when tested against ground-truth data.

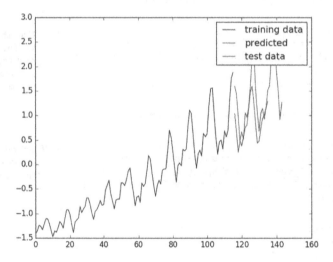

Figure 10.7 If the algorithm uses previously predicted results to make further predictions, then the general trend matches well, but not specific bumps.

You can use time-series predictors to reproduce realistic fluctuations in data. Imagine predicting market boom-and-bust cycles based on the tools you've learned so far. What are you waiting for? Grab some market data, and learn your own predictive model!

10.5 *Application of recurrent neural networks*

Recurrent neural networks are meant to be used with sequential data. Because audio signals are a dimension lower than video (linear signal versus two-dimensional pixel array), it's a lot easier to get started with audio time-series data. Consider how much speech recognition has improved over the years: it's becoming a tractable problem!

Like the audio histogram analysis you conducted in chapter 5 on clustering audio data, most speech recognition preprocessing involves representing the sound into a chromagram of sorts. Specifically, a common technique is to use a feature called *mel-frequency cepstral coefficients* (MFCCs). A good introduction is outlined in this blog post: http://mng.bz/411F.

Next, you'll need a dataset to train your model. A few popular ones include the following:

- LibriSpeech: www.openslr.org/12
- TED-LIUM: www.openslr.org/7
- VoxForge: www.voxforge.org

An in-depth walkthrough of a simple speech-recognition implementation in Tensor-Flow using these datasets is available online: https://svds.com/tensorflow-rnn-tutorial.

10.6 Summary

- A recurrent neural network (RNN) uses information from the past. That way, it can make predictions using data with high temporal dependencies.
- TensorFlow comes with RNN models out of the box.
- Time-series prediction is a useful application for RNNs because of temporal dependencies in the data.

Sequence-to-sequence models for chatbots

> **This chapter covers**
> - Examining sequence-to-sequence architecture
> - Vector embedding of words
> - Implementing a chatbot by using real-world data

Talking to customer service over the phone is a burden for both the customer and the company. Service providers pay a good chunk of money to hire these customer service representatives, but what if it's possible to automate most of this effort? Can we develop software to interface with customers through natural language?

The idea isn't as farfetched as you might think. Chatbots are getting a lot of hype because of unprecedented developments in natural language processing using deep-learning techniques. Perhaps, given enough training data, a chatbot could learn to navigate the most commonly addressed customer problems through natural conversations. If the chatbot were truly efficient, it could not only save the company money by eliminating the need to hire representatives, but even accelerate the customer's search for an answer.

In this chapter, you'll build a chatbot by feeding a neural network thousands of examples of input and output sentences. Your training dataset is a pair of English utterances; for example, if you ask, "How are you?" the chatbot should respond, "Fine, thank you."

> **NOTE** In this chapter, we're thinking of *sequences* and *sentences* as interchangeable concepts. In our implementation, a sentence will be a sequence of letters. Another common approach is to represent a sentence as a sequence of words.

In effect, the algorithm will try to produce an intelligent natural language response to each natural language query. You'll be implementing a neural network that uses two primary concepts taught in previous chapters: multiclass classification and recurrent neural networks (RNNs).

11.1 Building on classification and RNNs

Remember, *classification* is a machine-learning approach to predict the category of an input data item. Furthermore, multiclass classification allows for more than two classes. You saw in chapter 4 how to implement such an algorithm in TensorFlow. Specifically, the cost function between the model's prediction (a sequence of numbers) and the ground truth (a one-hot vector) tries to find the distance between two sequences by using the cross-entropy loss.

NOTE A one-hot vector is like an all-zero vector, except one of the dimensions has a value of 1.

In this case, implementing a chatbot, you'll use a variant of the cross-entropy loss to measure the difference between two sequences: the model's response (which is a sequence) against the ground truth (which is also a sequence).

EXERCISE 11.1

In TensorFlow, you can use the cross-entropy loss function to measure the similarity between a one-hot vector, such as (1, 0, 0), and a neural network's output, such as (2.34, 0.1, 0.3). On the other hand, English sentences aren't numeric vectors. How can you use the cross-entropy loss to measure the similarity between English sentences?

ANSWER

A crude approach would be to represent each sentence as a vector by counting the frequency of each word within the sentence. Then compare the vectors to see how closely they match up.

You may recall that RNNs are a neural network design for incorporating not only input from the current time step, but also state information from previous inputs. Chapter 10 covered these in great detail, and they'll be used again in this chapter. RNNs represent input and output as time-series data, which is exactly what you need to represent sequences.

A naïve idea is to use an out-of-the-box RNN to implement a chatbot. Let's see why this is a bad approach. The input and output of the RNN are natural language sentences, so the inputs $(x_t, x_{t-1}, x_{t-2}, \ldots)$ and outputs $(y_t, y_{t-1}, y_{t-2}, \ldots)$ can be sequences of words. The problem in using an RNN to model conversations is that the RNN produces an output result immediately. If your input is a sequence of words (*How, are, you*), the first output word will depend on only the first input word. The output sequence item y_t of the RNN couldn't look ahead to future parts of the input sentence to make a decision; it would be limited by knowledge of only previous input sequences $(x_t, x_{t-1}, x_{t-2}, \ldots)$. The naïve RNN model tries to come up with a response to the user's query before they've finished asking it, which can lead to incorrect results.

Instead, you'll end up using two RNNs: one for the input sentence and the other for the output sequence. After the input sequence is finished being processed by the first RNN, it'll send the hidden state to the second RNN to process the output sentence. You can see the two RNNs labeled Encoder and Decoder in figure 11.1.

Seq2seq model overview

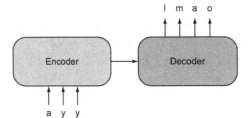

Figure 11.1   Here's a high-level view of your neural network model. The input *ayy* is passed into the encoder RNN, and the decoder RNN is expected to respond with *lmao*. These are just toy examples for your chatbot, but you could imagine more-complicated pairs of sentences for the input and output.

We're bringing concepts of multiclass classification and RNNs from previous chapters into designing a neural network that learns to map an input sequence to an output sequence. The RNNs provide a way of encoding the input sentence, passing a summarized state vector to the decoder, and then decoding it to a response sentence. To measure the cost between the model's response and the ground truth, we look to the function used in multiclass classification, the cross-entropy loss, for inspiration.

This architecture is called a *sequence-to-sequence (seq2seq) neural network architecture*. The training data you use will be thousands of pairs of sentences mined from movie scripts. The algorithm will observe these dialogue examples and eventually learn to form responses to arbitrary queries you might ask it.

> **EXERCISE 11.2**
> What other industries could benefit from a chatbot?
>
> **ANSWER**
> One example is a conversation partner for young students as an educational tool to teach various subjects such as English, math, and even computer science.

By the end of the chapter, you'll have your own chatbot that can respond somewhat intelligently to your queries. It won't be perfect, because this model always responds the same way for the same input query.

Suppose, for example, that you're traveling to a foreign country without any ability to speak the language. A clever salesman hands you a book, claiming it's all you need to respond to sentences in the foreign language. You're supposed to use it like a dictionary. When someone says a phrase in the foreign language, you can look it up, and the book will have the response written out for you to read aloud: "If someone says *Hello*, you say *Hi*."

Sure, it might be a practical lookup table for small talk, but can a lookup table get you the correct response for arbitrary dialogue? Of course not! Consider looking up the question "Are you hungry?" The answer to that question is stamped in the book and will never change.

The lookup table is missing state information, which is a key component in dialogue. In your seq2seq model, you'll suffer from a similar issue; but it's a good start! Believe it or not, as of 2017, hierarchical state representation for intelligent dialogue still isn't the norm; many chatbots start out with these seq2seq models.

11.2 Seq2seq architecture

The seq2seq model attempts to learn a neural network that predicts an output sequence from an input sequence. Sequences are a little different from traditional vectors, because a sequence implies an ordering of events.

Time is an intuitive way to order events: we usually end up alluding to words related to time, such as *temporal, time series, past,* and *future*. For example, we like to say that RNNs propagate information to *future time* steps. Or, RNNs capture *temporal dependencies*.

NOTE RNNs are covered in detail in chapter 10.

The seq2seq model is implemented using multiple RNNs. A single RNN cell is depicted in figure 11.2; it serves as the building block for the rest of the seq2seq model architecture.

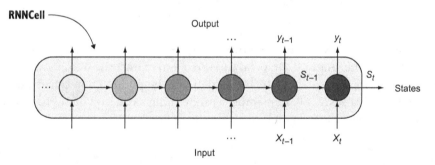

Figure 11.2 The input, output, and states of an RNN. You can ignore the intricacies of exactly how an RNN is implemented. All that matters is the formatting of your input and output.

First, you'll learn how to stack RNNs on top of each other to improve the model's complexity. Then you'll learn how to pipe the hidden state of one RNN to another RNN, so that you can have an "encoder" and "decoder" network. As you'll begin to see, it's fairly easy to start using RNNs.

After that, you'll get an introduction to converting natural language sentences into a sequence of vectors. After all, RNNs understand only numeric data, so you'll absolutely need this conversion process. Because a *sequence* is another way of saying "a list of tensors," you need to make sure you can convert your data accordingly. For example, a sentence is a sequence of words, but words aren't tensors. The process of converting words to tensors or, more commonly, vectors is called *embedding*.

Last, you'll put all these concepts together to implement the seq2seq model on real-world data. The data will come from thousands of conversations from movie scripts.

You can hit the ground running with the following code listing. Open a new Python file, and start copying listing 11.1 to set up constants and placeholders. You'll define the shape of the placeholder to be [None, seq_size, input_dim], where None means the size is dynamic because the batch size may change, seq_size is the length of the sequence, and input_dim is the dimension of each sequence item.

Listing 11.1 Setting up constants and placeholders

```
import tensorflow as tf          ◁──┐ All you need is
                                      TensorFlow.

input_dim = 1                     ◁── Dimension of
seq_size = 6                          each sequence
                                      element

                                      Maximum
                                      length of
                                      sequence

input_placeholder = tf.placeholder(dtype=tf.float32,
                                   shape=[None, seq_size, input_dim])
```

To generate an RNN cell like the one in figure 11.2, TensorFlow provides a helpful LSTMCell class. Listing 11.2 shows how to use it and extract the outputs and states from the cell. Just for convenience, the listing defines a helper function called make_cell to set up the LSTM RNN cell. Remember, just defining a cell isn't enough: you also need to call tf.nn.dynamic_rnn on it to set up the network.

Listing 11.2 Making a simple RNN cell

```
def make_cell(state_dim):
    return tf.contrib.rnn.LSTMCell(state_dim)   ◁── Check out the tf.contrib.rnn
                                                    documentation for other
                                                    types of cells, such as GRU.

with tf.variable_scope("first_cell") as scope:
    cell = make_cell(state_dim=10)                   There will be two
    outputs, states = tf.nn.dynamic_rnn(cell,   ◁──  generated results:
                                                     outputs and states.
                          input_placeholder,   ◁──┐ This is the
                          dtype=tf.float32)          input sequence
                                                     to the RNN.
```

You might remember from previous chapters that you can improve a neural network's complexity by adding more and more hidden layers. More layers means more parameters, and that likely means the model can represent more functions; it's more flexible.

You know what? You can stack cells on top of each other. Nothing is stopping you. Doing so makes the model more complex, so perhaps this two-layered RNN model will perform better because it's more expressive. Figure 11.3 shows two cells stacked together.

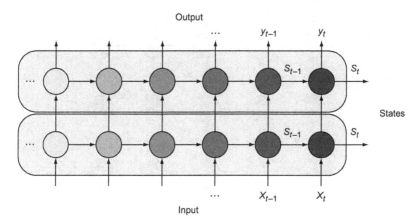

Figure 11.3   You can stack RNN cells to form a more complicated architecture.

WARNING   The more flexible the model, the more likely that it'll overfit the training data.

In TensorFlow, you can intuitively implement this two-layered RNN network. First, you create a new variable scope for the second cell. To stack RNNs together, you can pipe the output of the first cell to the input of the second cell. The following listing shows how to do exactly this.

Listing 11.3   Stacking two RNN cells

```
with tf.variable_scope("second_cell") as scope:      ⟵  Defining a variable scope
    cell2 = make_cell(state_dim=10)                        helps avoid runtime errors
    outputs2, states2 = tf.nn.dynamic_rnn(cell2,           due to variable reuse.
                                          outputs,     ⟵  Input to this cell will be
                                          dtype=tf.float32)    the other cell's output.
```

What if you wanted four layers of RNNs? Or 10? For example, figure 11.4 shows four RNN cells stacked atop each other.

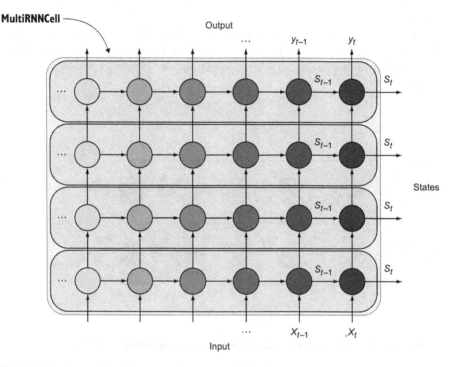

Figure 11.4   TensorFlow lets you stack as many RNN cells as you want.

A useful shortcut for stacking cells that the TensorFlow library supplies is called `MultiRNNCell`. The following listing shows how to use this helper function to build arbitrarily large RNN cells.

Listing 11.4   Using `MultiRNNCell` to stack multiple cells

```
def make_multi_cell(state_dim, num_layers):
    cells = [make_cell(state_dim) for _ in range(num_layers)]
    return tf.contrib.rnn.MultiRNNCell(cells)

multi_cell = make_multi_cell(state_dim=10, num_layers=4)
outputs4, states4 = tf.nn.dynamic_rnn(multi_cell,
                                      input_placeholder,
                                      dtype=tf.float32)
```

> The for-loop syntax is the preferred way to construct a list of RNN cells.

So far, you've grown RNNs vertically by piping outputs of one cell to the inputs of another. In the seq2seq model, you'll want one RNN cell to process the input sentence, and another RNN cell to process the output sentence. To communicate between the two cells, you can also connect RNNs horizontally by connecting states from cell to cell, as shown in figure 11.5.

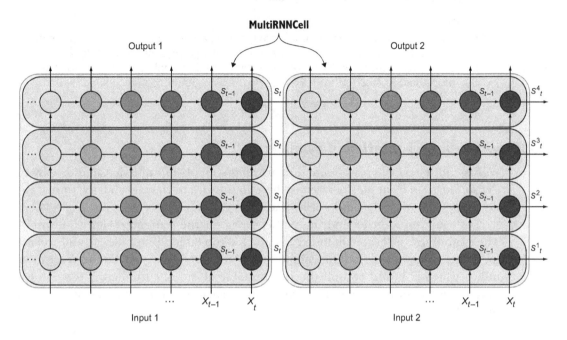

Figure 11.5 You can use the last states of the first cell as the next cell's initial state. This model can learn mapping from an input sequence to an output sequence. The model is called *seq2seq*.

You've stacked RNN cells vertically and connected them horizontally, vastly increasing the number of parameters in the network! Is this utter blasphemy? Yes. You've built a monolithic architecture by composing RNNs every which way. But there's a method to this madness, because this insane neural network architecture is the backbone of the seq2seq model.

As you can see in figure 11.5, the seq2seq model appears to have two input sequences and two output sequences. But only input 1 will be used for the input sentence, and only output 2 will be used for the output sentence.

You may be wondering what to do with the other two sequences. Strangely enough, the output 1 sequence is entirely unused by the seq2seq model. And, as you'll see, the input 2 sequence is crafted using some of output 2 data, in a feedback loop.

Your training data for designing a chatbot will be pairs of input and output sentences, so you'll need to better understand how to embed words into a tensor. The next section covers how to do so in TensorFlow.

EXERCISE 11.3
Sentences may be represented by a sequence of characters or words, but can you think of other sequential representations of sentences?

ANSWER
Phrases and grammatical information (verbs, nouns, and so forth) could both be used. More frequently, real applications use *natural language processing* (NLP) lookups to standardize word forms, spellings, and meanings. One example of a library that does this translation is *fastText* from Facebook (https://github.com/facebookresearch/fastText).

11.3   *Vector representation of symbols*

Words and letters are symbols, and converting symbols to numeric values is easy in TensorFlow. For example, let's say you have four words in your vocabulary: $word_0$: *the*; $word_1$: *fight*; $word_2$: *wind*; and $word_3$: *like*.

Let's say you want to find the embeddings for the sentence "Fight the wind." The symbol *fight* is located at index 1 of the lookup table, *the* at index 0, and *wind* at index 2. If you want to find the embedding of the word *fight*, you have to refer to its index, which is 1, and consult the lookup table at index 1 to identify the embedding value. In our first example, each word is associated with a number, as shown in figure 11.6.

Word	Number
the	17
fight	22
wind	35
like	51

Figure 11.6   A mapping from symbols to scalars

The following listing shows how to define such a mapping between symbols and numeric values using TensorFlow code.

Listing 11.5   Defining a lookup table of scalars

```
embeddings_0d = tf.constant([17, 22, 35, 51])
```

Or maybe the words are associated with vectors, as shown in figure 11.7. This is often the preferred method of representing words. You can find a thorough tutorial on vector representation of words in the official TensorFlow docs: http://mng.bz/35M8.

Word	Vector
the	[1, 0, 0, 0]
fight	[0, 1, 0, 0]
wind	[0, 0, 1, 0]
like	[0, 0, 0, 1]

Figure 11.7 A mapping from symbols to vectors

You can implement the mapping between words and vectors in TensorFlow, as shown in the following listing.

Listing 11.6 Defining a lookup table of 4D vectors

```
embeddings_4d = tf.constant([[1, 0, 0, 0],
                             [0, 1, 0, 0],
                             [0, 0, 1, 0],
                             [0, 0, 0, 1]])
```

This may sound over the top, but you can represent a symbol by a tensor of any rank you want, not just numbers (rank 0) or vectors (rank 1). In figure 11.8, you're mapping symbols to tensors of rank 2.

Word	Tensor
the	[[1, 0], [0, 0]]
fight	[[0, 1], [0, 0]]
wind	[[0, 0], [1, 0]]
like	[[0, 0], [0, 1]]

Figure 11.8 A mapping from symbols to tensors

The following listing shows how to implement this mapping of words to tensors in TensorFlow.

Listing 11.7 Defining a lookup table of tensors

```
embeddings_2x2d = tf.constant([[[1, 0], [0, 0]],
                               [[0, 1], [0, 0]],
                               [[0, 0], [1, 0]],
                               [[0, 0], [0, 1]]])
```

The embedding_lookup function provided by TensorFlow is an optimized way to access embeddings by indices, as shown in the following listing.

Listing 11.8   Looking up the embeddings

```
ids = tf.constant([1, 0, 2])
lookup_0d = sess.run(tf.nn.embedding_lookup(embeddings_0d, ids))
print(lookup_0d)

lookup_4d = sess.run(tf.nn.embedding_lookup(embeddings_4d, ids))
print(lookup_4d)

lookup_2x2d = sess.run(tf.nn.embedding_lookup(embeddings_2x2d, ids))
print(lookup_2x2d)
```

◁── **Embeddings lookup corresponding to the words *fight, the,* and *wind***

In reality, the embedding matrix isn't something you ever have to hardcode. These listings are for you to understand the ins and outs of the `embedding_lookup` function in TensorFlow, because you'll be using it heavily soon. The embedding lookup table will be learned automatically over time by training the neural network. You start by defining a random, normally distributed lookup table. Then, TensorFlow's optimizer will adjust the matrix values to minimize the cost.

EXERCISE 11.4

Follow the official TensorFlow word2vec tutorial to get more familiar with embeddings: www.tensorflow.org/tutorials/word2vec.

ANSWER

This tutorial will teach you to visualize the embeddings using TensorBoard.

11.4   *Putting it all together*

The first step in using natural language input in a neural network is to decide on a mapping between symbols and integer indices. Two common ways to represent sentences is by a sequence of *letters* or a sequence of *words*. Let's say, for simplicity, that you're dealing with sequences of letters, so you'll need to build a mapping between characters and integer indices.

NOTE The official code repository is available at the book's website (www.manning.com/books/machine-learning-with-tensorflow) and on GitHub (http://mng.bz/EB5A). From there, you can get the code running without needing to copy and paste from the book.

The following listing shows how to build mappings between integers and characters. If you feed this function a list of strings, it'll produce two dictionaries, representing the mappings.

Listing 11.9 Extracting character vocab

```
def extract_character_vocab(data):
    special_symbols = ['<PAD>', '<UNK>', '<GO>', '<EOS>']
    set_symbols = set([character for line in data for character in line])
    all_symbols = special_symbols + list(set_symbols)
    int_to_symbol = {word_i: word
                        for word_i, word in enumerate(all_symbols)}
    symbol_to_int = {word: word_i
                        for word_i, word in int_to_symbol.items()}

    return int_to_symbol, symbol_to_int

input_sentences = ['hello stranger', 'bye bye']          ◁──┐ List of input
                                                              │ sentences for
output_sentences = ['hiya', 'later alligator']   ◁─────┐     │ training

input_int_to_symbol, input_symbol_to_int =              List of corresponding
    extract_character_vocab(input_sentences)            output sentences for
                                                        training

output_int_to_symbol, output_symbol_to_int =
    extract_character_vocab(output_sentences
```

Next, you'll define all your hyperparameters and constants in listing 11.10. These are usually values you can tune by hand through trial and error. Typically, greater values for the number of dimensions or layers result in a more complex model, which is rewarding if you have big data, fast processing power, and lots of time.

Listing 11.10 Defining hyperparameters

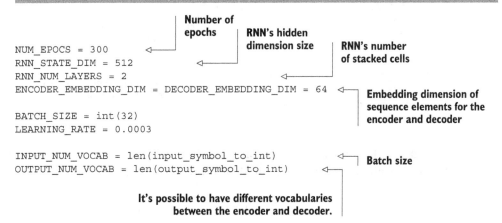

```
NUM_EPOCS = 300                         ◁──┘ Number of epochs
RNN_STATE_DIM = 512                  ◁────── RNN's hidden dimension size
RNN_NUM_LAYERS = 2                ◁────── RNN's number of stacked cells
ENCODER_EMBEDDING_DIM = DECODER_EMBEDDING_DIM = 64  ◁── Embedding dimension of
                                                       sequence elements for the
BATCH_SIZE = int(32)                                   encoder and decoder
LEARNING_RATE = 0.0003

INPUT_NUM_VOCAB = len(input_symbol_to_int)     ◁──┐ Batch size
OUTPUT_NUM_VOCAB = len(output_symbol_to_int)  ◁───┘
```

It's possible to have different vocabularies between the encoder and decoder.

Let's list all placeholders next. As you can see in listing 11.11, the placeholders nicely organize the input and output sequences necessary to train the network. You'll have to track both the sequences and their lengths. For the decoder part, you'll also need to compute the maximum sequence length. The None value in the shape of these placeholders means the tensor may take on an arbitrary size in that dimension. For example, the batch size may vary in each run. But for simplicity, you'll keep the batch size the same at all times.

Listing 11.11   Listing placeholders

```
# Encoder placeholders
encoder_input_seq = tf.placeholder(          Sequence of integers for
    tf.int32,                                the encoder's input
    [None, None],                            Shape is batch-size ×
    name='encoder_input_seq'                 sequence length
)

encoder_seq_len = tf.placeholder(            Lengths of sequences
    tf.int32,                                in a batch
    (None,),                                 Shape is dynamic because the
    name='encoder_seq_len'                   length of a sequence can change
)

# Decoder placeholders
decoder_output_seq = tf.placeholder(         Sequence of integers for
    tf.int32,                                the decoder's output
    [None, None],                            Shape is batch-size ×
    name='decoder_output_seq'                sequence length
)

decoder_seq_len = tf.placeholder(            Lengths of sequences
    tf.int32,                                in a batch
    (None,),                                 Shape is dynamic because the
    name='decoder_seq_len'                   length of a sequence can change
)

max_decoder_seq_len = tf.reduce_max(         Maximum length of a decoder
    decoder_seq_len,                         sequence in a batch
    name='max_decoder_seq_len'
)
```

Let's define helper functions to construct RNN cells. These functions, shown in the following listing, should appear familiar to you from the previous section.

Listing 11.12   Helper functions to build RNN cells

```
def make_cell(state_dim):
    lstm_initializer = tf.random_uniform_initializer(-0.1, 0.1)
    return tf.contrib.rnn.LSTMCell(state_dim, initializer=lstm_initializer)

def make_multi_cell(state_dim, num_layers):
    cells = [make_cell(state_dim) for _ in range(num_layers)]
    return tf.contrib.rnn.MultiRNNCell(cells)
```

You'll build the encoder and decoder RNN cells by using the helper functions you've just defined. As a reminder, we've copied the seq2seq model for you in figure 11.9, to visualize the encoder and decoder RNNs.

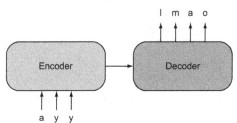

Seq2seq model overview

Figure 11.9 The seq2seq model learns a transformation between an input sequence to an output sequence by using an encoder RNN and a decoder RNN.

Let's talk about the encoder cell part first, because in listing 11.13 you'll build the encoder cell. The produced states of the encoder RNN will be stored in a variable called `encoder_state`. RNNs also produce an output sequence, but you don't need access to that in a standard seq2seq model, so you can ignore it or delete it.

It's also typical to convert letters or words in a vector representation, often called *embedding*. TensorFlow provides a handy function called `embed_sequence` that can help you embed the integer representation of symbols. Figure 11.10 shows how the encoder input accepts numeric values from a lookup table. You can see it in action at the beginning of listing 11.13.

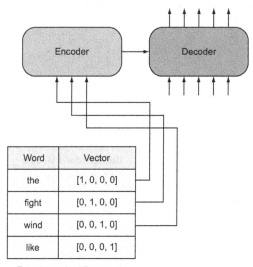

Encoder embedding matrix

Figure 11.10 The RNNs accept only sequences of numeric values as input or output, so you'll convert your symbols to vectors. In this case, the symbols are words, such as *the*, *fight*, *wind*, and *like*. Their corresponding vectors are associated in the embedding matrix.

Listing 11.13   Encoder embedding and cell

```
# Encoder embedding

encoder_input_embedded = tf.contrib.layers.embed_sequence(
    encoder_input_seq,
    INPUT_NUM_VOCAB,
    ENCODER_EMBEDDING_DIM
)
```

Input seq of numbers
(row indices)

Rows of embedding
matrix

Columns of
embedding matrix

```
# Encoder output

encoder_multi_cell = make_multi_cell(RNN_STATE_DIM, RNN_NUM_LAYERS)

encoder_output, encoder_state = tf.nn.dynamic_rnn(
    encoder_multi_cell,
    encoder_input_embedded,
    sequence_length=encoder_seq_len,
    dtype=tf.float32
)

del(encoder_output)
```

You don't need to
hold on to that value.

The decoder RNN's output is a sequence of numeric values representing a natural language sentence and a special symbol to represent that the sequence has ended. You'll label this end-of-sequence symbol as <EOS>. Figure 11.11 illustrates this process. The input sequence to the decoder RNN will look similar to the decoder's output sequence, except instead of having the <EOS> (end of sequence) special symbol at the end of each sentence, it will have a <GO> special symbol at the front. That way, after the decoder reads its input from left to right, it starts out with no extra information about the answer, making it a robust model.

Seq2seq model overview

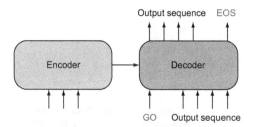

Output sequence   EOS

Encoder → Decoder

GO   Output sequence

Figure 11.11   The decoder's input is prefixed with a special <GO> symbol, whereas the output is suffixed by a special <EOS> symbol.

Listing 11.14 shows how to correctly perform these slicing and concatenating operations. The newly constructed sequence for the decoder's input will be called decoder_input_seq. You'll use TensorFlow's tf.concat operation to glue together matrices. In the listing, you define a `go_prefixes` matrix, which will be a column vector containing only the `<GO>` symbol.

Listing 11.14 Preparing input sequences to the decoder

> Crops the matrix by ignoring
> the very last column

```
decoder_raw_seq = decoder_output_seq[:, :-1]
go_prefixes = tf.fill([BATCH_SIZE, 1], output_symbol_to_int['<GO>'])
decoder_input_seq = tf.concat([go_prefixes, decoder_raw_seq], 1)
```

**Creates a column vector
of <GO> symbols**

**Concatenates the <GO> vector to
the beginning of the cropped matrix**

Now let's construct the decoder cell. As shown in listing 11.15, you'll first embed the decoder sequence of integers into a sequence of vectors, called `decoder_input_embedded`.

The embedded version of the input sequence will be fed to the decoder's RNN, so go ahead and create the decoder RNN cell. One more thing: you'll need a layer to map the output of the decoder to a one-hot representation of the vocabulary, which you call `output_layer`. The process of setting up the decoder starts out to be similar to that with the encoder.

Listing 11.15 Decoder embedding and cell

```
decoder_embedding = tf.Variable(tf.random_uniform([OUTPUT_NUM_VOCAB,
                                            DECODER_EMBEDDING_DIM]))
decoder_input_embedded = tf.nn.embedding_lookup(decoder_embedding,
                                            decoder_input_seq)

decoder_multi_cell = make_multi_cell(RNN_STATE_DIM, RNN_NUM_LAYERS)

output_layer_kernel_initializer =
    tf.truncated_normal_initializer(mean=0.0, stddev=0.1)
output_layer = Dense(
    OUTPUT_NUM_VOCAB,
    kernel_initializer = output_layer_kernel_initializer
)
```

Okay, here's where things get weird. You have two ways to retrieve the decoder's output: during training and during inference. The training decoder will be used only during training, whereas the inference decoder will be used for testing on never-before-seen data.

The reason for having two ways to obtain an output sequence is that during training, you have the ground-truth data available, so you can use information about the known output to help speed the learning process. But during inference, you have no ground-truth output labels, so you must resort to making inferences by using only the input sequence.

The following listing implements the training decoder. You'll feed `decoder_input`
`_seq` into the decoder's input, using `TrainingHelper`. This helper op manages the input to the decoder RNN for you.

Listing 11.16   Decoder output (training)

```
with tf.variable_scope("decode"):

    training_helper = tf.contrib.seq2seq.TrainingHelper(
        inputs=decoder_input_embedded,
        sequence_length=decoder_seq_len,
        time_major=False
    )

    training_decoder = tf.contrib.seq2seq.BasicDecoder(
        decoder_multi_cell,
        training_helper,
        encoder_state,
        output_layer
    )

    training_decoder_output_seq, _, _ = tf.contrib.seq2seq.dynamic_decode(
        training_decoder,
        impute_finished=True,
        maximum_iterations=max_decoder_seq_len
    )
```

If you care to obtain output from the seq2seq model on test data, you no longer have access to `decoder_input_seq`. Why? Well, the decoder input sequence is derived from the decoder output sequence, which is available only with the training dataset.

The following listing implements the decoder output op for the inference case. Here again, you'll use a helper op to feed the decoder an input sequence.

Listing 11.17   Decoder output (inference)

```
with tf.variable_scope("decode", reuse=True):
    start_tokens = tf.tile(
        tf.constant([output_symbol_to_int['<GO>']],
                    dtype=tf.int32),
        [BATCH_SIZE],
        name='start_tokens')

    inference_helper = tf.contrib.seq2seq.GreedyEmbeddingHelper(
        embedding=decoder_embedding,
        start_tokens=start_tokens,
        end_token=output_symbol_to_int['<EOS>']
    )
```

**Helper for
the inference
process**

```
inference_decoder = tf.contrib.seq2seq.BasicDecoder(
    decoder_multi_cell,
    inference_helper,                                      Basic
    encoder_state,                                         decoder
    output_layer
)
```

Performs dynamic decoding using the decoder

```
inference_decoder_output_seq, _, _ = tf.contrib.seq2seq.dynamic_decode(
    inference_decoder,
    impute_finished=True,
    maximum_iterations=max_decoder_seq_len
)
```

Compute the cost using TensorFlow's sequence_loss method. You'll need access to the inferred decoder output sequence and the ground-truth output sequence. The following listing defines the cost function in code.

Listing 11.18 Cost function

Renames the tensors for your convenience

```
training_logits =
    tf.identity(training_decoder_output_seq.rnn_output, name='logits')
inference_logits =
    tf.identity(inference_decoder_output_seq.sample_id, name='predictions')

masks = tf.sequence_mask(
    decoder_seq_len,                          Creates the
    max_decoder_seq_len,                      weights for
    dtype=tf.float32,                         sequence_loss
    name='masks'
)

cost = tf.contrib.seq2seq.sequence_loss(
    training_logits,                          Uses TensorFlow's
    decoder_output_seq,                       built-in sequence
    masks                                     loss function
)
```

Last, let's call an optimizer to minimize the cost. But you'll do one trick you might have never seen before. In deep networks like this one, you need to limit extreme gradient change to ensure that the gradient doesn't change too dramatically, a technique called *gradient clipping*. Listing 11.19 shows you how to do so.

EXERCISE 11.5
Try the seq2seq model without gradient clipping to experience the difference.

ANSWER
You'll notice that without gradient clipping, sometimes the network adjusts the gradients too much, causing numerical instabilities.

Listing 11.19 Calling an optimizer

```
optimizer = tf.train.AdamOptimizer(LEARNING_RATE)
                                                                    Gradient
gradients = optimizer.compute_gradients(cost)                      clipping
capped_gradients = [(tf.clip_by_value(grad, -5., 5.), var)   ◁┐
                    for grad, var in gradients if grad is not None]
train_op = optimizer.apply_gradients(capped_gradients)
```

That concludes the seq2seq model implementation. In general, the model is ready to be trained after you've set up the optimizer, as in the previous listing. You can create a session and run `train_op` with batches of training data to learn the parameters of the model.

Oh, right, you need training data from someplace! How can you obtain thousands of pairs of input and output sentences? Fear not—the next section covers exactly that.

11.5 *Gathering dialogue data*

The Cornell Movie Dialogues corpus (http://mng.bz/W28O) is a dataset of more than 220,000 conversations from more than 600 movies. You can download the zip file from the official web page.

> **WARNING**   Because there's a huge amount of data, you can expect the training algorithm to take a long time. If your TensorFlow library is configured to use only the CPU, it might take an entire day to train. On a GPU, training this network may take 30 minutes to an hour.

An example of a small snippet of back-and-forth conversation between two people (A and B) is the following:

> A: *They do not!*
>
> B: *They do too!*
>
> A: *Fine.*

Because the goal of the chatbot is to produce intelligent output for every possible input utterance, you'll structure your training data based on contingent pairs of conversation. In the example, the dialogue generates the following pairs of input and output sentences:

- "They do not!" → "They do too!"
- "They do too!" → "Fine."

For your convenience, we've already processed the data and made it available for you online. You can find it at www.manning.com/books/machine-learning-with-tensorflow or http://mng.bz/wWo0. After completing the download, you can run the following listing, which uses the `load_sentences` helper function from the GitHub repo under the `Concept03_seq2seq.ipynb` Jupyter Notebook.

Listing 11.20 Training the model

Loads the input sentences as a list of strings

Loads the corresponding output sentences the same way

```
input_sentences = load_sentences('data/words_input.txt')
output_sentences = load_sentences('data/words_output.txt')

input_seq = [
    [input_symbol_to_int.get(symbol, input_symbol_to_int['<UNK>'])
        for symbol in line]
    for line in input_sentences
]
```

Loops through the letters

Loops through the lines of text

```
output_seq = [
    [output_symbol_to_int.get(symbol, output_symbol_to_int['<UNK>'])
        for symbol in line] + [output_symbol_to_int['<EOS>']]
    for line in output_sentences
]
```

Appends the EOS symbol to the end of the output data

Loops through the lines

```
sess = tf.InteractiveSession()
sess.run(tf.global_variables_initializer())
saver = tf.train.Saver()
```

It's a good idea to save the learned parameters.

Loops through the epochs

```
for epoch in range(NUM_EPOCS + 1):

    for batch_idx in range(len(input_sentences) // BATCH_SIZE):
```

Loops by the number of batches

```
        input_data, output_data = get_batches(input_sentences,
                                              output_sentences,
                                              batch_idx)
```

Gets input and output pairs for the current batch

```
        input_batch, input_lenghts = input_data[batch_idx]
        output_batch, output_lengths = output_data[batch_idx]

        _, cost_val = sess.run(
            [train_op, cost],
            feed_dict={
                encoder_input_seq: input_batch,
                encoder_seq_len: input_lengths,
                decoder_output_seq: output_batch,
                decoder_seq_len: output_lengths
            }
        )
```

Runs the optimizer on the current batch

```
saver.save(sess, 'model.ckpt')
sess.close()
```

Because you saved the model parameters to a file, you can easily load it onto another program and query the network for responses to new input. Run the `inference_logits` op to obtain the chatbot response.

11.6 Summary

In this chapter, you built a real-world example of a seq2seq network, putting to work all the TensorFlow knowledge you learned in the previous chapters:

- You built a seq2seq neural network by putting to work all the TensorFlow knowledge you've acquired from the book so far.
- You learned how to embed natural language in TensorFlow.
- You used RNNs as a building block for a more interesting model.
- After training the model on examples of dialogue from movie scripts, you were able to treat the algorithm like a chatbot, inferring natural language responses from natural language input.

Utility landscape

This chapter covers

- Implementing a neural network for ranking
- Image embedding using VGG16
- Visualizing utility

A household vacuuming robot, like the Roomba, needs sensors to "see" the world. The ability to process sensory input enables robots to adjust their model of the world around them. In the case of the vacuum cleaner robot, the furniture in the room may change day to day, so the robot must be able to adapt to chaotic environments.

Let's say you own a futuristic housemaid robot, which comes with a few basic skills but also with the ability to learn new skills from human demonstrations. For example, maybe you'd like to teach it how to fold clothes.

Teaching a robot how to accomplish a new task is a tricky problem. Some immediate questions come to mind:

- Should the robot simply mimic a human's sequence of actions? Such a process is referred to as *imitation learning*.
- How do a robot's arms and joints match up to human poses? This dilemma is often referred to as the *correspondence problem*.

EXERCISE 12.1
The goal of imitation learning is for the robot to reproduce the action sequences of the demonstrator. This sounds good on paper, but what are the limitations of such an approach?

ANSWER
Mimicking human actions is a naive approach to learning from human demonstrations. Instead, the agent should identify the hidden goal behind a demonstration. For example, the goal when someone folds clothes is to flatten and compress them, which are concepts independent of a human's hand motions. By understanding why the human is producing their action sequence, the agent is better able to generalize the skill it's being taught.

In this chapter, you're going to model a task from human demonstrations while avoiding both imitation learning and the correspondence problem. Lucky you! You'll achieve this by studying a way to rank states of the world with a *utility function*, which is a function that takes a state and returns a real value representing its desirability. Not only will you steer clear of imitation as a measure of success, but you'll also bypass the complications of mapping a robot's set of actions to that of a human (the correspondence problem).

In the following section, you'll learn how to implement a utility function over the states of the world obtained through videos of human demonstrations of a task. The learned utility function is a model of preferences.

You'll explore the task of teaching a robot how to fold articles of clothing. A wrinkled article of clothing is almost certainly in a configuration that has never before been seen. As shown in figure 12.1, the utility framework has no limitations on the size of the state space. The preference model is trained specifically on videos of people folding T-shirts in various ways.

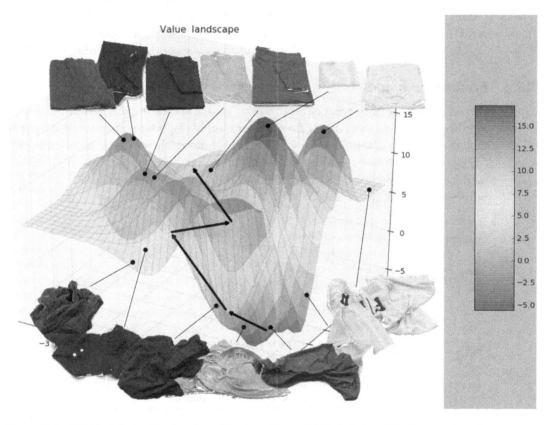

Figure 12.1 Wrinkled clothes in a less favorable state than well-folded clothes. This diagram shows how you might score each state of a piece of cloth; higher scores represent a more favorable state.

The utility function generalizes across states (wrinkled T-shirt in novel configuration versus folded T-shirt in familiar configuration) and reuses knowledge across clothes (T-shirt folding versus pants folding).

We can further illustrate the practical applications of a good utility function with the following argument: in real-world situations, not all visual observations are optimized toward learning a task. A teacher demonstrating a skill may perform irrelevant, incomplete, or even incorrect actions, yet humans are capable of ignoring the mistakes.

When a robot watches human demonstrations, you want it to understand the causal relationships that go into achieving a task. Your work enables the learning phase to be interactive, where the robot is actively skeptic of human behavior, to refine the training data.

To accomplish this, you first learn a utility function from a small number of videos to rank the preferences of various states. Then, when the robot is shown a new instance of a skill through human demonstration, it consults the utility function to verify that the expected utility increases over time. Lastly, the robot interrupts the human demonstration to ask whether the action was essential for learning the skill.

12.1   *Preference model*

We assume human preferences are derived from a *utilitarian* perspective, meaning a number determines the rank of items. For example, suppose you surveyed people to rank the fanciness of various foods (such as steak, hotdog, shrimp cocktail, and burger).

Figure 12.2 shows a couple of possible rankings between pairs of food. As you might expect, steak is ranked higher than hotdog, and shrimp cocktail higher than burger on the fanciness scale.

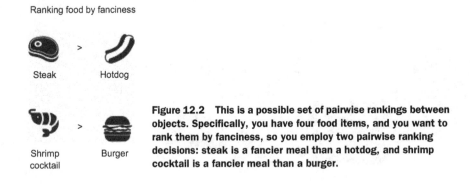

Ranking food by fanciness

Steak   Hotdog

Shrimp cocktail   Burger

Figure 12.2   This is a possible set of pairwise rankings between objects. Specifically, you have four food items, and you want to rank them by fanciness, so you employ two pairwise ranking decisions: steak is a fancier meal than a hotdog, and shrimp cocktail is a fancier meal than a burger.

Fortunately for the individuals being surveyed, not every pair of items needs to be ranked. For example, it might not be so obvious which is fancier between hotdog and burger, or between steak and shrimp cocktail. There's a lot of room for disagreement.

If a state s_1 has a higher utility than another state s_2, then the corresponding ranking is denoted $s_1 > s_2$, implying the utility of s_1 is greater than the utility of s_2.

Each video demonstration contains a sequence of n states $s_0, s_1, .., s_n$, which offers $n(n-1)/2$ possible ordered pairs ranking constraints. Let's implement our own neural network capable of ranking. Open a new source file, and use the following listing to import the relevant libraries. You're about to create a neural network to learn a utility function based on pairs of preferences.

Listing 12.1 Importing relevant libraries

```
import tensorflow as tf
import numpy as np
import random

%matplotlib inline
import matplotlib.pyplot as plt
```

To learn a neural network for ranking states based on a utility score, you'll need training data. Let's create dummy data to begin with. You'll replace it with something more realistic later. Reproduce the two-dimensional data in figure 12.3 by using listing 12.2.

Listing 12.2 Generating dummy training data

```
n_features = 2          ◁──┐ You'll generate two-dimensional data
                            so that you can easily visualize it.
                                                        The set of points that
                                                        should yield higher utility
def get_data():
    data_a = np.random.rand(10, n_features) + 1   ◁──┐ The set of points that
    data_b = np.random.rand(10, n_features)        ◁── are less preferred

    plt.scatter(data_a[:, 0], data_a[:, 1], c='r', marker='x')
    plt.scatter(data_b[:, 0], data_b[:, 1], c='g', marker='o')
    plt.show()

    return data_a, data_b

data_a, data_b = get_data()
```

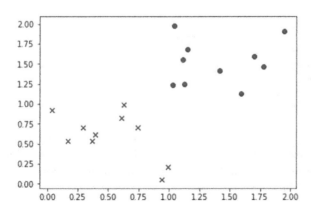

Figure 12.3 Example data that you'll work with. The circles represent more-favorable states, whereas the crosses represent less-favorable states. You have an equal number of circles and crosses because the data comes in pairs; each pair is a ranking, as in figure 12.2.

Next, you need to define hyperparameters. In this model, let's stay simple by keeping the architecture shallow. You'll create a network with just one hidden layer. The corresponding hyperparameter that dictates the hidden layer's number of neurons is the following:

```
n_hidden = 10
```

The ranking neural network will receive pairwise input, so you'll need to have two separate placeholders, one for each part of the pair. Moreover, you'll create a placeholder to hold the dropout parameter value. Continue by adding the following listing to your script.

Listing 12.3   Placeholders

```
                                                          Input placeholder for
                                                          preferred points

with tf.name_scope("input"):
    x1 = tf.placeholder(tf.float32, [None, n_features], name="x1")   ◄─┐
    x2 = tf.placeholder(tf.float32, [None, n_features], name="x2")   ◄──
    dropout_keep_prob = tf.placeholder(tf.float32, name='dropout_prob')

                                                          Input placeholder for
                                                          non-preferred points
```

The ranking neural network will contain only one hidden layer. In the following listing, you define the weights and biases, and then reuse these weights and biases on each of the two input placeholders.

Listing 12.4   Hidden layer

```
with tf.name_scope("hidden_layer"):
    with tf.name_scope("weights"):
        w1 = tf.Variable(tf.random_normal([n_features, n_hidden]), name="w1")
        tf.summary.histogram("w1", w1)
        b1 = tf.Variable(tf.random_normal([n_hidden]), name="b1")
        tf.summary.histogram("b1", b1)

    with tf.name_scope("output"):
        h1 = tf.nn.dropout(tf.nn.relu(tf.matmul(x1,w1) + b1),
    keep_prob=dropout_keep_prob)
        tf.summary.histogram("h1", h1)
        h2 = tf.nn.dropout(tf.nn.relu(tf.matmul(x2, w1) + b1),
    keep_prob=dropout_keep_prob)
        tf.summary.histogram("h2", h2)
```

The goal of the neural network is to calculate a score for the two inputs provided. In the following listing, you define the weights, biases, and fully connected architecture of the output layer of the network. You'll be left with two output vectors, s1 and s2, representing the scores for the pairwise input.

Listing 12.5 Output layer

```
with tf.name_scope("output_layer"):
    with tf.name_scope("weights"):
        w2 = tf.Variable(tf.random_normal([n_hidden, 1]), name="w2")
        tf.summary.histogram("w2", w2)
        b2 = tf.Variable(tf.random_normal([1]), name="b2")
        tf.summary.histogram("b2", b2)

    with tf.name_scope("output"):
        s1 = tf.matmul(h1, w2) + b2        Utility score
                                           of input x1
        s2 = tf.matmul(h2, w2) + b2        Utility score
                                           of input x2
```

You'll assume that when training the neural network, x1 should contain the less-favorable items. That means s1 should be scored lower than s2, meaning the difference between s1 and s2 should be negative. As the following listing shows, the loss function tries to guarantee a negative difference by using the softmax cross-entropy loss. You'll define a train_op to minimize the loss function.

Listing 12.6 Loss and optimizer

```
with tf.name_scope("loss"):
    s12 = s1 - s2
    s12_flat = tf.reshape(s12, [-1])

    cross_entropy = tf.nn.softmax_cross_entropy_with_logits(
                        labels=tf.zeros_like(s12_flat),
                        logits=s12_flat + 1)

    loss = tf.reduce_mean(cross_entropy)
    tf.summary.scalar("loss", loss)

with tf.name_scope("train_op"):
    train_op = tf.train.AdamOptimizer(0.001).minimize(loss)
```

Now, follow listing 12.7 to set up a TensorFlow session. This involves initializing all variables and preparing TensorBoard debugging by using a summary writer.

NOTE You used a summary writer before, at the end of chapter 2, when you were first introduced to TensorBoard.

Listing 12.7 Preparing a session

```
sess = tf.InteractiveSession()
summary_op = tf.summary.merge_all()
writer = tf.summary.FileWriter("tb_files", sess.graph)
init = tf.global_variables_initializer()
sess.run(init)
```

You're ready to train the network! Run `train_op` on the dummy data you generated to learn the parameters of the model.

Listing 12.8   Training the network

**Training dropout
keep_prob is 0.5.**

```
for epoch in range(0, 10000):
    loss_val, _ = sess.run([loss, train_op], feed_dict={x1:data_a, x2:data_b,
        dropout_keep_prob:0.5})
    if epoch % 100 == 0 :
        summary_result = sess.run(summary_op,
                            feed_dict={x1:data_a,
                                x2:data_b,
                                dropout_keep_prob:1})
        writer.add_summary(summary_result, epoch)
```

Preferred points

Non-preferred points

Testing dropout keep_prob should always be 1.

Finally, let's visualize the learned score function. As shown in the following listing, append two-dimensional points to a list.

Listing 12.9   Preparing test data

```
grid_size = 10
data_test = []
for y in np.linspace(0., 1., num=grid_size):
    for x in np.linspace(0., 1., num=grid_size):
        data_test.append([x, y])
```

Loops through the rows

Loops through the columns

You'll run the `s1` op on the test data to obtain utility values of each state, and visualize it as shown in figure 12.4. Use the following listing to generate the visualization.

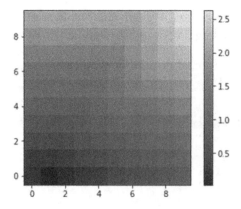

Figure 12.4   The landscape of scores learned by the ranking neural network

> **Listing 12.10 Visualize results**

```
def visualize_results(data_test):
    plt.figure()
    scores_test = sess.run(s1, feed_dict={x1:data_test, dropout_keep_prob:1})
    scores_img = np.reshape(scores_test, [grid_size, grid_size])
    plt.imshow(scores_img, origin='lower')
    plt.colorbar()

visualize_results(data_test)
```

Computes the utility of all the points

Reshapes the utilities to a matrix so you can visualize an image using Matplotlib

12.2 Image embedding

In chapter 11, you summoned the hubris to feed a neural network some natural language sentences. You did so by converting words or letters in a sentence into numeric forms, such as vectors. For example, each symbol (whether it's a word or letter) was embedded into a vector by using a lookup table.

EXERCISE 12.2

Why is a lookup table that converts a symbol into a vector representation called an embedding matrix?

ANSWER

The symbols are being embedded into a vector space.

Fortunately, images are already in a numeric form. They're represented as a matrix of pixels. If the image is grayscale, perhaps the pixels take on scalar values indicating luminosity. For colored images, each pixel represents color intensities (usually three: red, green, and blue). Either way, an image can easily be represented by numeric data structures, such as a tensor, in TensorFlow.

EXERCISE 12.3

Take a photo of a household object, such as a chair. Scale the image smaller and smaller until you can no longer identify the object. By what factor did you end up shrinking the image? What's the ratio of the number of pixels in the original image to the number of pixels in the smaller image? This ratio is a rough measure of redundancy in the data.

ANSWER

A typical 5 MP camera produces images at a resolution of 2560 × 1920, yet the content of that image might still be decipherable when you shrink it by a factor of 40 (resolution 64 × 48).

Feeding a neural network a large image, say of size 1280×720 (almost 1 million pixels), increases the number of parameters and, consequently, escalates the risk of overfitting the model. The pixels in an image are highly redundant, so you can try to somehow capture the essence of an image in a more succinct representation. Figure 12.5 shows the clusters formed in a two-dimensional embedding of images of clothes being folded.

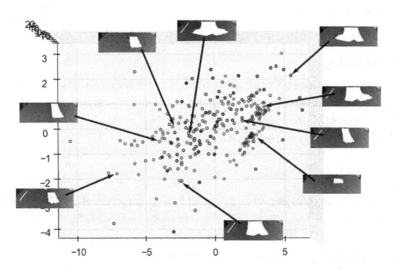

Figure 12.5   Images can be embedded into much lower dimensions, such as 2D as shown here. Notice that points representing similar states of a shirt occur in nearby clusters. Embedding images allows you to use the ranking neural network to learn a preference between the states of a piece of cloth.

You saw in chapter 7 how to use autoencoders to reduce the dimensionality of images. Another common way to accomplish low-dimensional embedding of images is by using the penultimate layer of a deep convolutional neural network image classifier. Let's explore the latter in more detail.

Because designing, implementing, and learning a deep image classifier isn't the primary focus of this chapter (see chapter 9 for CNNs), you'll instead use an off-the-shelf pretrained model. A common go-to image classifier that many computer vision research papers cite is called *VGG16*.

Many online implementations of VGG16 exist for TensorFlow. We recommend using the one by Davi Frossard (www.cs.toronto.edu/~frossard/post/vgg16/). You can download the vgg16.py TensorFlow code and the vgg16_weights.npz pretrained model parameters from his website or, alternatively, from the book's website (www.manning .com/books/machine-learning-with-tensorflow) or GitHub repo (https://github.com/ BinRoot/TensorFlow-Book).

Figure 12.6 is a depiction of the VGG16 neural network from Frossard's page. As you see, it's a deep neural network, with many convolutional layers. The last few are the usual fully connected layers, and, finally, the output layer is a 1,000-dimensional vector indicating the multiclass classification probabilities.

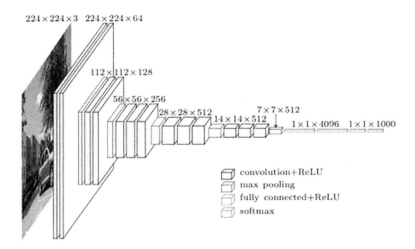

Figure 12.6 **The VGG16 architecture is a deep convolutional neural network used for classifying images. This particular diagram is from www.cs.toronto.edu/ ~frossard/post/vgg16/.**

Learning how to navigate other people's code is an indispensable skill. First, make sure you have vgg16.py and vgg16_weights.npz downloaded, and test that you're able to run the code by using python vgg16.py my_image.png.

> **NOTE** You might need to install SciPy and Pillow to get the VGG16 demo code to run without issues. You can download both via pip.

Let's start by adding TensorBoard integration to visualize what's going on in this code. In the main function, after creating a session variable sess, insert the following line of code:

```
my_writer = tf.summary.FileWriter('tb_files', sess.graph)
```

Now, running the classifier once again (python vgg16.py my_image.png) will generate a directory called tb_files, to be used by TensorBoard. You can run TensorBoard to visualize the computation graph of the neural network. The following command runs TensorBoard:

```
$ tensorboard --logdir=tb_files
```

Open TensorBoard in your browser, and navigate to the Graphs tab to see the computation graph, as shown in figure 12.7. Notice that with a quick glance, you can immediately get an idea of the types of layers involved in the network: the last three layers are fully connected dense layers, labeled fc1, fc2, and fc3.

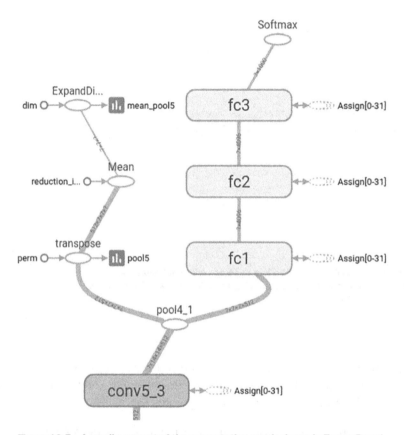

Figure 12.7   A small segment of the computation graph shown in TensorBoard for the VGG16 neural network. The topmost node is the softmax operator used for classification. The three fully connected layers are labeled fc1, fc2, and fc3.

12.3 *Ranking images*

You'll use the VGG16 code in the previous section to obtain a vector representation of an image. That way, you can rank two images efficiently in the ranking neural network designed in section 12.1.

Consider videos of shirt-folding, as shown in figure 12.8. You'll process videos frame by frame to rank the states of the images. That way, in a novel situation, the algorithm can understand whether the goal of cloth-folding has been reached.

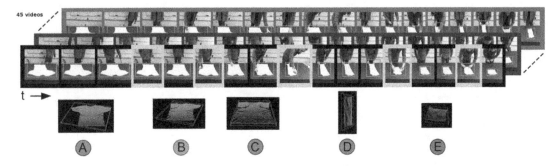

Figure 12.8 Videos of folding a shirt reveal how the cloth changes form through time. You can extract the first state and the last state of the shirt as your training data to learn a utility function to rank states. Final states of a shirt in each video should be ranked with a higher utility than those shirts near the beginning of the video.

First, download the cloth-folding dataset from http://mng.bz/eZsc. Extract the zip. Keep note of where you extract it; you'll call that location DATASET_DIR in the code listings.

Open a new source file, and begin by importing the relevant libraries in Python.

Listing 12.11   Importing libraries

```
import tensorflow as tf
import numpy as np
from vgg16 import vgg16
import glob, os
from scipy.misc import imread, imresize
```

For each video, you'll remember the first and last images. That way, you can train the ranking algorithm by assuming the last image is of a higher preference than the first image. In other words, the last state of cloth-folding brings you to a higher-valued state than the first state of cloth-folding. The following listing shows an example of how to load the data into memory.

Listing 12.12   Preparing the training data

```
DATASET_DIR = os.path.join(os.path.expanduser('~'), 'res',
    'cloth_folding_rgb_vids')                              ◁── Directory of
NUM_VIDS = 45                                                   downloaded files

def get_img_pair(video_id):
    img_files = sorted(glob.glob(os.path.join(DATASET_DIR, video_id,
    '*.png')))
    start_img = img_files[0]
    end_img = img_files[-1]                              ◁── Gets the starting
    pair = []                                                and ending image
                                                             of a video
```

Number of videos to load ⟶ NUM_VIDS = 45

```
    for image_file in [start_img, end_img]:
        img_original = imread(image_file)
        img_resized = imresize(img_original, (224, 224))
        pair.append(img_resized)
    return tuple(pair)

start_imgs = []
end_imgs= []
for vid_id in range(1, NUM_VIDS + 1):
    start_img, end_img = get_img_pair(str(vid_id))
    start_imgs.append(start_img)
    end_imgs.append(end_img)
print('Images of starting state {}'.format(np.shape(start_imgs)))
print('Images of ending state {}'.format(np.shape(end_imgs)))
```

Running listing 12.12 results in the following output:

```
Images of starting state (45, 224, 224, 3)
Images of ending state (45, 224, 224, 3)
```

Use the following listing to create an input placeholder for the image that you'll be embedding.

Listing 12.13   Placeholder

```
imgs_plc = tf.placeholder(tf.float32, [None, 224, 224, 3])
```

Copy over the ranking neural network code from listings 12.3–12.7; you'll reuse it to rank images. Then prepare the session in the following listing.

Listing 12.14   Preparing the session

```
sess = tf.InteractiveSession()
sess.run(tf.global_variables_initializer())
```

Next, you'll initialize the VGG16 model by calling the constructor. Doing so, as shown next, loads all the model parameters from disk to memory.

Listing 12.15   Loading the VGG16 model

```
print('Loading model...')
vgg = vgg16(imgs_plc, 'vgg16_weights.npz', sess)
print('Done loading!')
```

Next, let's prepare training and testing data for the ranking neural network. As shown in listing 12.16, you'll feed the VGG16 model your images, and then you'll access a layer near the output (in this case, fc1) to obtain the image embedding.

In the end, you'll have a 4,096-dimensional embedding of your images. Because there are a total of 45 videos, you'll split some for training and some for testing:

- Train
  - Start-frame size: (33, 4096)
  - End-frame size: (33, 4096)
- Test
  - Start-frame size: (12, 4096)
  - End-frame size: (12, 4096)

Listing 12.16 Preparing data for ranking

```
start_imgs_embedded = sess.run(vgg.fc1, feed_dict={vgg.imgs: start_imgs})
end_imgs_embedded = sess.run(vgg.fc1, feed_dict={vgg.imgs: end_imgs})


idxs = np.random.choice(NUM_VIDS, NUM_VIDS, replace=False)
train_idxs = idxs[0:int(NUM_VIDS * 0.75)]
test_idxs = idxs[int(NUM_VIDS * 0.75):]


train_start_imgs = start_imgs_embedded[train_idxs]
train_end_imgs = end_imgs_embedded[train_idxs]
test_start_imgs = start_imgs_embedded[test_idxs]
test_end_imgs = end_imgs_embedded[test_idxs]


print('Train start imgs {}'.format(np.shape(train_start_imgs)))
print('Train end imgs {}'.format(np.shape(train_end_imgs)))
print('Test start imgs {}'.format(np.shape(test_start_imgs)))
print('Test end imgs {}'.format(np.shape(test_end_imgs)))
```

With your training data ready for ranking, let's run `train_op` an epoch number of times. After training the network, run the model on the test data to evaluate your results.

Listing 12.17 Training the ranking network

```
train_y1 = np.expand_dims(np.zeros(np.shape(train_start_imgs)[0]), axis=1)
train_y2 = np.expand_dims(np.ones(np.shape(train_end_imgs)[0]), axis=1)
for epoch in range(100):
    for i in range(np.shape(train_start_imgs)[0]):
        _, cost_val = sess.run([train_op, loss],
                        feed_dict={x1: train_start_imgs[i:i+1,:],
                                   x2: train_end_imgs[i:i+1,:],
                                   dropout_keep_prob: 0.5})
    print('{}. {}'.format(epoch, cost_val))
    s1_val, s2_val = sess.run([s1, s2], feed_dict={x1: test_start_imgs,
                                                   x2: test_end_imgs,
                                                   dropout_keep_prob: 1})
    print('Accuracy: {}%'.format(100 * np.mean(s1_val < s2_val)))
```

Notice that the accuracy approaches 100% over time. Your ranking model learns that the images that occur at the end of the video are more favorable than the images that occur near the beginning.

Just out of curiosity, let's see the utility over time of a single video, frame by frame, as shown in figure 12.9. The code to reproduce figure 12.9 requires loading all the images in a video, as outlined in listing 12.18.

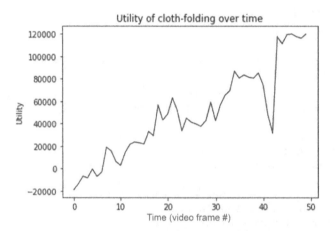

Figure 12.9   The utility increases over time, indicating the goal is being accomplished. The utility of the cloth near the beginning of the video is near 0, but it dramatically increases to 120,000 units by the end.

Listing 12.18   Preparing image sequences from video

```
def get_img_seq(video_id):
    img_files = sorted(glob.glob(os.path.join(DATASET_DIR, video_id,
     '*.png')))
    imgs = []
    for image_file in img_files:
        img_original = imread(image_file)
        img_resized = imresize(img_original, (224, 224))
        imgs.append(img_resized)
    return imgs

imgs = get_img_seq('1')
```

You can use your VGG16 model to embed the images, and then run the ranking network to compute the scores, as shown in the following listing.

Listing 12.19   Computing the utility of images

```
imgs_embedded = sess.run(vgg.fc1, feed_dict={vgg.imgs: imgs})
scores = sess.run([s1], feed_dict={x1: imgs_embedded,
                                   dropout_keep_prob: 1})
```

Visualize your results to reproduce figure 12.9.

Listing 12.20 Visualizing utility scores

```
from matplotlib import pyplot as plt
plt.figure()
plt.title('Utility of cloth-folding over time')
plt.xlabel('time (video frame #)')
plt.ylabel('Utility')
plt.plot(scores[-1])
```

12.4 Summary

- You can rank states by representing objects as vectors and learning a utility function over such vectors.
- Because images contain redundant data, you used the VGG16 neural network to reduce the dimensionality of your data so that you can use the ranking network with real-world images.
- You learned how to visualize the utility of images over time in a video, to verify that the video demonstration increases the utility of the cloth.

You've finished your TensorFlow journey! The 12 chapters of this book approached ML from different angles; but together, they taught you the concepts required to master these skills:

- Formulating an arbitrary real-world problem into a machine-learning framework
- Understanding the basics of many machine-learning problems
- Using TensorFlow to solve these machine-learning problems
- Visualizing a machine-learning algorithm, and speaking the lingo

12.5 What's next?

Because the concepts taught in this book are timeless, the code listings should be, too. To ensure the most up-to-date library calls and syntax, we actively manage a GitHub repository at https://github.com/BinRoot/TensorFlow-Book. Please feel free to join the community there and file bugs or send us pull requests.

> **TIP** TensorFlow is in a state of rapid development, so more functionality will become available all the time!

If you're thirsty for more TensorFlow tutorials, we know exactly what might interest you:

- *Reinforcement learning (RL)*—An in-depth series of blog posts by Arthur Juliani on using RL in TensorFlow: http://mng.bz/C17q.
- *Natural language processing (NLP)*—An essential TensorFlow guide to modern neural network architectures in NLP, by Thushan Ganegedara: http://mng.bz/2Kh7.

- *Generative adversarial networks (GAN)*—An introductory study of generative versus discriminative models in machine learning (using TensorFlow), by John Glover at AYLIEN: http://mng.bz/o2gc.
- *Web tool*—Tinker with a simple neural network to visualize the flow of data: http://playground.tensorflow.org.
- *Video lectures*—Basic introduction and hands-on demos using TensorFlow, on the Google Cloud Big Data and Machine Learning Blog: http://mng.bz/vb7U.
- *Open source projects*—Follow along with the most recently updated TensorFlow projects on GitHub: http://mng.bz/wVZ4

appendix
Installation

You can install TensorFlow in a couple of ways. This book assumes you'll be using Python 3 for every chapter unless otherwise stated. The code listings abide by Tensor-Flow v1.0, but the accompanying source code on GitHub will always be up to date with the latest version (https://github.com/BinRoot/TensorFlow-Book/). This appendix covers one of these installation methods that works on all platforms, including Windows. If you're familiar with UNIX-based systems (such as Linux or macOS), feel free to use one of the installation approaches in the official documentation: www.tensorflow.org/get_started/os_setup.html.

Without further ado, let's install TensorFlow by using a Docker container.

A.1 *Installing TensorFlow by using Docker*

Docker is a system for packaging software dependencies to keep everyone's installation environment identical. This standardization helps limit inconsistencies between computers. It's a relatively recent technology, so let's go through how to use it.

> **TIP** You can install TensorFlow in many ways other than using a Docker container. Visit the official documentation for more details on installing Tensor-Flow: www.tensorflow.org/get_started/os_setup.html.

A.1.1 *Installing Docker on Windows*

Docker works only on 64-bit Windows (7 or above) with virtualization enabled. Fortunately, most consumer laptops and desktops easily satisfy this requirement. To check whether your computer supports Docker, open Control Panel, click System and Security, and then click System. Here, you can see the details about your Windows machine, including processor and system type. If the system is 64-bit, you're almost good to go.

The next step is to check whether your processor can support virtualization. On Windows 8 or higher, you can open the Task Manager (Ctrl-Shift-Esc) and click the Performance tab. If Virtualization shows up as Enabled, you're all set. (See figure A.1.) For Windows 7, you should use the Microsoft Hardware-Assisted Virtualization Detection Tool (http://mng.bz/cBlu).

Now that you know whether your computer can support Docker, let's install the Docker Toolbox located at www.docker.com/products/docker-toolbox. Run the downloaded setup executable, and accept all the defaults by clicking Next in the dialog boxes. After the toolbox is installed, run the Docker Quickstart Terminal.

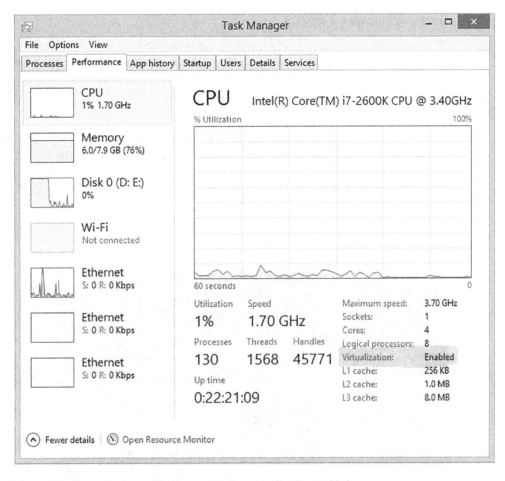

Figure A.1 Ensure that your 64-bit computer has virtualization enabled.

A.1.2 *Installing Docker on Linux*

Docker is officially supported on several Linux distributions. The official Docker documentation (https://docs.docker.com/engine/installation/linux/) contains tutorials for Arch Linux, CentOS, CRUX Linux, Debian, Fedora, Frugalware, Gentoo, Oracle Linux, Red Hat Enterprise Linux, openSUSE, and Ubuntu. Docker is native to Linux, so there's typically no problem installing it.

A.1.3   *Installing Docker on macOS*

Docker works on macOS 10.8 Mountain Lion or newer. Install the Docker Toolbox from www.docker.com/products/docker-toolbox. After installation, open the Docker Quickstart Terminal from the Applications folder or the Launchpad.

A.1.4   *How to use Docker*

Run the Docker Quickstart Terminal. Next, launch the TensorFlow binary image by using the following command in the Docker terminal, as shown in figure A.2:

```
$ docker run -p 8888:8888 -p 6006:6006 b.gcr.io/tensorflow/tensorflow
```

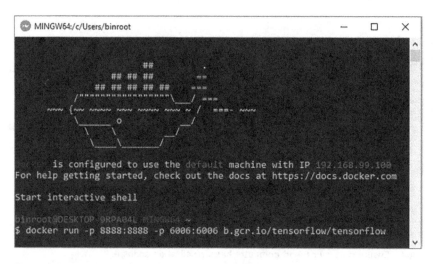

Figure A.2   Running the official TensorFlow container

TensorFlow will now be accessible from a Jupyter Notebook via a local IP address. The IP can be found by using the `docker-machine ip` command, as shown in figure A.3.

Open a browser and navigate to http://<YOUR_IP_ADDRESS>:8888 to start using TensorFlow. In our case, the URL was http://192.168.99.100:8888. Figure A.4 shows the Jupyter Notebook accessed through a browser.

You can press Ctrl-C or close the terminal window to stop running the Jupyter Notebook. To rerun it, follow the steps in this section again.

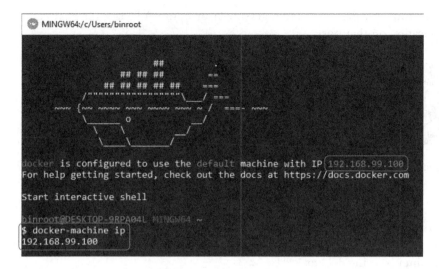

Figure A.3 Docker's IP address can be found using the `docker-machine ip` command or can be found in the intro text under the ASCII whale.

Figure A.4 You can interact with TensorFlow through a Python interface called Jupyter.

If you run into the error message shown in figure A.5, Docker is already using an application on that port.

```
binroot@DESKTOP-9RPA04L MINGW64 ~
$ docker run -p 8888:8888 -p 6006:6006 b.gcr.io/tensorflow/tensorflow
C:\Program Files\Docker Toolbox\docker.exe: Error response from daemon:
driver failed programming external connectivity on endpoint tender_allen
 (ab6dcf2455a5704f8f2911ac53ea946deb3ed939864c30e8fe867c2f5c88a63d): Bin
d for 0.0.0.0:8888 failed: port is already allocated.
```

Figure A.5   A possible error message from running the TensorFlow container

To resolve this issue, you can either switch the port or quit the intruding Docker containers. Figure A.6 shows how to list all containers by using docker ps and then kill the container by using docker kill.

```
binroot@DESKTOP-9RPA04L MINGW64 ~
$ docker ps
CONTAINER ID          IMAGE
62904e0a4489          b.gcr.io/tensorflow/tensorflow

binroot@DESKTOP-9RPA04L MINGW64 ~
$ docker kill 62904e0a4489
62904e0a4489
```

Figure A.6   Listing and killing a Docker container to get rid of
the error message in figure A.5

A.2   *Installing Matplotlib*

Matplotlib is a cross-platform Python library for plotting 2D visualizations of data. Generally, if your computer can successfully run TensorFlow, it'll have no trouble installing Matplotlib. Install it by following the official documentation at http://matplotlib.org/users/installing.html.

index

MORE TITLES FROM MANNING

Deep Learning with Python
by François Chollet

> ISBN: 9781617294433
> 384 pages
> $49.99
> November 2017

Deep Learning with R
by François Chollet
  with J. J. Allaire

> ISBN: 9781617295546
> 384 pages
> $49.99
> January 2018

Keras in Motion
by Dan Van Boxel

> Course duration: 2h 4m
> 55 exercises
> $49.99

For ordering information go to www.manning.com